BUSINESS ISSUES, COMPETITION AND ENTREPRENEURSHIP

STRUCTURED FINANCIAL PRODUCTS AND FINANCIAL ENGINEERING

A TAX AVOIDANCE INVESTIGATION

BUSINESS ISSUES, COMPETITION AND ENTREPRENEURSHIP

BUSINESS ISSUES, COMPETITION AND ENTREPRENEURSHIP

STRUCTURED FINANCIAL PRODUCTS AND FINANCIAL ENGINEERING

A TAX AVOIDANCE INVESTIGATION

LENORA OSBORNE
EDITOR

nova publishers
New York

Library of Congress Cataloging-in-Publication Data

ISBN: 978-1-63463-785-5

Published by Nova Science Publishers, Inc. † New York

CONTENTS

PREFACE

Chapter 1 - For the last decade, the U.S. Senate Permanent Subcommittee on Investigations has presented case histories showing how financial institutions, law firms, accountants, and others have designed and implemented complex financial structures to take advantage of and, at times, abuse or violate U.S. tax statutes, securities regulations, and accounting rules.[1] This investigation offers yet another detailed case study of how two financial institutions – Deutsche Bank AG and Barclays Bank PLC – developed structured financial products called MAPS and COLT, two types of basket options, and sold them to one or more hedge funds, including Renaissance Technologies LLC and George Weiss Associates, that used them to avoid federal taxes and leverage limits on buying securities with borrowed funds. While that type of option product was identified as abusive in a public memorandum by the Internal Revenue Service (IRS) in 2010, taxes have yet to be collected on many of the basket option transactions and its use to circumvent federal leverage limits has yet to be analyzed or halted.

The basket option contracts examined by the Subcommittee investigation were used by at least 13 hedge funds to conduct over $100 billion in securities trades, most of which were short- term transactions and some of which lasted only seconds. Yet the resulting short-term profits were frequently cast as long-term capital gains subject to a 20% tax rate (previously 15%) rather than the ordinary income tax rate (currently as high as 39%) that would otherwise apply to investors in hedge funds engaged in daily trading. While the banks styled the trading arrangement as an "option" under which profits from short-term trades would be treated as long- term capital gains, in essence, the banks loaned the hedge funds money to finance their trading and allowed them to trade for themselves in highly leveraged positions in the banks' proprietary accounts and reap the resulting profits. The banks offering the "options" benefited from the financing, trading, and other fees charged to the hedge funds initiating the trades. In the end, the trading conducted by the hedge funds using the basket option accounts was virtually indistinguishable from the trading conducted by hedge funds using their own brokerage accounts, and provided no justification for treating the resulting short-term trading profits as long-term capital gains.

The facts indicate that the basket option structures examined in this investigation were devised by sophisticated financial firms to allow clients to circumvent federal taxes and leverage limits. The structures rested on two fictions. The first was that the bank, rather than the hedge fund, owned the assets being traded in the designated option accounts, even though the hedge fund bought and sold the assets, was exposed to all significant risks and rewards, and profited from the trading, with little input from the bank serving as the nominal owner of the assets. In effect, the structure purported to enable the hedge fund to purchase an "option" on its own trading activity, an arrangement that makes no economic sense outside of an effort to bypass federal taxes and leverage limits. The second fiction was that the profits from the trades controlled by the hedge fund could be treated as long-term capital gains, even for trades lasting seconds. That fiction depended upon the hedge fund claiming that the profits came from exercising the "option" rather than from executing the underlying trades. In fact, the "option" functioned as little more than a fictional derivative, permitting the hedge fund to cast short-term capital gains as long-term gains and authorizing financing at levels otherwise legally barred for a customer's U.S. brokerage account.

The basket options sold by Deutsche Bank AG starting in 1998, and by Barclays Bank PLC since 2002, produced a total of more than $35 billion in trading profits, of which at least $34 billion came from options exercised after more than one year. Most of those profits came from assets which were held for less than one year but which were treated by the hedge funds holding the options as having produced long-term capital gains taxable at the lower long-term capital gains rate. The options were also used by the participating hedge funds to trade on borrowed funds using a leverage ratio of as much as 20:1, versus the much lower federal leverage limit of 2:1 that normally applies to brokerage accounts held by U.S. broker-dealers for their clients. These financially engineered products – which relied on high volume trading, leveraged funds, and artificially lowered tax rates to produce their profits – warrant greater attention from federal tax, securities, and banking regulators to prevent their continued misuse.

Chapter 2 - Statement of Senator Carl Levin, Chairman, Senate Permanent Subcommittee on Investigations.

Chapter 3 - Testimony of Steven M. Rosenthal, Senior Fellow, Urban-Brookings Tax Policy Center.

Chapter 4 - Statement of Marty Malloy, Managing Director, Barclays.

Chapter 5 - Joint Testimony of Barry Bausano, President, and Satish Ramakrishna, Managing Director, Deutsche Bank Securities,Inc.

Chapter 6 - Joint Statement of Peter F. Brown, Co-CEO, Mark Silber, CFO, and Jonathan Mayers, Counsel, Renaissance Technologies LLC.

Chapter 7 - Statement of Gerard LaRocca, Chief Administrative Officer, Barclays.

In: Structured Financial Products ...
Editor: Lenora Osborne
ISBN: 978-1-63463-785-5

Chapter 1

ABUSE OF STRUCTURED FINANCIAL PRODUCTS: MISUSING BASKET OPTIONS TO AVOID TAXES AND LEVERAGE LIMITS[*]

Permanent Subcommittee on Investigations

I. EXECUTIVE SUMMARY

For the last decade, the U.S. Senate Permanent Subcommittee on Investigations has presented case histories showing how financial institutions, law firms, accountants, and others have designed and implemented complex financial structures to take advantage of and, at times, abuse or violate U.S. tax statutes, securities regulations, and accounting rules.[1] This investigation offers yet another detailed case study of how two financial institutions – Deutsche Bank AG and Barclays Bank PLC – developed structured financial products called MAPS and COLT, two types of basket options, and sold them to one or more hedge funds, including Renaissance Technologies LLC and George Weiss Associates, that used them to avoid federal taxes and leverage limits on buying securities with borrowed funds. While that type of option product was identified as abusive in a public memorandum by the Internal Revenue Service

---

[*] This is an edited, reformatted and augmented version of a Majority and Minority Staff Report of the Senate Committee on Homeland Security and Governmental Affairs, Permanent Subcommittee on Investigations, issued July 22, 2014.

(IRS) in 2010, taxes have yet to be collected on many of the basket option transactions and its use to circumvent federal leverage limits has yet to be analyzed or halted.

The basket option contracts examined by the Subcommittee investigation were used by at least 13 hedge funds to conduct over $100 billion in securities trades, most of which were short- term transactions and some of which lasted only seconds. Yet the resulting short-term profits were frequently cast as long-term capital gains subject to a 20% tax rate (previously 15%) rather than the ordinary income tax rate (currently as high as 39%) that would otherwise apply to investors in hedge funds engaged in daily trading. While the banks styled the trading arrangement as an "option" under which profits from short-term trades would be treated as long- term capital gains, in essence, the banks loaned the hedge funds money to finance their trading and allowed them to trade for themselves in highly leveraged positions in the banks' proprietary accounts and reap the resulting profits. The banks offering the "options" benefited from the financing, trading, and other fees charged to the hedge funds initiating the trades. In the end, the trading conducted by the hedge funds using the basket option accounts was virtually indistinguishable from the trading conducted by hedge funds using their own brokerage accounts, and provided no justification for treating the resulting short-term trading profits as long-term capital gains.

The facts indicate that the basket option structures examined in this investigation were devised by sophisticated financial firms to allow clients to circumvent federal taxes and leverage limits. The structures rested on two fictions. The first was that the bank, rather than the hedge fund, owned the assets being traded in the designated option accounts, even though the hedge fund bought and sold the assets, was exposed to all significant risks and rewards, and profited from the trading, with little input from the bank serving as the nominal owner of the assets. In effect, the structure purported to enable the hedge fund to purchase an "option" on its own trading activity, an arrangement that makes no economic sense outside of an effort to bypass federal taxes and leverage limits. The second fiction was that the profits from the trades controlled by the hedge fund could be treated as long-term capital gains, even for trades lasting seconds. That fiction depended upon the hedge fund claiming that the profits came from exercising the "option" rather than from executing the underlying trades. In fact, the "option" functioned as little more than a fictional derivative, permitting the hedge fund to cast short-term capital gains as long-term gains and authorizing financing at levels otherwise legally barred for a customer's U.S. brokerage account.

The basket options sold by Deutsche Bank AG starting in 1998, and by Barclays Bank PLC since 2002, produced a total of more than $35 billion in trading profits, of which at least $34 billion came from options exercised after more than one year. Most of those profits came from assets which were held for less than one year but which were treated by the hedge funds holding the options as having produced long-term capital gains taxable at the lower long-term capital gains rate. The options were also used by the participating hedge funds to trade on borrowed funds using a leverage ratio of as much as 20:1, versus the much lower federal leverage limit of 2:1 that normally applies to brokerage accounts held by U.S. broker-dealers for their clients. These financially engineered products – which relied on high volume trading, leveraged funds, and artificially lowered tax rates to produce their profits – warrant greater attention from federal tax, securities, and banking regulators to prevent their continued misuse.

A. Subcommittee Investigation

To conduct this investigation, the Subcommittee subpoenaed, collected, and reviewed over 1.5 million pages of documents from Deutsche Bank AG (Deutsche Bank), Barclays Bank PLC (Barclays), Renaissance Technologies Corporation LLC (RenTec), George Weiss Associates (George Weiss), and BDO Seidman, RenTec's accountant. The Subcommittee obtained additional information from these entities through information requests and a review of publicly available information. The Subcommittee also participated in 23 interviews and briefings involving current and former employees from those financial institutions. In addition, the Subcommittee gathered documents, obtained information, and received briefings from a number of federal agencies and related parties. The Subcommittee also spoke with academic and other tax experts concerning the tax treatment of basket options. Deutsche Bank, Barclays, RenTec, George Weiss, and the agencies all cooperated with Subcommittee requests for information.

B. Investigation Overview

The Subcommittee investigation examined the basket option financial products designed and promoted by Deutsche Bank and Barclays. It also examined how the hedge funds that entered into basket option contracts with those two banks actually used those contracts to make investments, looking in particular at the two largest participants, RenTec and George Weiss.

Purchasing a Basket Option. The basket option contracts were designed and issued by the sponsoring bank and held by the option holder. In the cases examined by the Subcommittee, the option holder was always a hedge fund. Typically, to initiate the transaction, the hedge fund client entered into a contract with the bank to purchase an "option" on the performance of an unspecified basket of assets placed in a designated account. The referenced account was opened in the name of the bank and operated as the bank's own proprietary trading account. All assets were purchased in the name of the bank.

To reduce trading risk, the option contract normally set a few basic parameters for the assets that could be purchased for the account, but otherwise provided wide discretion over the assets to be selected. The hedge fund was required to deposit into the account a cash "premium," which typically consisted of funds representing about 10% of the total capital to be invested in the account and functioned as collateral for the account. The sponsoring bank financed the other 90% of the capital to be invested, and the hedge fund paid financing fees on that financed amount. The designated account then used the funds from the premium and credit extension to conduct trades until the option holder exercised the option. If at the time the option was exercised, the securities in the referenced account had produced a profit, the bank had to pay those profits to the hedge fund holding the option, after subtracting fees for certain trading, financing, and other expenses.

In the basket option contracts examined by the Subcommittee, the bank always appointed the general partner of the hedge fund client to act as the investment advisor for the trading account holding the referenced assets during the duration of the option. Once appointed, the investment adviser exercised complete control over the securities included in the option account, designing its own trading strategy and using the bank's own facilities to execute the trades. In some cases reviewed by the Subcommittee, the investment advisor used algorithms to engage in a high volume of trading, executing more than 100,000 transactions per day. Many of those trading positions lasted minutes, and the overall composition of the securities basket changed on a second-to-second basis. One basket option account later reviewed by the U.S. Securities and Exchange Commission (SEC) was found to have experienced 129 million orders in a year. In other cases, the investment adviser purchased securities whose positions remained unchanged for weeks, but all of the basket option accounts reviewed by the Subcommittee were dominated by short-term trading involving assets held less than one year.

By acting as the investment adviser, the hedge fund – the option holder – became the party that actually controlled the trading strategy, the timing of trades, and what assets were selected for the referenced account. The hedge fund was also exposed to all significant rewards and risks associated with the trading. The banks claimed that the hedge funds did not bear 100% of the risk of loss, because the banks provided so-called "gap" protection in the event of a catastrophic market failure. That risk was so small, however, that despite, for example, hundreds of millions of trades that took place in the more than 60 basket options held by RenTec over a decade, including during the worst financial crisis in a generation, neither bank was ever required to satisfy a loss due to a market failure.

To further minimize the gap risk, the option contract contained several provisions designed to limit trading losses in the account to the 10% premium provided by the hedge fund. The key provision accomplished that objective by specifying a loss threshold – sometimes called a "barrier" or "knockout" amount – which if reached would cause the option to cease to exist, or "knockout," and trigger the ability of the bank to liquidate the account assets.

During the period of the option, the securities transactions were executed in the name of the bank and the resulting securities were held in the bank's proprietary trading account. The accompanying profits or losses also remained within the account until the option was exercised. The hedge fund chose when to exercise the option. Although the options reviewed by the Subcommittee often had three-year terms and the hedge funds claimed they wanted longer-term financing arrangements, the hedge funds often exercised the options shortly after 12 months. In all cases examined by the Subcommittee, the option accounts paid the profits to the hedge fund option holder.

Deutsche Bank developed its basket option product in 1998, naming it the Managed Account Product Structure (MAPS). Over the next 15 years, Deutsche Bank sold 156 MAPS options, of which 96 had terms greater than one year. At their peak, those 96 options had assets with a total initial notional value of about $60 billion. Deutsche Bank sold the MAPS options to 13 hedge funds, including 36 to RenTec. Of those 36 option contracts, the first 29 had terms greater than one year. The MAPS options sold to RenTec produced profits for that hedge fund totaling about $17 billion. The MAPS options sold to all 13 hedge funds produced revenues for Deutsche Bank totaling about $570 million. The Barclays' basket options product was developed in 2002, at the request of RenTec, and was named COLT. Barclays sold 43 COLT options to RenTec, of which 31 had terms greater than one year. At their peak, those 31 COLT options had assets with a total initial notional value of about $62 billion. The COLT options produced trading profits for RenTec totaling about $18.5 billion. They also produced revenues for Barclays totaling about $655 million.

Claiming Long-Term Capital Gains. With respect to basket options that were exercised more than one year after the option was created, the hedge funds holding those options claimed that any short-term trading profits earned within the option period could be recast as long-term capital gains for U.S. tax purposes after the option was exercised. They claimed that even trades that had lasted a few seconds or were executed the day before the option was exercised could be treated as long-term capital gains, although the lower capital gains tax rate was explicitly intended to reward holding a security for more than one year.

The basket option contracts administered by Deutsche Bank and Barclays over the last ten years produced profits utilizing hundreds of millions of trades, with 97% of the assets held for less than 6 months, yet the trading profits were treated by the hedge funds as long-term gains. In one SEC examination report that reviewed some of those options, the SEC estimated that, during a four-year period from April 2003 through October 2007, five hedge funds utilizing MAPS options, including RenTec, had "saved a total of $779 million in taxes by exercising the option after one year."[2] Another SEC examination report on the COLT option, used by RenTec over a five-year period from 2002 to 2007, found that the hedge fund had used it to "defer $140 million of taxes."[3] The resulting total of $919 million does not take into account other taxes avoided or deferred by hedge funds using basket options from 1999 through March 2003, or from November 2007 to the present.

Although the Subcommittee does not have the information needed to estimate the total amount of taxes avoided through use of the basket options examined during this investigation, specific data supplied by the banks with respect to RenTec, the largest basket option user, suggests that the basket options may have been used to treat short-term capital gains as long-term capital gains, resulting in estimated tax avoidance of more than $6 billion. This chart provides the data used to arrive at that estimate.

RenTec Basket Options Held for More than One Year 2000-2013

Bank	Number of Options	Cash Payments to Settle Options*	Premiums Paid by RenTec	Cash Payments Less Premiums	Estimated Tax Difference between LTCG Rate and STCG Rate[1]
Barclays[2]	31	$24.5	$6.2	$18.3	$3.6
Deutsche Bank	29	$20.8	$4.8	$15.9	$3.2
Total	60	$45.3	$11.0	$34.2	$6.83

*All dollar figures in billions of dollars.

1. LTCG stands for Long-Term Capital Gains (rate was 15% until 2013, 20% thereafter); STCG stands for Short-Term Capital Gains (used rate of 35%). The difference between the two was calculated at 20% for options exercised prior to 2013, and at 15% thereafter.
2. Table excludes three RenTec options at Barclays, despite being in effect for over one year, because they are unexercised.
3. Total does not reflect any other income, deductions, credits, or other tax matters that might affect RenTec's tax liability.

Source: Tables produced by Deutsche Bank (DB-PSI 00052588) and Barclays (BARCLAYS-PSI-748604). Prepared by U.S. Senate Permanent Subcommittee on Investigations, July 2014.

Disallowing Abusive Basket Options. In 2010, the IRS issued a Generic Legal Advice Memorandum (GLAM) which found that basket options referencing accounts with ever- changing assets did not function as true option contracts, and that investors had to recognize the trading gains and losses in the designated accounts when they occurred, rather than at the time the alleged "option" was finally exercised. The IRS advised that investors could not use the basket option contracts to justify applying the long-term capital gains tax rate to what were really short-term gains.

Despite learning of the GLAM when it was issued in 2010, and interpreting it as applying to the COLT basket options it offered, Barclays continued to sell COLT options to RenTec for the next two years. In contrast, after the GLAM was issued, Deutsche Bank suspended issuing new MAPS basket options, although it continued to administer multiple option accounts already trading assets. In 2012, Deutsche Bank began offering them again, but only with options whose terms lasted less than one year and contractually required all profits to be reported as short-term capital gains. In 2013, Barclays revised its basket option contract so that it, too, offered only basket options with terms that lasted less than one year and could not be used to claim long-term capital gains.

According to information provided by RenTec to the Subcommittee, the IRS notified the hedge fund in 2012, that the IRS had reviewed some of its basket option trading activity and intended to disallow long-term capital gains treatment of basket option profits from trades lasting less than 12 months. The IRS also proposed an assessment of additional taxes for certain tax years. RenTec submitted a letter in opposition, and the matter is apparently now awaiting review by the IRS' internal Office of Appeals.

Circumventing Federal Leverage Limits. In addition to using basket options to reduce taxes on their short-term capital gains, the hedge funds used them to obtain financing for securities trades far in excess of what federal leverage limits allow. Federal leverage limits were established in response to the stock market crash of 1929, when securities purchased on borrowed funds magnified stock market losses and caused failures of, not only the stock speculators, but also the banks and broker-dealers that lent them money. Federal "margin rules" were enacted to impose a leverage limit of 2:1 on brokerage accounts opened by U.S. broker- dealers for their customers. In contrast, because the participating banks seemingly lent money to their own accounts, the basket option accounts examined by the Subcommittee provided the hedge fund option holders with leverage ratios as high as 20:1. RenTec indicated in one document that it had been unable to attain such high leverage levels in any other setting. While federal financial regulators are aware of ongoing efforts to bypass federal leverage limits through derivative and structured financial products, including basket options, they have not taken the steps necessary to obtain meaningful data on the extent of the leverage problem, gauge the resulting systemic risks, or develop ways to curb abuses.

C. Findings of Fact

Based upon the Subcommittee investigation, this Report makes the following findings of fact.

1. **Profiting from Basket Options.** Between 1998 and 2013, Deutsche Bank AG sold basket option products to 13 hedge funds, while

Barclays Bank PLC sold them to one hedge fund, together leading to over $100 billion in securities trades and tens of billions of dollars in profits, most of which came from trades that lasted less than 12 months in duration, but were treated by the hedge funds as producing long-term capital gains. The basket options also produced financing, trading, and other fee revenue for the banks totaling $570 million for Deutsche Bank and $655 million for Barclays.

2. **Turning a Blind Eye.** Deutsche Bank AG and Barclays Bank PLC were aware of the questionable tax status of their basket option structures for many years prior to the issuance of the 2010 IRS advisory memorandum, but continued to sell the product.
3. **Claiming Short-Term Trading Profits as Long-Term Capital Gains.** Over a fourteen-year period from 1999 to 2013, one hedge fund, Renaissance Technologies LLC, held 60 basket option contracts for more than one year, used them to carry out an investment strategy utilizing hundreds of millions of trades, virtually all of which lasted less than 12 months, and characterized the vast majority of the resulting $34 billion in trading profits as long-term capital gains.
4. **Ceding Control.** Although the investments in the basket option trading accounts were held in the name of the banks, Deutsche Bank and Barclays routinely hired the option holder – the hedge fund – as the investment adviser for the accounts and ceded control of their accounts to the option holder, which traded the account for its own benefit.
5. **Assessing Risk.** Although Deutsche Bank and Barclays claimed the basket option structure was a valid derivative in part because it carried financial risk for the bank, Barclays downplayed that risk both internally and in reports to its U.K. regulator when it benefited the banks' interests.
6. **Avoiding Leverage Limits.** By opening the basket option accounts in their own names and supplying their own funds to those accounts as financing for the trades controlled by their hedge fund clients, Deutsche Bank and Barclays enabled the hedge funds to attain a leverage ratio of as high as 20:1, despite the much lower federal leverage limit of 2:1 intended to prevent systemic risk.
7. **Producing a Low Audit Rate.** While, in 2010, the IRS determined that basket options were being misused and, in 2012, proposed additional tax liability for one hedge fund, the Government Accountability Office has determined that 99% of the tax returns filed

by large partnerships with assets exceeding $100 million have not been audited by the IRS. This extremely low auditing rate may embolden large partnerships such as hedge funds to employ abusive tax structures.

8. **Failing to Enforce Leverage Limits.** Although federal financial regulators have long been aware that derivative and structured financial products, including basket options, are being used to circumvent federal leverage limits, they have taken little or no action to limit those practices and enforce the statutory limits on purchasing securities with borrowed funds.

D. Recommendations

Based upon the Subcommittee investigation and findings of fact, the Report makes the following recommendations.

1. **Collect Additional Taxes Owed on Basket Option Profits.** The IRS should audit the hedge funds that used Deutsche Bank or Barclays basket option products, disallow any characterization of profits from trades lasting less than 12 months as long-term capital gains, and collect from those hedge funds any unpaid taxes.
2. **Stop Bank Participation in Abusive Tax Structures.** To end bank involvement with abusive tax structures, federal financial regulators, as well as Treasury and the IRS, should intensify their warnings against, scrutiny of, and legal actions to penalize bank participation in tax-motivated transactions.
3. **Revamp TEFRA.** Treasury and the IRS should revamp the Tax Equity and Fiscal Responsibility Act (TEFRA) regulations to reduce impediments to audits of large partnerships like hedge funds, and Congress should consider amendments to TEFRA to facilitate those audits.
4. **Stop Circumvention of Leverage Limits.** The Financial Stability Oversight Council, working with other agencies, should establish new reporting and data collection mechanisms to enable financial regulators to analyze the use of derivative and structured financial products to circumvent federal leverage limits on purchasing securities with borrowed funds, gauge the systemic risks, and develop preventative measures.

II. BACKGROUND

This chapter provides an overview of the nature, mechanics, and tax and securities implications of derivatives, options, and basket options. It also reviews key tax principles and provisions, a 1999 statutory change that attempted to stop option abuses, and the IRS' decision making related to basket options.

A. General Description of Derivatives

A financial "derivative" is a broad term covering a variety of different financial instruments, all of which share the common property that their value is dependent upon an underlying asset.[4] Derivatives can take numerous forms, including options, swaps, futures, forwards, structured debt obligations, and others.[5] Derivatives can also be traded in two different ways: some are traded through standardized instruments over exchanges, while others are traded privately through individualized contracts, also called "over-the-counter," "bilateral," or "bespoke" derivatives.[6]

Derivatives can be used to trade for profit, alter the risk-reward profile of some other asset, or make risky and sometimes leveraged bets on the future value of equities, options, bonds, interest rates, companies, or even financial markets as a whole.[7] Also, they are often used by large banks to hedge or reduce financial risks related to a variety of complex transactions.[8] Derivatives can also be designed to operate in tandem, and combinations of options, forwards, swaps, or more esoteric transactions can be used to engineer economic returns equivalent to any single derivative or to ownership of the underlying positions.[9]

(1) Taxes, Leverage Limits, and Transparency Problems

A derivative is, in essence, a financial bet. In many cases, it allows the derivative holder to obtain the same economic effect as if the holder owned the relevant financial instrument, such as a bond or shares of stock. However, instead of owning the instrument, the derivative holder can derive value by referencing the instrument and bet that it will go up or down in value.

Economically identical positions may sometimes be treated differently for tax purposes depending upon the nature of the financial instrument at issue. Derivatives can enable a taxpayer to elect a form of ownership that defers payment of taxes and characterizes income in the form most advantageous to the taxpayer.[10] Differences in the tax treatment of derivatives versus other types of financial instruments can also lead to market inefficiencies. First, resources may be wasted paying for tax planning on two economically equivalent positions.[11] Second, using derivatives to minimize the payment of tax may result in needlessly complex financial arrangements, and inefficient taxes in other areas to make up for the lost revenues.[12] Despite those problems, derivatives continue in some cases to receive more favorable tax treatment than other financial instruments.[13]

Derivatives have been used by taxpayers in the past to take advantage of "economic imperfections in the tax law" and lower their taxes.[14] In 2008, for example, the Subcommittee identified a situation in which U.S. financial institutions were using derivatives to assist hedge funds in avoiding taxes owed on U.S. stock dividends. The Subcommittee found that the banks were designing and engaging in swap transactions with those hedge funds to disguise stock dividend payments and avoid paying millions of dollars in dividend taxes each year.[15]

Derivative instruments may also be used to circumvent federal leverage limits.[16] Federal securities laws and financial regulations currently impose restrictions on the use of credit to purchase securities.[17] Those restrictions were developed after highly leveraged securities transactions contributed to the stock market crash of 1929, and imposed losses, not only on stock speculators, but also on the banks and broker-dealers responsible for lending them funds.[18] Today, derivatives can be used to create more highly leveraged trading positions than otherwise permitted under current law, including by putting up significantly less collateral for a derivative trade than permitted for a direct purchase of a security.[19]

The extension of credit for securities transactions between customers and broker-dealers is governed by Regulation T.[20] Regulation T applies to customer accounts of U.S. broker- dealers and sets the margin requirements for stocks bought by customers on credit and used as collateral for the loan. Margin refers to the portion of the purchase price that the customer must deposit in cash as initial equity in the customer's securities trading account.[21] Those funds serve as collateral for the broker-dealer executing securities trades for the customer.[22] Under Regulation T, U.S. broker-dealers offering a U.S. prime brokerage account[23] to a client may lend that client up to 50% of the total price for stock purchases, but no more.[24]

Some market participants use various arrangements, including derivatives and structured financial products, to establish leveraged securities positions that far exceed Regulation T's margin limits. For example, in the case of a hedge fund with a basket option account in which a bank has agreed to lend 90% of the funds to be invested, the hedge fund could pay a premium of $1,000 to the bank and gain access to $10,000 for trading in the market. Because the bank supposedly owns the securities in the option account, it is supposedly supplying funds to that account for its own trading, rather than lending money to the hedge fund, even though the hedge fund is conducting the trading and taking all of the profits. By using this "option" account rather than a regular prime brokerage account, the hedge fund and the bank claim they can circumvent the leverage limits in Regulation T.[25]

Some derivative transactions may also create transparency problems. For example, a derivative may provide an opportunity for a purchaser to avoid the ownership reporting requirements under the securities laws. Schedule 13D requires any person with a beneficial ownership interest of more than 5% of any class of publicly traded securities in a company to report that interest in a filing to the SEC.[26] A purchaser who wants to acquire more than 5% of a company may delay reporting the transaction to the SEC by using a swap transaction to achieve the economic equivalent of owning that portion of the shares.[27]

These leverage and transparency problems have been known for many years, but neither the SEC, bank regulators, nor the new Financial Stability Oversight Council have obtained the data needed to fully analyze the extent of leverage in the U.S. financial system, gauged the nature and extent of the systemic risks, or taken action to address the impact of derivatives and structured financial products on federal leverage limits and disclosure obligations.

(2) Options

An option is a form of derivative transaction. In general terms, an option is a "contract between two parties that gives the holder of the option the right but not the obligation to buy from (in the case of a call option) or sell to (in the case of a put option) the issuer of the option a specified amount of property … at a fixed price and specified time."[28] In the case of options on stock or other types of equity, an option on the underlying equity is a "contract that gives the holder of the option the right, but not the obligation, to buy from or to sell to the counterparty to the contract … a specified number of shares of [an underlying] equity security, at a fixed price."[29]

The forms and terms of options can vary greatly. A "European style" option, for example, can be exercised by the buyer only on a specified date, while an "American style" option can be exercised by the buyer any time prior to the final date on which the option expires.[30] The option buyer pays the option seller a "premium" for the option, which can vary with the terms of the option.[31] This premium is usually paid at the start of the option and is the potential profit for the option seller.[32] Options also have a "strike price," which is the price specified in the option contract at which the buyer may purchase the underlying property when exercising the option.[33] The final day on which an option may be exercised is generally called the "exercise date" or "maturity date."[34] Options are often priced using the Black-Scholes model, which takes into account several factors including the volatility of the price of the underlying assets, the duration of the option, and the strike price as compared to the market price of the underlying assets.[35]

Options and other derivatives can be used as tools to manage risk, especially in the prices of raw materials or in financial transactions that must be hedged to avoid losses.[36] Options can also be used speculatively to profit from securities transactions and even obtain leverage beyond the amount permitted by federal margin regulations.[37] For example, an option may have a premium of only $5 on a stock that costs $100 a share. A purchaser with $1,000 could then buy 10 shares of the stock or options on 200 shares of the same stock.

(3) Basket Options on a Basket of Securities

A basket option is typically an over-the-counter or negotiated derivative transaction between an option seller and buyer on an underlying set of assets. The structure investigated by the Subcommittee involved cash-settled basket options on a designated account containing an ever-changing basket of securities. When exercised, the option was settled with a cash payment to the option holder rather than providing the option holder with the assets in the basket. The amount of the cash payment reflected the profits earned on the basket as of the date the option was exercised.

The option buyer – which in the cases examined by the Subcommittee was always a hedge fund – purchased the option on the performance of the basket of securities which were held in a proprietary trading account– called a "managed account" – belonging to the option seller, the bank.[38] Although the account is opened in the name of the bank, the hedge fund served as the investment advisor to the managed account through an investment advisory agreement with the bank. In that role, the hedge fund had the exclusive right and discretion to determine what assets were purchased for and sold from the bank's account, subject to basic guidelines to reduce risk specified in the investment advisory agreement.[39] In the confirmation stating the terms of the option, the managed account was defined to include all of the assets and only the assets selected by the hedge fund, subject to the investment advisory agreement guidelines.[40]

For each basket option, the managed account served dual roles. In its first role, the account was described as serving as the reference for the option, so that the performance of the assets in the account determined the amount of gain or loss that the hedge fund realized when it exercised the option. In its second role, the managed account was described as serving as a "hedge" for the bank that sold the option, with the profits from the trades made in the account available to pay what was owed to the hedge fund when the hedge fund exercised the option.[41]

Since the hedge fund's gain or loss under the option was determined by the gain or loss in the managed account, as long as the bank executed all of the trade orders made by the hedge fund as the Investment Advisor, the value of the holdings in the managed account would match and cover the cost of any gain due to the hedge fund when the option was exercised.[42] Both Deutsche Bank and Barclays told the Subcommittee that they always executed the trades directed by the hedge fund acting as the Investment Advisor to ensure sufficient funds to pay off the option when exercised and to ensure the banks remained economically neutral with respect to the trading activity conducted by the hedge fund, acting as both Investment Advisor and option holder.[43]

In addition, in many of the basket options examined by the Subcommittee, the option buyer, the hedge fund, paid a cash premium equal to about 10% of the funds intended to be invested from the managed account and the bank then provided financing for the remaining 90%, charging interest on the funds provided by the bank. In other words, if the hedge fund paid a $1 million premium into the basket option account, the bank could deposit another $9 million into the account, giving the hedge fund, as Investment Advisor, a total of $10 million to invest, while charging interest on the $9 million loaned to the account. This financing arrangement greatly increased the amount of funds that the hedge fund, as Investment Advisor, had available to invest. It also magnified the potential investment profits or losses from the managed account.

Upon exercise, the hedge fund benefited from the option if the value of the securities in the managed account increased during the option period, while its risk of loss was limited to the amount of the premium it had paid to the bank. In other words, to continue the earlier example, if the account began experiencing losses, the hedge fund's losses would be limited to the $1 million premium it had deposited into the account. In contrast to the hedge fund which conducted the trades and benefited from the resulting profits or losses, the bank benefited from the option transaction primarily from fee revenues generated from the financing and trading fees it charged to the option holder for the trading activity in the managed account. The bank also benefitted from the revenues generated from its ability to lend out securities contained in the managed account.

The hedge fund also supposedly benefited from a certain amount of compensation paid by the bank for performing investment advisory services for the managed account. That compensation in at least one case was substantially below the standard hedge fund fees charged in the market for years, presumably because the hedge fund was investing on behalf of itself and not for the bank. For example, for years, RenTec was paid a minimal fixed fee by both Deutsche Bank and Barclays for acting as an Investment Advisor to basket options accounts at those institutions. Moreover, the banks did not pay the fee separately. Instead, the fee was subtracted from the option account's trading profits that would otherwise have been paid to the hedge fund upon exercise of the option. In 2008, Deutsche Bank increased the fee to give it the appearance of being in the range of a standard fee, but continued to deduct it from the trading profits in the option account. By agreeing to subtract the investment advisory fee from the trading profits otherwise owed to the hedge fund investors upon exercise of the option, the hedge fund's compensation was essentially limited to the total amount of profits produced by the trading strategy it directed.

Basket Option Advantages. A basket option constructed according to the terms just described are alleged to create several advantages for the buyer and the seller. First, because the option purports to act as a synthetic derivative product rather than as the direct trading of a portfolio of real assets, the option buyer pays only a small premium to participate in the trading of the assets. Second, the option enables the option buyer to gain financing for its securities investments far in excess of the Regulation T limits on leverage that would apply if it had purchased the securities directly through a prime brokerage account.[44] Essentially, Regulation T limits the leverage in a margin account to a ratio of 2:1, while the basket options arrangements reviewed by the Subcommittee generated a leverage ratio of as much as 20:1.

Third, the banks claimed that the basket options shifted the risk of short-term catastrophic market events from the option buyer to the option seller. Normally, the owner of a brokerage account bears the entire risk of losses on its holdings and can be forced to satisfy margin calls on its account or go into default. In a basket option structure, however, the option buyer's loss is limited under the basket options contracts to the amount of its premium. For example, if a hedge fund paid a $1 million premium, and the bank supplied $9 million in additional financing, even if the account losses exceeded $1 million, the hedge fund's loss would be capped at that amount. At the same time, the basket option contracts included provisions that permitted the banks to terminate any option in which substantial losses began to accumulate prior to exhausting the entire premium, thereby minimizing the risk of loss to the bank.[45] If the securities in the managed account dropped in value by more than the premium, despite provisions included in the option contract to preclude such additional losses, the option ceased to exist ("knocked out") and the option holder received nothing, while the option seller, in this case a major bank, bore the remainder of any additional loss.

The option seller benefits from the basket option arrangement through receipt of the premium and, in the case where the seller also provides financing for the purposes of leverage, from fees paid in exchange for the loans.[46] It also earns fees from executing transactions for the managed account which, in the case of high volume trading, can be substantial. In addition, the option seller can protect against any financial loss by hedging the option through the managed account and using the profits from the transactions in that account to cover any gains owed to the option buyer.

Potential Tax, Leverage, and Transparency Abuses. Basket options are vulnerable to the same tax, leverage, and transparency abuses identified above for derivatives generally. Of particular concern in the Subcommittee's investigation is abuse of basket options to avoid tax. Option buyers have used the basket option structure to characterize short-term trading profits from the daily trading activity in the managed account as long-term capital gains for tax purposes. Option buyers have claimed that those profits were entitled to long-term capital gains treatment, because the option itself was held open for more than one year and thereby lowered the tax rate an investor had to pay on the gains paid out upon the exercise of the option. Option buyers have also claimed that they were not required to recognize any taxable gain from dividends paid on securities in the managed account until the option is exercised, despite the fact that the option buyer was credited with the gains from those dividends prior to any exercise of the option. In addition to those tax abuses, basket options can be used to circumvent the leverage limits in Regulation T and the reporting requirements in Schedule 13D, as indicated earlier.

B. Overview of Tax Principles

To understand the tax issues raised by basket options, it is useful to review key tax principles involving the taxation of capital gains and stock dividends; an existing tax code section, Section 1260, that sought to stop the use of abusive derivatives, including options; and the judicial doctrine warning taxpayers against elevating form over substance to avoid taxation. Also relevant is a 2010 IRS advisory memorandum determining that basket option arrangements did not entitle the option holders to treat their short-term trading profits as long-term capital gains.

(1) Short and Long-Term Capital Gains Tax Treatment

Because basket options involve the trading of securities, one key tax issue involves the taxation of capital gains, and whether those gains should be taxed at the short or long-term rate. A related issue is when the gains are realized.

The profit realized from the sale of a capital asset is known as a capital gain.[47] Capital assets include stocks, options, bonds, precious metals, and real property held for investment.[48] When such an asset is sold, the difference between the amount paid for the asset and the amount for which it is sold is a capital gain.[49] When an asset is owned by a taxpayer for one year or less and sold, the gain is considered a "short-term" capital gain, and when the asset is held for more than a year at the time of sale, the gain is classified as a "long-term" capital gain.[50]

Long-term and short-term capital gains have long been taxed at different rates for individuals under the Internal Revenue Code.[51] To encourage long-term investments in the economy, the tax code has applied more favorable tax rates to longer term investments held by individuals, while short-term capital gains have been taxed at the taxpayer's ordinary income tax rate.[52] For example, if a taxpayer's ordinary income were taxed at a marginal rate of 35%, the taxpayer would pay that same tax rate on any short-term capital gains. In contrast, any long-term capital gains reported by the individual would currently be taxed at a rate of 20%. The level of the reduced rate for long-term capital gains has fluctuated since the introduction of personal income taxes in 1913.[53] During the period 2008 to 2012, for example, the long-term capital gains tax rate was 15%.[54]

Timing of Income. For federal income tax purposes, a "realization" event – an event in which a taxpayer realizes income – is required to determine the amount of taxable income from a capital asset that must be reported on a tax return. The Supreme Court described realization events as "undeniable accessions to wealth, clearly realized, and over which the taxpayers have complete dominion."[55] A taxpayer generally may not choose the timing of income to minimize the taxpayer's tax burden.[56] In other words, a taxpayer has realized and must report taxable income whenever the taxpayer sells a financial instrument, such as shares of stock, and experiences a financial gain.

In the case of derivatives, realization events under I.R.C. §1001 can occur at several different times. Often derivatives, such as options, are considered open transactions, which are not taxed during their life, but are instead taxed at a realization event, usually when the option is exercised or sold.[57] Other sections of the tax code mandate realization events, such as requirements that certain financial instruments be assigned a market value ("marked to market") on a regular or annual basis.[58] Additionally, even if the realization of income from a capital asset could otherwise be deferred, events that represent material or fundamental changes to that asset can result in an immediate realization event that requires the taxpayer to report the gain or loss on the taxpayer's tax return.[59]

Taxation of Hedge Fund Investors. Hedge funds are often organized as limited partnerships. Typically, the general partner of the hedge fund acts as the investment advisor and administers the fund, while investors provide the capital for the fund and hold limited partnership interests. Because the funds are taxed as partnerships, they are not taxed at the entity level, like a corporation, and are instead treated as pass-through entities for tax purposes. In other words, taxes owed by the partnership are not paid by the partnership, but are instead passed on to each individual partner who becomes responsible for paying any taxes owed. Because hedge funds are not taxed at the entity or fund level, the fund distributes to its investors their proportionate share of the fund's gains and losses for tax purposes. Investors are required to report the gains or losses on their individual tax returns based upon the character of the income or gain earned by the fund. Investors pay taxes on the gains or losses at the short-term capital gains rate if the investment was held by the fund for a year or less, and taxes at the long-term capital gains rate if the fund held the investment for more than one year.

(2) Taxation of Stock Dividends

Because basket options involve the trading of securities, another key tax issue involves the taxation of stock dividends.

Dividends Generally. A dividend is a distribution by a corporation of a portion of its earnings to its stockholders, with the amount to be distributed based upon the number of shares held by each stockholder. If the dividend recipient is a U.S. person, at the end of the calendar year, the recipient must report all dividends received on the recipient's tax return as part of that taxpayer's taxable income.[60] Under the tax code, U.S. stock dividends are treated as ordinary income and taxed at the ordinary income tax rate, unless they fall into a special category of "qualified dividends" in which case they are taxed at a 0%, 15%, or 20% rate depending on the tax bracket of the taxpayer.

Dividend Withholding. Different rules apply to stock dividends paid by U.S. corporations to nonresident alien individuals or non-U.S. corporations, partnerships, or other entities ("non-U.S. persons"). Dividends paid to non-U.S. persons that are not connected with a U.S. business are subject to a tax rate of 30%, absent a tax treaty between United States and the non-U.S. person's country of residence setting a lower rate.[61]

U.S. tax law also requires the 30% tax to be "deducted and withheld at the source" of the dividend payment being made to the non-U.S. person.[62] The purpose of this requirement is to ensure that the tax owed on the dividend payment is withheld and remitted to the IRS, before the dividend payment leaves the United States, since the United States is generally without authority to compel collection of U.S. taxes outside of its borders.[63]

The tax code's tax withholding regime for U.S. stock dividends has been in place for decades.[64] The law requires the U.S. withholding agent to withhold the appropriate amount of tax from the dividend payment and remit the withheld amount to the IRS, before sending the rest of the dividend payment to the non-U.S. recipient.

Dividends and Basket Options. The dividend and capital gains tax requirements apply to all transactions involving securities. In the case of the basket options examined in this investigation, if a stock held in an options trading account were to pay a dividend, that dividend was typically paid to the bank in whose name the stock was held. The bank then credited the dividend amount to the appropriate options account, increasing the total amount of trading profits in that account.

Some basket options proponents claim, as explained earlier, that the basket option arrangement enables the option holder to treat those stock dividends as incorporated into the option's overall gains, which can qualify as long-term capital gains if the option is exercised more than one year from inception. Some also claim that including the dividends in the option's overall gains could enable the hedge fund's investors to defer paying tax on the dividends to a year later than the year in which the dividends were paid, depending upon when the option is exercised. In addition, some might claim that the option arrangement could enable a non-U.S. hedge fund to claim a lower tax rate than the 30% withholding rate that applies to some dividends paid to non-U.S. persons. Each of those claims depends upon the validity of the option structure, and whether or not preferential tax treatment should be given to dividends that are paid into an option account compared to dividends that are paid into a regular brokerage account without a basket option structure.

If the IRS were to disregard the option structure, treat the hedge funds as owning the underlying securities, and take note of the dividends paid by the hedge funds to their non-U.S. partners, the IRS might determine that the banks or the hedge funds failed to meet their withholding obligations and seek to collect the taxes that should have been withheld, plus interest and penalties.

(3) Section 1260

During the 1990s, after some investors attempted to use derivatives, including options on hedge funds, to convert short-term trading profits into long-term capital gains subject to a lower tax rate, Congress enacted a new tax code provision, Section 1260, to stop the practice.[65] While that tax code provision demonstrated Congressional intent to stop abusive derivatives, including abusive options, its provisions were drawn narrowly to stop the problematic tax schemes then under scrutiny and have not since been expanded by regulation to capture similarly abusive structures. Nevertheless, Section 1260 provides historical context in analyzing the use of basket options to avoid taxes on short-term capital gains.

The abusive derivatives used prior to enactment of Section 1260 often involved an investment bank and hedge fund.[66] The goal of the strategy was to permit an investor in a hedge fund to convert their short-term gains from the hedge fund into long-term gains. The investment bank designed the derivative so that it functioned like an ownership interest in the hedge fund, with its value linked to the hedge fund's investment performance. The bank marketed the derivative to clients as an alternative to investing directly in the hedge fund.[67] To "hedge" its derivative, the investment bank became the partner in the hedge fund.[68] The strategy sought to allow the investment bank's clients to take advantage of the hedge fund's high pre-tax returns from short-term trading activity (which would normally be treated as short-term capital gains) using a derivative that would be held for over a year, contending that after the derivative was cashed out, the short-term trading profits could be treated as long-term capital gains.[69] At the time, the strategy was estimated to produce an 8% tax savings on the investment activity.[70]

In 1999, to stop the abuses, Congress enacted Section 1260. Section 1260 treats the profits from the "constructive ownership" of specified "financial assets" as ordinary income, not long-term capital gains.[71] The conference report from the House of Representatives explained that, without Section 1260: "[i]nvestors may enter into forward contracts, notional principal contracts, and other similar arrangements with respect to property that provides the investor with the same or similar economic benefits as owning the property directly but with potentially different tax consequences."[72] The conference report also explained that Section 1260 would limit "the amount of long-term capital gain a taxpayer could recognize from certain derivative contracts ('constructive ownership transactions') … to the amount of such gain the taxpayer would have recognized if the taxpayer held the financial asset directly during the term of the derivative contract."[73]

Section 1260 defined "constructive ownership" as applying to one of four types of transactions in which the taxpayer:

> "(A) holds a long position under a notional principal contract with respect to the financial asset,
>
> (B) enters into a forward or futures contract to acquire the financial asset,
>
> (C) is the holder of a call option, and is the grantor of a put option, with respect to the financial asset and such options have substantially equal strike prices and substantially contemporaneous maturity dates, or
>
> (D) to the extent provided in regulations prescribed by the Secretary, enters into one or more other transactions (or acquires one or more positions) that have substantially the same effect as a transaction described in any of the preceding subparagraphs."[74]

The statute also defined "financial asset" as an equity interest in any pass-thru entity (like an interest in a partnership), and authorized the IRS to write regulations to expand the definition of "financial asset" to cover stocks and bonds. Despite the statute's broad intent to stop taxpayers from misusing derivatives, including options, to treat short-term trading profits as long-term capital gains, the IRS has not used the regulatory authority granted in Section 1260 to capture transactions that are substantially similar to, but distinct from, those specified in the provision. So for example, while basket options mirror the abusive schemes prohibited by Section 1260, Treasury has not issued regulations that clearly capture basket options as one of the abusive structures prohibited by the provision.

According to some experts, it was understood at the time that option structures could continue to get around this section of the tax code by using a variety of strategies.[75] Despite the enactment of Section 1260, some financial institutions and hedge funds continued to market derivative strategies, including options, to transform short-term trading profits into long-term capital gains.

(4) Substance over Form Doctrine

It has long been a principle of federal tax law that the substance of a transaction, and not its form, will determine the federal income tax consequences of the transaction.[76] In 1924, in one of its earliest articulations of the substance over form doctrine, the Supreme Court said: "Questions of taxation must be determined by viewing what was actually done, rather than the declared purpose of the participants. ... [W]hen applying … income [tax] laws … we must regard matters of substance and not mere form."[77]

According to the Joint Committee on Taxation of the U.S. Congress, while a taxpayer's legal right "to decrease the amount of what otherwise would be his taxes, or altogether avoid them, by means which the law permits cannot be doubted," the court "applied the sham transaction doctrine to deny the tax benefits" when the taxpayer's activity circumvents the purpose of the tax code.[78] One of the judicial doctrines used to deny such tax advantaged transactions designed to circumvent the Internal Revenue Code is the substance over form doctrine.[79] Again, according to the Joint Committee on Taxation: "The concept of the substance over form doctrine is that the tax results of an arrangement are better determined based on the underlying substance rather than an evaluation of the mere formal steps by which the arrangement was undertaken." [80]

The substance over form judicial doctrine permits the IRS to re-characterize a transaction according to its actual substance.[81] According to a leading tax expert, "to permit the true nature of a transaction to be disguised by mere formalisms which exist solely to alter tax liabilities would seriously impair the effective administration of the tax policies of Congress."[82] Under rulings of the Supreme Court, the substance over form doctrine allows the IRS and the courts to look holistically at a transaction to understand its nature and bypass any titles or formalities used to disguise the transaction for tax purposes.[83] For example, the IRS may apply the substance over form doctrine in analyzing whether a derivative, such as an option, should more properly be analyzed as a direct investment in the underlying or referenced assets through the use of "a disguised agency arrangement" with a counterparty, since the derivative can be used to achieve economic returns indistinguishable from the direct investment in the underlying physical security.[84]

Step Transaction Doctrine. The step transaction doctrine is a corollary of the substance over form doctrine. It treats a series of separate transactions as a single transaction if the separate transactions were, in substance, steps that were intended to be "integrated" and "focused" toward a result to avoid taxation.[85] According to the Joint Committee on Taxation: "In determining whether to invoke the step transaction doctrine, the courts have looked to two primary factors: (1) the intent of the taxpayer, and (2) the temporal proximity of the separate steps."[86] Courts have held that the doctrine should not apply if the taxpayer can show that at the time the first of a series of steps was undertaken, the taxpayer did not intend to affect the other steps.[87] Courts have also held that the step transaction doctrine may apply even if a taxpayer can identify a valid business purpose. As one appeals court stated: "'[A] legitimate business goal does not grant [a] taxpayer carte blanche to subvert Congressionally mandated tax patterns.'"[88]

(5) 2010 IRS Basket Options Memorandum

On November 12, 2010, the IRS issued Generic Legal Advice Memorandum (GLAM) No. AM2010-005, determining that an option used to purchase a basket of securities that is essentially managed by the taxpayer holding the option should not be treated as an option for tax purposes.[89] Instead, the taxpayer should be treated as owning the securities underlying the alleged option and pay the taxes owed on any capital gains.

GLAMs are issued by the Associate Chief Counsel of the IRS to provide authoritative legal opinions to IRS personnel on matters relevant to administering the federal tax code. While the IRS does not use or cite GLAMs as legal precedent in court, they provide authoritative information on the agency's views of key tax issues.[90]

The 2010 GLAM addressed an options structure involving a foreign bank and a hedge fund whose general partner had been made the investment advisor in charge of creating and trading the basket of securities that was the focus of the option. In the fact pattern set out in the GLAM, the hedge fund entered into an options contract with the foreign bank, with the option payoff equal to the gains produced by a "dynamic" basket of securities, also called the "Reference Basket."[91] The fact pattern described in the GLAM was analogous to the basket option structures at Deutsche Bank and Barclays examined in this investigation.

In the GLAM, the IRS concluded: (1) the contract did not function like an option, and should not be treated as an option; and (2) the taxpayer should be treated as the owner of the underlying securities, because it had control over the securities, had the full opportunity for gain, and bore the substantial risk of loss.[92] Refusing to elevate form over substance, the IRS rejected the contract's formalistic invocation of an option and determined instead that the hedge fund, in substance, owned the securities underlying the Reference Basket.[93] The GLAM observed that, to determine ownership of stock, the most relevant factors courts have considered are the ability to sell shares, the power to vote, the right to receive dividends, and the opportunity for gain and risk of loss.[94] The IRS concluded that the hedge fund had most of those attributes and should be treated as the tax owner of the securities in the basket, because the hedge fund had the opportunity for full gain, bore the substantial risk of loss, and had complete control over the securities in the basket.[95] It also noted that the hedge fund bore the risk of loss up to its entire premium.[96] Even though the securities were held in the name of the foreign bank, the GLAM determined that the foreign bank did not bear substantial risk for the basket of securities, because it had rights to liquidate the securities or force risk-reducing trades.[97]

In essence, like this Report, the IRS determined that the basket option contracts had created fictional derivatives that should be disregarded for tax purposes.

III. Basket Option Case Studies

The financial institutions that most extensively promoted and used the basket option structure from 1998 to 2013, were Deutsche Bank, Barclays, and hedge funds RenTec and George Weiss. The Subcommittee's case studies involving their actions illustrate how basket options have been used to circumvent taxes and federal leverage limits.

A. Basket Option Participants

(1) Deutsche Bank

Deutsche Bank AG (Deutsche Bank) was founded in 1870 and is headquartered in Frankfurt, Germany.[98] Deutsche Bank is the largest bank in

Germany and one of the largest financial institutions in the world.[99] It had total assets of over $2.2 trillion as of December 31, 2013.[100] As of December 31, 2012, Deutsche Bank employed about 100,000 people on a full- time basis and operated over 3,000 branches worldwide in 72 countries, with nearly 50% of its employees located in Germany.[101] Deutsche Bank is a global investment bank and offers a wide variety of investment, financial, and related products and services to private individuals, corporate entities, and institutional clients around the world.

Deutsche Bank has offices in major centers including London and New York City.[102] It has eight major entities in the United States.[103] Deutsche Bank AG New York Branch deals with derivatives trading and standard deposit and currency transactions; the New York Branch, along with almost all other U.S. entities, is Deutsche Bank AG's subsidiary.[104] Other subsidiaries include Deutsche Bank Securities Inc., a SEC-registered broker dealer and investment advisor, and Deutsche Bank Trust Corporation, a bank holding company.[105]

Deutsche Bank offers financial products and services for corporate and institutional clients along with business and high net worth clients.[106] Services include global banking; corporate finance; sales, trading and structuring of financial products; mergers and acquisitions; and investment and wealth management.[107]

Jürgen Fitschen and Anshu Jain are the current co-Chief Executive Officers of Deutsche Bank and were appointed to those positions in 2011.[108] Mr. Jain was previously head of Deutsche Bank's investment banking group.[109] In the United States, Jacques Brand has been the Chief Executive Officer of Deutsche Bank in North America since 2012.[110] He was previously the Global Head of Investment Banking Coverage and Advisory in Deutsche Bank's Corporate Banking and Securities division.[111]

Deutsche Bank Non-Prosecution Agreement. About ten years ago, Deutsche Bank became the subject of a series of investigations focused on its participation in abusive tax shelters from 1996 through 2002, which aided and abetted evasion of an estimated $5.9 billion in U.S. income taxes.[112] On December 21, 2010, Deutsche Bank and the U.S. Attorney for the Southern District of New York executed a non-prosecution agreement (NPA) related to the bank's involvement with the abusive tax shelters.[113] Under the agreement, the bank paid more than $550 million to the United States,[114] and the U.S. Attorney and the U.S. Department of Justice (DOJ) agreed not to prosecute Deutsche Bank criminally for participating in abusive tax shelters benefiting its clients from 1997 to 2005, provided the bank met certain requirements.[115]

Those requirements included Deutsche Bank's continued cooperation with the DOJ in its tax shelter prosecutions, and appointment of an independent expert to oversee bank reforms to ensure the bank stopped participating in transactions used to defraud the IRS.[116] The NPA also banned Deutsche Bank's involvement with any pre-packaged tax products, which were the type of tax shelters that led to the criminal proceedings.[117] Bart Schwartz was selected to serve as the independent expert to monitor Deutsche Bank's actions.[118] In that position, Mr. Schwartz was responsible for evaluating the implementation and effectiveness of the bank's compliance measures.[119] Under the terms of the NPA, the government was also authorized to prosecute the bank for a violation of the NPA or to extend the tenure of the independent expert.[120]

During the multiple years in which the NPA was negotiated, the bank apparently made no mention of the MAPS product. As explained later, after a Federal Reserve Bank examination identified concerns with the MAPS product in 2012, Deutsche Bank, at the insistence of the Federal Reserve, brought the product to the attention of the U.S. Attorney for the Southern District of New York in connection with the NPA.[121] The bank contacted the U.S. Attorney's Office in August 2012, and engaged in several followup discussions and meetings.[122] Aside from those contacts, the Subcommittee is unaware of what, if any, actions were taken by the U.S. Attorney's Office in response. The NPA is still in effect.[123]

(2) Barclays

Barclays Public Limited Company (BPLC) was founded in 1690, and is a public limited company based in London.[124] Barclays is one of the largest banks in the United Kingdom. It has total assets of nearly $2.2 trillion as of December 31, 2013.[125] Barclays provides financial services in over 50 countries and employs approximately 140,000 people.[126] Since the closure of the U.K. Financial Services Authority (FSA) in 2013, Barclays is now regulated by the United Kingdom's Prudential Regulation Authority and Financial Conduct Authority.[127] In the United States, BPLC is a bank holding company that possesses nearly £1.5 trillion in consolidated assets and owns multiple U.S. entities, including Barclays Bank PLC New York Branch (BBPLC) and Barclays Capital Inc. (BCI), which is a registered broker-dealer.[128] Its five core lines of business are: (1) fixed income securities products such as mortgage-backed securities, (2) fixed income rates, (3) liquid equities products, (4) prime services such as margin and securities lending, and (5) fixed income credit.[129]

BCI is the market access point for customers for all Barclays' U.S. secured financing.[130] It provides secured financing through its prime services business, which includes both a fixed income repurchase agreement desk and an equity financing desk within BCI.[131] BBPLC serves as the consolidation point within the Barclays group for all funding in U.S. dollars.[132] It has access to the discount window at the Federal Reserve Bank of New York, and it is funded through external, unsecured financing from BPLC.[133]

Sir David Walker has been the Barclays Group Chairman since 2012.[134] He was previously the Chief Executive Officer of Morgan Stanley.[135] In addition, Antony Jenkins replaced Bob Diamond as the bank's Chief Executive Officer after the bank became the subject of a number of investigations into its business practices.[136] Some of those investigations examined the bank's participation in tax avoidance schemes.[137] In February 2012, for example, the U.K. Treasury stopped a "high-street bank," understood to be Barclays, from implementing what they called "highly abusive" tax avoidance schemes that could have resulted in the loss of some £500 million in public revenue.[138]

Salz Review. In response to the multiple investigations and negative public reaction, in July 2012, Barclays' leadership commissioned what it called the Salz Review, named after Sir Anthony Salz, a prominent British solicitor who headed the effort.[139] The stated objective of the effort was to get an independent review of Barclays' business practices and determine "what went wrong."[140] The reviewers reported to a non-executive committee at Barclays.[141] The Salz Review described the bank culture as one of "winning at all costs" and prizing the "cleverness" of employees who took "robust positions with regulators ... [and followed] the letter rather than the spirit of the rules."[142] Among other findings, the Salz Review stated that "a culture developed within Barclays, quite possibly derived originally from the investment bank, which came across to some as being … arrogant and aggressive."[143]

The bank drew particular criticism for abusive tax structures that were deemed "insensitive to changing political and public expectations around tax."[144] When confronted by regulators about tax avoidance issues, the bank's Structured Capital Markets (SCM) Group and the bank at large were "more willing than its peers to challenge outsiders and less willing to cede ground."[145] Among other tax products, SCM devised and administered the COLT options structure under examination by the Subcommittee.[146]

In 2013, Barclays responded to the Salz Review by instituting "Project Transform," a project that sought to review and implement changes in many of the bank's divisions to steer away from future regulatory violations.[147] Many of the changes instituted through the project were a direct result of the recommendations of the Salz Review, including an overhaul of Barclays' corporate values and the implementation of risk-reduction strategies in its business transactions.[148]

In addition, in another response to the Salz Review, Barclays terminated the SCM group in February 2013.[149] CEO Antony Jenkins' speech to the news media at the time explained "[t]here are some areas [at SCM] that relied on sophisticated and complex structures, where transactions were carried out with the primary objective of accessing the tax benefits. Although this was legal, going forward such activity is incompatible with our purpose. We will not engage in it again."[150]

(3) Renaissance Technologies Corporation LLC

Founded in 1982, Renaissance Technologies Corporation LLC (RenTec), a Delaware limited liability corporation, is a SEC-registered investment adviser.[151] Its main headquarters is in East Setauket, New York, while its administrative offices are in New York City.[152] As of March 31, 2014, its combined holdings exceeded $41 billion.[153]

RenTec was founded by James Simons who had previously served as a code breaker for the United States military and then headed the mathematics department at SUNY-Stony Brook.[154] The current co-CEOs are Peter Brown and Bob Mercer.[155] The current Chief Financial Officer, Chief Compliance Officer, and Chief Legal Officer is Mark Silber.[156] The current Chief Operating Officer is James Rowen.

RenTec is a closely held corporation. Presently, all of RenTec shareholders are current or former employees of the firm.[157] In addition, currently, 70% of RenTec shares are held by the five members of RenTec's Executive Committee and their respective family trusts.[158]

RenTec makes use of mathematical and statistical methods to create its investment programs.[159] It generally employs an overall strategy referred to as statistical arbitrage (StatArb) to identify market inefficiencies and take advantage of them.[160] In practice, this investment strategy often involves engaging in a very high volume of trading in order to take advantage of small differences in prices between related stocks.[161]

In order to be able to constantly adjust its trading model and implement its strategy, RenTec employs a large number of employees with doctorates and training in advanced mathematics, physics, and computer science.[162] According to RenTec, over 90 members of RenTec's staff hold doctorates in mathematics and other scientific disciplines.

RenTec currently controls four funds. They are the Medallion Fund (Medallion), Renaissance Institutional Equities Fund (RIEF), Renaissance Institutional Futures Fund (RIFF), and Renaissance Institutional Diversified Alpha Funds (RIDA).[163]

Renaissance Medallion Fund. Of the four RenTec funds, only the Medallion Fund made use of the basket option structure. The Medallion Fund is the name given to a collection of related master and feeder funds, as well as a number of subsidiaries, established by RenTec to implement a proprietary algorithmic investment strategy.[164] The fund was started in 1988.[165]

The Medallion Fund consists of five domestic and two foreign feeder funds, all of which are controlled by RenTec in its role as general partner of each fund.[166] These separate feeder funds were used to accommodate different types of investors: RenTec employees, non-RenTec employees, accredited and non-accredited investors, and foreign investors who do not pay taxes as U.S. persons, among other types.[167] Outside of the basket option structures, the Medallion feeder funds invest through six subsidiaries, structured to gain access to certain markets.[168]

The Medallion feeder funds hold ownership interests as limited partners in five Medallion master funds which RenTec controls as either the general partner or designated investment advisor.[169] One of those master funds, Medallion Holdings Ltd., is the holding company for nine trading subsidiaries.[170] Those subsidiaries "were formed to trade in various markets around the world."[171] Three of the subsidiaries are no longer active.[172]

The Medallion funds were initially open to outside investors, but by 1993, RenTec management began to remove all outside investors and limit interest holders in the fund to only employees and family members.[173] As of March 31, 2009, over 99% of the funds in the Medallion master and feeder funds were composed of firm capital and capital provided by current and former RenTec employees.[174]

(4) George Weiss Associates

George Weiss Associates, Inc. was founded in 1978, by its namesake George Weiss.[175] It served as the manager of a George Weiss proprietary capital fund until 1997, as an investment advisor to that fund from 1997 to 2005, and then as a provider of office space to the new advisor, Weiss Multi-

Strategy Advisers LLC, from 2006 to the present.[176] In 1996, the holding company GWA, LLC was founded to provide key George Weiss Associates employees with investment opportunities in the firm's proprietary portfolio.[177]

GWA, LLC held direct or indirect ownership interests in five entities: Weiss Multi- Strategy Advisers LLC, Weiss Special Operations LLC, Weiss Transportation Services LLC, Weiss Investment Management Services LLC, and OGI Associates LLC.[178] Four of those entities are organized in Connecticut, and the fifth, Weiss Investment Management Services LLC, is organized in New York.[179] Of those entities, OGI Associates LLC executes direct proprietary trading under the management of Weiss Multi-Strategy Advisers.[180] The company initially began by investing in utility bonds with the objective of identifying electricity utilities that had been mispriced relative to their returns.[181] Through the 1990s, the Weiss funds expanded to include management of corporate funds and a variety of internationally traded instruments such as sovereign debt and various currencies.[182]

Because their trading strategy involved identifying market inefficiencies, the Weiss strategies sought and engaged in leveraged trading in order to magnify their returns.[183] When George Weiss became involved with basket options at Deutsche Bank in 2003, it purchased them for GWA, LLC directly and organized a separate entity run by GWA personnel, Quaker Partners LLC, to take on the role of the investment advisor in the basket options transactions.[184]

During the period reviewed by the Subcommittee, the head of George Weiss Associates was George Weiss. The Chief Operating Officer (COO) was Frederick Doucette.

B. Evolution of Basket Options

As explained earlier, during the 1990s, several banks and hedge funds began exploring ways in which options could be written on a hedge fund's own trading strategy, while also avoiding Section 1260's 1999 prohibition on abusive derivatives, including options. At that time, a number of hedge funds were also using trading strategies that benefited from high leverage levels. The banks and hedge funds went through several different structures before settling on the basket options examined in this investigation.

Initial RBC Structure. The first basket option structure appears to have been designed between 1996-1997, by the Royal Bank of Canada (RBC). That year, according to George Weiss employees, RBC marketed a basket option structure using a derivative option on a managed trading account to circumvent the leverage restrictions in Regulation T.[185] The option enabled a hedge fund, who was the option holder, to act as the investment advisor to the account set up by the bank. The bank also provided financing to add funds to the trading account, charged a high financing rate, and required the hedge fund to pay financing on the maximum possible leverage, regardless of the amount actually used.[186]

Introduction of Deutsche Bank MAPS. A few years later, Deutsche Bank developed and marketed a less costly structure it named Managed Account Product Structure (MAPS). The MAPS basket option product at Deutsche Bank evolved from a similar product called MAIDS, which was initially designed by National Westminster Bank (NatWest).[187] In 1998 - 1999, Deutsche Bank acquired NatWest Securities, including the team that had worked on the MAIDS transaction and brought over almost the entire group to help Deutsche Bank establish its Global Prime Services business.[188] At Deutsche Bank, the team continued to refine the MAPS structure, using Deutsche Bank's trading platform to create effective monitoring and risk mitigation systems that would allow a basket option holder to place orders and execute trades directly through Deutsche Bank's proprietary trading accounts.[189]

George Weiss Participation in Basket Options. The Weiss funds became involved with MAPS basket options as a result of their focus on low-volatility utility stocks.[190] According to George Weiss, the funds noticed that they had very consistent, but very low positive returns, generally in the range of only a few percentage points.[191] As a result, the Weiss funds sought out ways to obtain leverage in order to magnify the gains from their strategy.[192] While the funds realized that leverage would also lead to increased losses in bad years, they viewed the overall successful performance and general stability of their funds as justification for the use of high leverage.[193]

Beginning in the early 1990s, the Weiss funds sought various financing mechanisms to increase their trading leverage. Initially, the funds became a specialist market maker in stocks traded at the Philadelphia Stock Exchange.[194] That structure allowed the funds to obtain leverage in the realm of twenty times on certain equities: ten times long and ten times short.[195] However, those leverage levels were limited to certain types of equities and did not extend to any over-the-counter (OTC) trades.[196]

According to George Weiss, sometime during 1996 to 1997, RBC approached the George Weiss funds with its basket option strategy, which

George Weiss readily accepted.[197] George Weiss told the Subcommittee that the RBC structure enabled George Weiss to act as the investment advisor to the bank's proprietary account, and obtain leverage up to twenty times the premium that George Weiss paid into the account. However, as noted above, the bank charged a very high financing fee.[198] George Weiss continued using the RBC arrangement until 2003.[199]

In 2003, according to George Weiss, the company was approached by representatives of Deutsche Bank with a new basket option structure that Deutsche Bank had developed.[200] This structure was the same MAPS structure that Deutsche Bank was offering to other hedge funds, and George Weiss became interested because it offered high leverage at a much lower financing rate than RBC.[201] Ultimately, between the years 2003 and 2006, George Weiss purchased from Deutsche Bank a total of ten MAPS basket options with terms exceeding one year involving trading assets with an initial total notional value of about $2.8 billion.[202] The last six options were exercised by George Weiss in May 2010.[203]

RenTec Participation in Basket Options. RenTec became interested in the basket option structure due to its development of a computer-based trading strategy using complex algorithms, which required high volume trading and benefited from leverage to amplify its returns. That trading strategy led RenTec to search for a financing arrangement that could accommodate both high volume trading and significant leverage.

During the 1990s, RenTec used a joint back office (JBO) arrangement with Bear Stearns to increase its leverage beyond Regulation T margin restrictions permitting a maximum leverage level of 2:1.[204] Under federal rules, JBO arrangements were allowed leverage levels up to 7.6:1.[205] In 1999, Deutsche Bank approached RenTec with the MAPS product.[206] According to RenTec, Deutsche Bank marketed it as a product that offered superior leverage as well as loss protection at a relatively low cost.[207]

RenTec purchased its first MAPS option in 2000, followed by additional options in 2002.[208] Later, several Deutsche Bank employees who worked with RenTec on the basket option structure moved over to RenTec, including operations personnel, management, and legal counsel.[209] Since 2000, RenTec has purchased from Deutsche Bank a total of 29 basket options with terms exceeding one year, involving trading assets with a total initial notional value of about $46 billion and profits totaling about $15.9 billion.[210] All of the basket options were utilized by RenTec's Medallion funds employing their proprietary algorithmic strategy.

Barclays COLT Options. In 2002, RenTec introduced the basket option concept to Barclays.[211] According to RenTec, Barclays initially approached them to expand Barclays' U.S based business. RenTec told the Subcommittee that, because RenTec wanted to spread its counterparty credit risk with multiple banks, [212] it agreed to do business with Barclays, but only if the bank could develop a basket options type structure.[213] Contemporaneous internal Barclays communications indicate that RenTec pushed Barclays to create its own basket options structure, informing the bank that it would move its accounts elsewhere if Barclays did not provide it with a basket options structure.[214] To accommodate RenTec, Barclays created the COLT structure, which used a separate Barclays entity, Palomino Ltd., and a two-tiered options structure to execute trades for RenTec.[215] Since 2002, RenTec has purchased from Barclays a total of 31 basket options with terms exceeding one year, involving trading assets with a total initial notional value of about $62 billion and profits totaling about $18.3 billion.[216]

Options After 2010 GLAM. In late 2010, the IRS issued its Generic Legal Advice Memorandum (GLAM) advising that basket options were not true options and could not be used to treat short-term trading profits as long-term capital gains.[217] In response, Deutsche Bank placed a moratorium on issuing new basket options, but continued to administer multiple existing option accounts. In 2012, Deutsche Bank resumed offering basket options, but used a revised version whose term lasted less than one year and whose contract required the option holder to report any gains as short-term capital gains.[218] In contrast, even after the 2010 GLAM, Barclays continued to offer basket options to RenTec until 2013, when it also revised its basket options contract to offer only short-dated options with term lasting less than a year.[219]

According to information supplied by RenTec to the Subcommittee, in 2012, the IRS sent what are commonly known as "60-Day Letters" to RenTec, notifying the hedge fund that the IRS intended to disallow long-term capital gains treatment of basket option profits from option trades lasting less than 12 months and proposing an assessment of additional taxes for certain tax years. RenTec responded with what is known as a "Protest of the 60-Day Letters," indicating that it disagreed with the IRS analysis. According to RenTec, the matter is apparently now awaiting review by the IRS internal Office of Appeals.[220]

Overall Basket Option Statistics. Altogether, as indicated earlier, Deutsche Bank sold MAPS basket options to 13 different hedge funds.[221]

RenTec was the largest MAPS client, and George Weiss was the second largest.[222] Deutsche Bank used the original MAPS structure from approximately 2000 to the end of 2007, writing over one hundred options that were used to purchase trading assets with a notional value in excess of $75 billion.[223] In 2008, Deutsche Bank restructured the MAPS option, and its hedge fund clients stopped purchasing new basket option contracts, except for RenTec.[224] From 2002 to 2012, Barclays provided COLT basket options solely to RenTec.[225]

The following chart summarizes some of the key data on the MAPS and COLT basket options activity over the past 15 years.

Total Basket Options Sold by Deutsche Bank and Barclays 1998-2014

Bank	Name of Product	All Basket Options*				Basket Options Executed after One Year		
		Total Number Sold[1]	Revenue for Bank	Number Sold to RenTec[1]	Profits Generated for RenTec	Total Number Sold	Total Initial Notional Value	Number Sold to RenTec
Deutsche Bank	MAPS	156	$571	36	$16,969	96	$60,446	29
Barclays	COLT	43	$655	43	$18,484	31	$61,925	31
Total		199	$1,121	79	$35,453	127	$122,371	60

*All dollar amounts in millions.

1. Two Deutsche Bank and four Barclays options are outstanding, of which three Barclays options have lasted over one year.

Source: Tables produced by Deutsche Bank (DB-PSI-00052577-582, DB-PSI-00052586-587, and

DB-PSI-0005588-590) and submissions by Barclays (BARCLAYS-PSI-018114-116, BARCLAYS-PSI-748604, and

PSI-Barclays-22-000005-114.

Prepared by U.S. Senate Permanent Subcommittee on Investigations, July 2014.

C. Development of MAPS and COLT

Deutsche Bank and Barclays developed their basket option structures in different ways and at different times. Although the Barclays structure was developed later and in response to the Deutsche Bank structure, it is discussed first due to greater simplicity.

(1) Barclays' COLT Structure

Barclays developed the COLT basket option structure in 2002, at the request of RenTec, and it was used solely by that hedge fund over the next decade. The COLT structure was designed and administered by the bank's Structured Capital Markets (SCM) group until 2013, when Barclays disbanded that group for involvement with overly aggressive tax strategies.[226]

Under the COLT structure, Barclays created a Cayman Island Special Purpose Entity (SPE) named Palomino Ltd.[227] Palomino was a shell corporation controlled by Barclays; it had no full time employees or physical offices of its own.[228] Its directors and officers were Barclays employees who worked for other Barclays entities.[229] Each basket option account was opened in the name of Palomino, which was the nominal owner of all of the account assets. The accounts were opened as prime brokerage accounts with Barclays Capital Inc. in the United States and by Barclays Capital Securities Limited in the United Kingdom.[230]

In connection with each COLT option, Palomino hired RenTec to be its investment advisor under an Investment Management Agreement that gave RenTec the exclusive right and the "full" discretion without the need to consult with Barclays to execute transactions directly into the Palomino prime brokerage accounts in the United States and United Kingdom, subject to general guidelines specified in the agreement.[231] While RenTec representatives told the Subcommittee that they merely recommended or suggested trades to Palomino,[232] given the company's shell status, the extraordinary number of daily trade executions, and the provisions in the option contracts, the facts indicate that all transactions in the accounts were actually fully controlled by RenTec.

After the accounts were opened and the Investment Management Agreement signed, Palomino sold options on the performance of the accounts to the U.S. branch of Barclays Bank PLC, which in turn sold identical options to Badger Holding LP (Badger), a shell entity set up in 2004 and fully controlled by RenTec.[233] Like Palomino, Badger had no employees or physical offices of its own. Prior to Badger, RenTec used a company called Bass

Equities Ltd. (Bass), which was originally incorporated in Bermuda.[234] Badger was later incorporated in the United States.[235] Badger served as the official option holder for the COLT options on behalf of RenTec.[236]

The COLT options were generally established with three-year terms, meaning that the option holder could exercise the option at any time prior to the maturity date which was three years after the option was established.[237] RenTec representatives told the Subcommittee that one of the benefits of the option structure was that it gave the hedge fund access to long-term financing.[238] In many of the COLT options reviewed by the Subcommittee, however, the option holder – RenTec – exercised the option shortly after 12 months.

RenTec purchased multiple COLT options, some of which were in effect at the same time. In that case, the assets referenced by each option were not separately managed or accounted for, but pooled together in a single trading account of which each option represented a proportional share.[239]

As previously noted, the algorithmic strategy employed by RenTec's Medallion Funds was more effective with a high trading volume. RenTec accordingly conducted tens of thousands of trades per day using the prime brokerage accounts designated in the basket option contracts.

To execute the trades, Barclays gave RenTec direct market access through its proprietary trading software, enabling RenTec to place trade orders instantly into the market and receive immediate executions.[240] "The trade is done within milliseconds …."[241] In almost all instances, the trades were placed and executed by computer from RenTec's facilities, using its algorithms to initiate and execute the trades through the bank's proprietary trading software. The trades were typically executed with no human intervention on either side, except when RenTec personnel adjusted the algorithm parameters.[242] The executed positions were held in the designated option accounts in the name of Palomino and were immediately reported to Barclays.[243] All positions were reconciled daily for both Barclays and RenTec.[244]

The value of the COLT options was linked to the performance of the assets held in the designated accounts, consisting of all trading positions resulting from executions made by RenTec for those accounts.[245] The options included a commitment by Barclays to provide financing for the accounts that, based upon the amount of the initial premium provided by Badger, could reach a leverage level of up to 20:1.[246] Because all marketable trade orders made by RenTec were immediately executed and the assets assigned to the designated accounts, those accounts also were described in documents and by Barclays personnel as providing a hedge for Palomino and, ultimately, for Barclays.

Under the Investment Management Agreement, if the value of the referenced assets in the designated accounts were to fall by an amount equal to the premium provided by Badger, the options would terminate. As explained earlier, this provision was called a "knockout." If a knockout occurred, Barclays, through Palomino and with the assistance of RenTec, could liquidate the assets in the account to minimize losses.[247] The bank was required to bear any losses that exceeded the premium.

By entering into the basket option arrangement, while RenTec placed its initial premium at risk, Barclays bore the catastrophic risk (also called the "gap risk") associated with the option accounts. According to Barclays and RenTec, that catastrophic risk applied to a situation in which market conditions deteriorated so rapidly that all of the premium paid by RenTec was lost and Barclays was unable to sell the remaining assets from the Palomino accounts quickly enough to cover losses in excess of the premium.[248] Barclays included several features in the basket options structure to ensure that it faced little or no real risk, including provisions giving the bank the right to liquidate the account assets once the losses exhausted the premium amount.[249] Moreover, in more than ten years of operation, in which the COLT options not only experienced millions of trades as detailed below but also operated throughout the worst financial crisis to affect the market in generations, no knockout event ever took place. In fact, the facts indicate that no losses took place in any year with respect to any COLT option.

If the options were exercised rather than knocking out, RenTec, through Badger, received a cash settlement equal to the gains made from the trading activity in the designated account minus the cost of financing, trading, and structuring fees charged by Barclays.[250] Those cash payments were made routinely to RenTec as it exercised various basket options over the years.

For its role as investment advisor to the trading accounts, RenTec, through Badger, received a nominal amount of compensation from Palomino. Barclays, through Palomino, paid Badger a fixed fee equal to about $600,000.[251] Barclays did not provide the promised fee separately; instead it subtracted the fee amount from the trading profits otherwise payable to RenTec, through Badger, upon exercise of the relevant option.[252] By agreeing to allow the investment advisory fee to be subtracted from the option profits, RenTec essentially agreed to forego any additional compensation and instead limit its returns to the trading profits in each option account.

Barclays also entered into tax indemnity agreements with RenTec as part of the COLT transactions.[253] In the agreements, RenTec promised to reimburse Barclays for any tax exposure that Barclays might suffer as a result of entering into the COLT transaction, such as being required to pay penalties for failing to withhold taxes in its role as withholding agent for the option accounts.[254] In other words, under the tax indemnification agreement, Barclays would not have to pay any tax penalties levied on it in connection with the COLT options.

The overall effect of this arrangement was that RenTec received all of the gains resulting from its trading orders, while Barclays remained economically neutral to the designated accounts. Barclays instead made money from its financing, trading, and structuring fees.[255]

The following chart provides a simplified diagram demonstrating how the COLT basket options structure was intended to work.

(2) Deutsche Bank MAPS

In contrast to Barclays which used a single option structure over time, over the years, Deutsche Bank developed two different types of basket option structures under the MAPS name. The first was used from 1998 through the end of 2007. The second was used from 2008 to 2010, but the bank ceased offering it after the IRS issued its basket options GLAM in November 2010. In 2012, Deutsche Bank began offering the revised MAPS structure again, but limited the duration of the option to less than one year.

(a) Original MAPs

From 1998 to 2007, Deutsche Bank sold basket options on the performance of assets held in designated option accounts within Deutsche Bank propriety accounts, with the trading controlled by the hedge funds that purchased the options. Like COLT, Deutsche Bank hired as the investment advisor for the option accounts an entity related to the hedge fund that purchased the option. Like COLT, Deutsche Bank also gave the hedge fund entity discretionary authority without having to consult with the bank to execute trading transactions directly, using Deutsche Bank's trading platform and proprietary account. Similar to the Investment Management Agreement between Barclays and RenTec, Deutsche Bank and the hedge funds executed Investment Advisory Agreements which included certain limits and guidelines on what could be selected for the accounts.[256]

Like COLT, the MAPS options were generally established with three-year terms, meaning that the option holder could exercise the option at any time prior to the maturity date which was three years after the option was established.[257] In many of the MAPS options reviewed by the Subcommittee, however, as with COLT, the option holder exercised the option shortly after 12 months.

Also like COLT, to execute the trades, Deutsche Bank gave the hedge fund direct market access through its proprietary trading software, enabling the hedge fund to place trading orders and obtain immediate executions. Typically, those trade orders were placed and executed by computers controlled by the hedge fund and bank, with no human intervention on either side. The executed positions were then held in the designated account and reported immediately to Deutsche Bank. All positions were reconciled daily for both Deutsche Bank and the hedge fund.[258] Like Barclays, Deutsche Bank told the Subcommittee that the bank executed every trade order made by a hedge fund with a MAPS account that was within the guidelines established in the Investment Advisory Agreement.[259]

Like COLT, if a hedge fund purchased multiple MAPS options at the same time, prior to 2008, the assets referenced by each option were not separately managed or accounted for, but were part of a single pooled account of which each option represented a proportional share.[260]

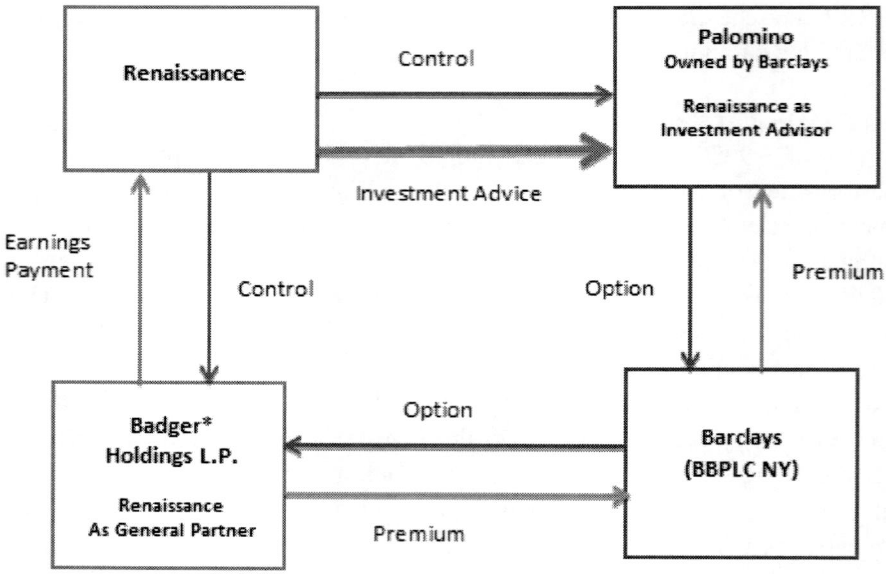

* Early options were purchased through Bass, a non-US corporate entity, prior to switching to Badger.

Figure 1. A simplified diagram outlining the COLT transaction.

Similar to the Barclays options, Deutsche Bank committed to providing financing for each account that would produce a high degree of leverage many times larger than the premium paid by the hedge fund and charged a financing fee for that leverage to the option holder.[261] Because the investment advisor, which in every case was the hedge fund that purchased the option, executed the trades directly into the Deutsche Bank's proprietary account, that account was also described by Deutsche Bank personnel as serving as a hedge for the option for Deutsche Bank.

When the hedge fund exercised the option, it received a cash settlement equal to the gains made from its trading minus the cost of financing and trade execution fees charged by the bank. In addition, the hedge fund was typically paid a nominal amount of compensation by Deutsche Bank for acting as the investment advisor to the option accounts. For example, in the case of RenTec, from 2000 to 2007, Deutsche Bank paid the hedge fund a fixed fee as low as $100,000 per option.[262] Like Barclays, however, Deutsche Bank did not pay the fee separately but instead subtracted it from the option trading profits that would otherwise have been paid to the hedge fund upon exercising the option.[263]

Like COLT, the MAPS options were designed to provide catastrophic risk loss protection to the hedge fund, but also to minimize possible losses to the bank. If the value of the assets in the options account were to drop below a specified level, generally reflecting a loss equal to a certain percentage of the premium paid by the option holder, it could cause one or more of the options in the pool to hit thresholds that would trigger certain actions within the account. Unlike Barclays, Deutsche Bank set the knockout level at a point where the option purchaser would have some premium remaining, resulting in both the investment advisor and the bank maintaining an interest in the liquidation of the account.[264] At the initial level, called a "notice level," the investment advisor maintained control of the account, but was required to initiate a reduction in the portfolio assets and in the account leverage in order to reduce risk.[265] If the value continued to fall, Deutsche Bank could take over the account and liquidate the assets.[266] If the liquidation resulted in leftover premium, that leftover amount would be returned to the option holder; otherwise, the bank would bear any losses exceeding the premium.[267]

The accounts of the two largest users of this version of the MAPS options, RenTec and George Weiss, which purchased and held the options from 2000 to 2007, never experienced any losses or knockout events. Instead, every option, every year, provided a cash payment to the hedge fund that exercised the option.

(b) Revised MAPS

Starting at the end of 2007, following what was known in the hedge fund industry as the "Quant Quake," Deutsche Bank decided to revise the general terms of the MAPS option.[268] In August 2007, several hedge funds which used similar statistical arbitrage strategies based on computer models suffered significant losses in a relatively short amount of time due to the high correlation of their strategies, despite the fact that the market remained overall neutral during the event.[269] Those hedge funds experienced big losses, even though the rest of the market was stable. The Quant Quake event demonstrated that hedge funds employing the same statistical arbitrage strategies ran a risk called "duplication," in which models all reacting in the same manner could drive other models to mimic the same behavior leading to widespread, unexpected losses.[270] In an interview with the Subcommittee, Barclays Director of Credit Risk, Lansford Dyer, said: "The only real risk I worry about, for a fund similar to RenTec, is duplication risk, the risk funds running the same strategies start affecting each other."[271]

Following the Quant Quake, Deutsche Bank personnel reviewed the basket options structure for risk, legal, and compliance issues, including tax, as well as how Deutsche Bank might earn a greater financial return on the MAPS options. At the same time, RenTec became concerned that provisions in its Investment Advisory Agreement with Deutsche Bank did not clearly define which party would be responsible for controlling the liquidation of assets in the managed account if Deutsche Bank were forced to unwind an option.

The new MAPs structure was completed by late 2008. It included a number of significant changes. First, Deutsche Bank began to subdivide each option's referenced assets and place each set of assets in a separate sub-account, rather than grouping them in one large pooled account. This subdivision meant that, although the referenced assets continued to be traded through one proprietary account, they were tracked separately and assets could be identified as belonging to a particular option, where previously it had not been possible to determine which assets belonged to which option.[272]

Second, the new options had separate investment guidelines for each sub-account as well as continuing to maintain general guidelines for the overall structure. Third, the bank switched from American style options to European style options, meaning the options could no longer be exercised at any time prior to the maturity date, but only on a specified exercise date.

Fourth, under the revised MAPS structure, instead of a fixed fee, the investment advisor was paid a performance fee equal to 2% of the trading gains, which was higher than the prior fee, but was still subtracted from the trading profits in the option account.[273] Fifth, Deutsche Bank changed the formula used to calculate the premium paid by the hedge fund purchasing the option.[274]

Finally, in response to RenTec's concerns, Deutsche Bank and RenTec negotiated new liquidation terms under which, if an option were terminated by the bank without cause and if RenTec determined the liquidation could harm its other holdings, then RenTec had the right to decide whether it wanted to control the liquidation of the account.[275]

The following chart provides a simplified diagram demonstrating how the restructured MAPS basket options were intended to work.

In designing the restructured MAPS option, Deutsche Bank negotiated with RenTec about a number of the terms. Deutsche Bank also initiated negotiations with George Weiss about switching to the revised MAPS structure. Ultimately, however, Deutsche Bank did not enter into any new MAPS transactions with George Weiss.[276] According to the George Weiss Associates COO, Federick Doucette, George Weiss viewed the new structure as a sign that Deutsche Bank no longer had any real interest in continuing the MAPS structure.[277] Mr. Doucette told the Subcommittee that he believed the new structure had several provisions that lacked "any business purpose" and that Deutsche Bank had explained most of the new provisions as being necessary "for tax purposes."[278] In an email, George Weiss informed Deutsche Bank that several of the new requirements would forcibly change the way that George Weiss operated its business, noting for example that the lack of cross-collateralization could reduce George Weiss investments in MAPS by as much as 60% due to the need for additional liquidity to fund the remainder of the business.[279] After George Weiss was unable to negotiate changes to the revised structure, it decided to end its participation in MAPS.[280] No hedge fund other than RenTec purchased options using the new structure.

At the same time Deutsche Bank was making substantial changes to MAPS, the evidence indicates that very few changes were made to the COLT structure employed by Barclays. As one RenTec employee explained to the Subcommittee, Barclays was very easy to work with and its structure accommodated RenTec's needs. Moreover, as previously noted, RenTec provided Barclays with a tax indemnity agreement, in which RenTec promised to pay for any potential tax exposure that Barclays might suffer as a result of entering into the COLT transaction.[281]

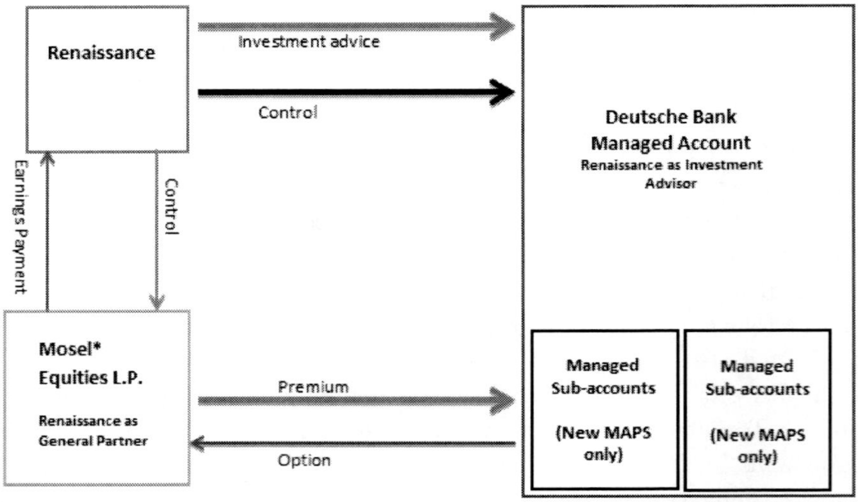

* Early options were purchased through Franconia, a non-US corporate entity, prior to switching to Mosel.

Figure 2. A simplified diagram outlining the MAPS transaction as conducted by RenTec.

(c) Current MAPS

The restructured MAPS option remained in place from 2009 through 2010, and was used by RenTec to purchase additional options.[282] In November 2010, after the IRS issued its Generic Legal Advice Memorandum (GLAM) on basket options, as indicated earlier, Deutsche Bank ceased writing new MAPS options for over a year. In 2012, Deutsche Bank resumed offering the restructured MAPS basket options. Those MAPS options, however, had been revised yet again. In the new format, the only MAPS options offered to RenTec had terms which lasted less than one year and contractually required all gains to be reported as short-term capital gains.[283] MAPS options lasting more than one year were no longer available.

In contrast to Deutsche Bank, Barclays continued to offer COLT options to RenTec, even after issuance of the IRS basket options GLAM in November 2010. It was not until two years later, in 2013, that Barclays revised its COLT structure so that it, too, offered only those basket options that were less than a year in length.[284]

D. Analysis of Basket Option Case Studies

A review of the basket option transactions involving Deutsche Bank, Barclays, RenTec, and George Weiss Associates demonstrates that although those financial products were styled as options, the terms, conditions, and day-to-day operation of the MAPS and COLT structures, the locus of control in each case, and who realized the profits from those arrangements undercut the structures' status as options and, more generally, as financial derivatives. Instead of options, the MAPS and COLT accounts functioned as highly leveraged prime brokerage accounts controlled by the so-called "option holders" who directed the trading and took the profits. Those basket option holders did not profit from a derivative activity, but directly from the trades they executed.

Although the option accounts and assets were held in the name of the banks, as investment advisors to the trading accounts, RenTec and George Weiss had the exclusive right and discretion to determine what assets were purchased and sold from each account, subject to basic risk reduction guidelines specified in the investment advisory agreements. The hedge funds told the Subcommittee that they were passive option buyers making mere "suggestions" or "recommendations" to assist the banks with their hedging activities, but, in reality, the hedge funds fully controlled the trading accounts used to determine the option payoffs, executed the trades made per day, and reaped the profits from those trades. Additionally, by characterizing the funds lent by the banks as money that the banks were depositing into their own accounts, the hedge funds used the basket option accounts to obtain leverage at far greater levels than otherwise allowed under federal law for prime brokerage accounts.

When RenTec took control of the option accounts at Deutsche Bank and Barclays, it employed a proprietary investment strategy that utilized a computer-based set of algorithms which was managed by over 90 professionals and required continual adjustments. The trading strategy used hundreds of thousands of short-term trades per day and produced an average of 26 to 39 million trades per year. In addition, that high-volume trading strategy caused rapid and significant turnover in the assets in the option accounts. The resulting, ever-changing basket of securities, controlled by RenTec as the investment advisor, continually modified the portfolio of assets supposedly supporting the option contracts. The constant changes not only undermine the notion of an option whose value was linked to a specific set of assets, but also could be seen as having given rise to realization events for tax purposes, further exposing the option's role as window-dressing to disguise direct securities trading by the company purporting to serve as a mere option holder.

In substance, the structures functioned as prime brokerage accounts with non-recourse financing that enabled the hedge funds to far exceed federal leverage limits on margin accounts, conduct non-stop, direct trades using the banks' trade execution software, and reap the resulting profits from their own trading activity. In the case of RenTec, the basket option contracts were not even administered as distinct, independent legal contracts, but were instead woven into an integrated trading strategy across multiple banks, multiple legal entities, and multiple accounts. This integrated strategy conducted hundreds of thousands of trades each day, yet RenTec used the basket option structure to characterize the resulting profits from the option related trades as long-term gains, saving billions of dollars in taxes over more than a decade.

Just as RenTec treated the management of the MAPS and COLT option accounts as components of a larger investment strategy, so too did the banks view and treat the individual option accounts as if they were part of a single large investment pool at each bank rather than trading specific securities within each option contract. For years, neither RenTec nor the banks tracked the basket option trading activity on an option-by-option basis, instead pooling the assets and profits. It was not until 2008, that Deutsche Bank began tracking asset performance on a per option basis, while Barclays has never tracked performance on a per option basis.

In late 2008, when Deutsche Bank revised the MAPS structure and limited the transactions to European style options that could be executed only on a fixed date, RenTec made clear its intention to use the MAPS accounts to maintain its access to cash on a short-term basis. RenTec did so by scheduling the options it purchased to produce exercise dates periodically throughout the year. RenTec then exercised those options on the pre-determined dates to obtain cash payments at regular intervals, and used the cash to support its business operations. This activity offers further evidence of the extent of the hedge fund's control over the option trading activities and profits to meet its financial needs, in contrast to a passive option holder waiting to see how a capital investment might pan out.

Each of these factors, RenTec's control over the trading strategy and related activities, high-volume trading and account turnover, integration of the accounts into a larger investment strategy, and use of the accounts to produce regular cash payments supporting its business operations, contradict a depiction of RenTec as a passive option holder awaiting derivative gains. The option structure functioned instead as a vehicle for RenTec to conduct direct trades with leverage at much higher levels than available in normal margin accounts, to aggregate and defer its gains, and to avoid billions of dollars in short-term capital gains taxes. The structure functioned the same way for George Weiss Associates.

(1) RenTec Utilization of the Basket Option Structure

Because RenTec was the longest and largest user of basket options studied by the Subcommittee, and entered into options with both Deutsche Bank and Barclays, its use of the basket option structures will be analyzed first.

(a) Disguising Trading Activity as an Option

Although Deutsche Bank and Barclays established proprietary accounts for the basket options, purportedly to hold assets that would serve as a hedge to cover the option payoffs, those accounts actually functioned as if they were RenTec's own prime brokerage trading accounts, with RenTec acting in the role of trader rather than option holder. The facts show RenTec had active and total control over the trading strategy and executions. Barclays, in an internal memorandum to its auditors, described RenTec as having so much control over the accounts that Barclays planned to remove from Barclays' financial statements the shell entity, Palomino Ltd., in whose name the accounts and assets were held. Further evidence that the accounts did not function as true options, or likely even as derivatives, is that RenTec managed the MAPS and COLT basket option accounts as components of one large investment pool, journaling assets between option accounts, rolling assets from expired to new option accounts, and shifting parts of its investment portfolio between different financial institutions. The resulting rapid asset turnover in the various option accounts meant that the options purchased by RenTec had no fixed assets and did not function as true options. The accounts existed simply to carry out RenTec's algorithmic trading strategy. In the end, for all practical purposes, the accounts functioned as over-leveraged prime brokerage accounts controlled by the hedge funds to produce trading profits rather than as accounts controlled by the banks to provide a hedge against an option contract.

(i) Controlling Trading Activity

Although the basket option accounts were opened in the name of Deutsche Bank and Barclays, RenTec, and only RenTec, controlled the investment decisions and trading activity undertaken in each account. Since 2000, RenTec was named as the investment advisor for all of the accounts referenced in the 79 basket options it purchased from the two banks, of which 60 have been exercised by RenTec after the one-year mark.[285] As the investment advisor, every direction by RenTec to buy or sell an asset in a particular option account served dual roles: the resulting portfolio of assets served as the reference assets to determine the ultimate value of the option and hold the profits from executed trades and, simultaneously, each transaction provided the assets described by Deutsche Bank and Barclays as the hedges created for the option contracts.

High Volume Trading. Trading records and other evidence indicate that RenTec used its discretion over the basket option accounts to conduct millions of high-volume trades for years. In response to a Subcommittee inquiry, RenTec estimated that the company conducted from 100,000 to 150,000 trades per day with each bank.[286] Those estimates of the daily trading activities at each bank yield a combined estimated average of 26-39 million trades per year through the option accounts.[287] Still another document, prepared by Barclays, described the trading activity of the Medallion Fund, the entity Renaissance used to implement the basket option transactions, as "very high frequency trader."[288]

While RenTec executives repeatedly told the Subcommittee that the company simply "suggested" or "recommended" trades to the banks for their hedge accounts,[289] it is difficult to credit that description of RenTec's actions given that it had the trading authority and electronic means to execute actual trades through the option accounts at its discretion and without consultation with the banks. Another factor is the sheer volume of trades that were actually executed on a minute-to-minute basis each day; it is difficult to understand how all of those trades were completed if RenTec were merely suggesting rather than executing the trades. It is also difficult to understand how the company offered "suggestions," since virtually all of the trade orders were initiated electronically, using RenTec's proprietary algorithms, and were executed immediately using the banks' trading software and direct market access, typically with no human intervention on either side.

Bearing the Rewards and Risks. Within the MAPS and COLT structures, RenTec bore all of the significant risks and rewards due the owner of the securities positions held in the option accounts. Subject to trading and financing costs, all of the profits accrued from the trading in each option account were paid to RenTec when the option was exercised. No portion of the trading profits was paid to either bank, which received only financing and fee income. In addition, except for catastrophic market events, RenTec bore all of the risks associated with the ownership of those assets. For example, any trading losses served to lower the value of the affected option account and lower the final option payoff when RenTec exercised the option. The only risk faced by the banks was a catastrophic market event that depleted the value of the option accounts, an event that never occurred for any RenTec options. One RenTec analyst wrote that, even if a threshold level were breached requiring bank assumption of losses in an option account, losses would be minimal since the portfolio was "well-diversified, market- neutral, and with low liquidity imbalance," and "could be liquidated slowly if required."[290]

Paying Ownership Costs. Further, RenTec bore the day-to-day costs associated with ownership of the assets in the option accounts, even though the assets were held in the name of the banks providing the accounts. Each option had a "trade confirmation," which is a written acknowledgment provided by the bank indicating that a trade has been completed, and which included details such as the date, price, commission, fees, and settlement terms of the trade. A section in the confirmation entitled, "Basket Cost" at Barclays and "Basket Income and Expenses" at Deutsche Bank, identified the account expenses and subtracted the costs directly from the account.[291] The costs charged to RenTec included trade transaction fees, including ticket charges and short sale borrowing fees, reflecting the costs incurred by the bank for completing each individual transaction executed in the account. Transaction fees are common expenses in a traditional client brokerage account, but are normally absent from proprietary trading accounts operated by the bank itself.[292] Similarly, the trade confirmations charged RenTec financing fees, which are common in client brokerage accounts, but not in a bank's own proprietary trading accounts.

The financing charges and transaction fees ultimately reduced the cash-settled payout to RenTec when it exercised the option on that account to withdraw its profits. Paying those daily trading and financing costs offer further evidence that the accounts did not operate as the banks' accounts to hedge the options, but as prime brokerage accounts for RenTec.

Disguising Control. At Deutsche Bank, a representation made by the option holder in some option confirmations appears to disguise RenTec's control over the option account.

When RenTec purchased an option, it did not hold the option in its own name, using instead one of its related entities. For the Deutsche Bank basket options, RenTec used a Bermuda corporation, named Franconia Equities Ltd., as the official option holder until 2007, when it replaced the company with a Delaware partnership named Mosel Equities LP (Mosel).[293]

RenTec served as the general partner of the Mosel partnership, and RenTec officials signed legal documents on behalf of Mosel. According to a recent ruling of the First Circuit Court of Appeals, under Delaware partnership law, "a partner 'is an agent of the partnership for the purpose of its business, purposes or activities,' and an act of a partner '... binds the partnership.'"[294] Under that ruling and Delaware law, since RenTec was the general partner of Mosel, it necessarily acted as an agent of Mosel.

At the same time, in the basket option transactions, RenTec served as the investment advisor for the Deutsche Bank accounts. In that role, RenTec determined what assets would be placed in the Deutsche Bank account which served as the reference for the option payoff, with full power to "supervise and direct the investment ... of all assets in the [Deutsche Bank] Account ... without prior consultation."[295]

The result was that Mosel, through its agent, RenTec, controlled the selection of assets for the account of the option seller, Deutsche Bank. However, in the option confirmations executed as part of the basket option transactions, Mosel represented that it would "not attempt to direct or influence the choice of investments in the Basket" of assets to be held in the Deutsche Bank option account.[296] But, as noted above, Mosel did "direct" the choice of investments through its agent RenTec. The representations made by Mosel in the confirmations for each transaction were fictions, using the formal structure of the transaction – Mosel's role as the official option holder – to disguise RenTec's control over the option holder as well as the option's trading activity.[297]

Fronting for the Hedge Fund. Not every Deutsche Bank affiliate felt comfortable using MAPS options. According to one Deutsche Bank employee, the bank's U.K. affiliate declined due to concerns that the MAPS structure involved the bank "fronting" for a hedge fund that was actually "actively trading" the assets in the option account.[298]

In a May 2008 email exchange involving Adrienne Browning, a Deutsche Bank tax counsel who was located in the United States and was handling the MAPS issue, and Steven Purvis, a Deutsche Bank colleague located in the United Kingdom, Ms. Browning asked if he remembered the rationale for Deutsche Bank UK deciding not to move ahead with a MAPS option that sounded very similar to the MAPS options used by RenTec. Ms. Browning wrote:

> "Do you remember ... What the analysis was for the following proposal: a MAPS (managed account) option, where the underlying assets were CFDs [Contract for Differences, a contract similar to a Total Return Swap] traded by DBL/UK. DBL would hire an investment advisor to trade the account, the assets of which are CFDs, and write an option on the account to a hedge fund. It is my understanding that we didn't do the trade due to UK regulatory/tax restrictions. Do you recall the rationale?"[299]

Mr. Purvis responded:

> "[W]hat you described faced some general objection where DB could be argued to have been effectively fronting for an unregulated fund, i.e., trading carried ostensibly in the name of DB as counterparty but the reality being that a third party fund was (a) actively trading and (b) DB on limited risk and (c) manager only partially subject to DB oversight. Not thought to be a good idea then and following the Soc. Gen. fiasco I imagine there would be even more twitching now."[300]

(ii) Informing Auditor of RenTec Control

At Barclays, some of the clearest and most direct evidence that RenTec controlled the COLT option accounts and bore the related rewards and risks from the trading in those accounts was Barclays' decision to remove the account assets from its balance sheet. Barclays carried out its decision by removing from its balance sheet the special purpose entity it had established, called Palomino Ltd., to hold the COLT basket option accounts on behalf of the bank. Removing Palomino, a shell corporation, from the balance sheet – an action called deconsolidation – in effect removed Palomino's assets from the balance sheet as well. When consulting with its auditor over making the change, Barclays justified taking that action by explaining how RenTec controlled Palomino and Palomino's accounts and received all of the significant rewards and risks associated with the account activity, as explained below.

Barclays removed Palomino from its balance sheet for accounting purposes in 2009, as part of a larger series of changes to its overall corporate structure.[301] Its action meant that the accounts and assets held in Palomino's name were no longer considered part of Barclays and no longer included in Barclays' financial statements, reducing Barclays' total assets by more than $4 billion.[302] This accounting approach mirrored the accounting treatment that the bank already provided for standard prime brokerage accounts holding client assets; it also mirrored how Prime Services, the Barclays division that dealt directly with RenTec, already handled the accounting for the majority of its client accounts.[303]

Barclays had begun considering the removal of the Palomino assets from its balance sheet in 2008, noting in an early analysis: "Generally, Palomino and Barclays do not share in any gains in the value of the account, because any such gains are paid away to Badger under the Options."[304] Badger was the shell entity established by RenTec to act as the official option holder on behalf of the hedge fund.

In June 2009, to obtain approval for the proposed deconsolidation from its auditor, PricewaterhouseCoopers (PWC), Barclays implemented several PWC recommendations to clarify that Palomino was controlled by and operated for the benefit of RenTec. First, Barclays amended the Palomino Articles of Association to "restrict the activities of Palomino to those it is currently engaged in under the COLT transaction,"[305] including to continue to work with RenTec. Second, Barclays entered into a side letter with RenTec in which its subsidiary, BBPLC, the sole owner of Palomino, "covenant[ed] that it shall not make any amendments or modifications to the Memorandum and Articles of Association of Palomino without … the prior written consent thereto of Renaissance."[306] According to Barclays and PWC, after taking those actions, Palomino could be considered a special purpose entity "set up for the benefit of Renaissance."[307] In a contemporaneous email, PWC also observed that the risk to Barclays from the Palomino option accounts was "remote," citing several "critical features of the agreement" related to the basket option accounts, including "trading parameters, the trigger points at which Barclays can control a wind-down, the ability to adjust the call premium such that if losses are incurred, more funds are injected, and the involvement of market risk in setting these parameters."[308]

PWC confirmed in writing to Barclays that the restrictions placed on Palomino ensured that Palomino existed only for the benefit of RenTec, citing in particular the restriction on the activities of Palomino resulting from the June 2009 amendments to the Palomino Articles of Association.[309] Among other matters, those amendments specified that only RenTec could serve as the trading manager for a Palomino account and that Palomino could hold prime brokerage accounts only through members of the Barclays group.[310] In addition, Palomino's owner, BBPLC, entered into the side letter with RenTec, promising not to further amend the Palomino Articles of Association without obtaining RenTec's prior approval, further demonstrating RenTec's control over Palomino.[311]

On June 24, 2009, Barclays sent a memorandum to PWC proposing to remove Palomino from the bank's balance sheet.[312] In that memorandum, to support the proposed deconsolidation, Barclays made the following statements regarding RenTec's control of Palomino, Palomino's COLT accounts, and the assets in those accounts:

- "Although BBPLC owns 100% of the ordinary shares of Palomino, RenTec has the power to govern the financial and operations decisions for its benefit due to decisions it makes over Palomino's activities under the IMA [Investment Management Agreement] ….
- Palomino was created solely to enable RenTec … to benefit … from its long- short statistical arbitrage strategy in an efficient manner (we understand that RenTec also obtains an additional tax benefit under the transactions as its profits on the Badger Options will generally be subject to tax at the long term capital gains rate of 15% rather than the ordinary income tax rate of 35%).
- The trading activities of Palomino in relation to the PB [Prime Brokerage] Accounts are managed solely by RenTec as the Trading Managers such that RenTec can obtain the majority of the benefits from Palomino's activities. ...
- [T]he PB [Prime Brokerage] Accounts are controlled by RenTec.
- RenTec is effectively entitled … to 100% of the benefits from Palomino's trading activates less any prime brokerage fees paid to BCI and BCSL in respect of the PB Accounts.
- Conclusion: Following the proposed amendments to the Articles and the entry into the Side Letter, RenTec controls the major activities of Palomino and is exposed to substantially all significant risks and rewards arising from the activities carried out through the PB Accounts, being the only permitted activities of Palomino."[313]

These statements, made by Barclays to its independent auditor to obtain approval for a significant accounting action, are strong evidence of the control RenTec exerted over Palomino and the option accounts.[314]

Although RenTec signed the side letter with Barclays and agreed to the amendments of the Palomino Articles of Association, a RenTec executive told the Subcommittee that RenTec did not fully understand the nature of what Barclays was doing and was not aware of the representations that Barclays had made to its auditor.[315] When informed of RenTec's assertions, Barclays counsel told the Subcommittee that RenTec was fully engaged in the bank's effort to remove Palomino from its balance sheet and knew the side letter was part of that effort. In a letter to the Subcommittee, Barclays counsel wrote in part:

- "[D]uring this deconsolidation process, Barclays was also engaged with Renaissance and its counsel.
- In the second quarter of 2009, Barclays had a series of telephone calls and e-mail and letter exchanges, and also exchanged drafts of documents, with Renaissance and their counsel that dealt with amendments to the Articles of Association and the drafting of a side letter.
- Mark Silber of Renaissance signed the Side Letter, and at least Jim Rowen and Renaissance outside Counsel Ed Cohen of Winston & Strawn were participants in these exchanges.
- … Barclays believes it made clear during these communications that its objective was to change the accounting treatment of Palomino, and Barclays believed that Renaissance understood that an accounting deconsolidation would be the logical result of these changes.
- … [Barclays understood] that RenTec confirmed to Barclays that it did not intend to consolidate Palomino under the applicable accounting standards.
- In connection with these discussions, Renaissance requested that Barclays confirm that its prior representations regarding the transaction were still true and correct, which Barclays did. Moreover, Renaissance cooperated with Barclays in negotiating and executing the required documents."[316]

Regarding the amendments to Palomino's Articles of Association, Barclays counsel wrote that, "Renaissance and their counsel reviewed the proposed amendments and confirmed they had no issues."[317] In addition, Barclay's counsel represented that, with respect to the side letter, "Barclays initially proposed that the provision relating to consent to further amendments to the Articles," and "Renaissance and its counsel provided Barclays with an initial draft of a letter that requested certain representations by Barclays, and the provision regarding amendments later was included in that Side Letter."[318]

Barclays disclosed the deconsolidation of Palomino from its financial statements in its 2009 Annual Report and stated the following:[319]

> **"Entities where the Group's interest exceeds 50% which are excluded from consolidation**
>
> Although the Group's interest in the equity voting rights in certain entities exceeds 50%, or it may have the power to appoint a majority of their Boards of Directors, they are excluded from consolidation because the Group either cannot direct the financial and operating policies of these entities, or on the grounds that another entity has a superior economic interest in them. Consequently, these entities are not deemed to be controlled by Barclays."

Barclays' SEC filing also included a table, excerpted below, with information in relation to such entities as required by the Companies Act 2006 Section 410(2)(b):

Country of Registration or Incorporation	Name	Percentage of ordinary share capital held %
Cayman Islands	Palomino Limited	100

Barclays, with its auditor's support, removed Palomino from its balance sheet, because the accounts and assets held in Palomino's name benefited RenTec, not the bank. In the documents sent to its auditor and disclosed in its annual reports and SEC filings, Barclays plainly stated that RenTec controlled the COLT accounts and bore "substantially all significant risks and rewards" arising from the account activities.[320] Barclay's statements offer yet more proof that RenTec, rather than the banks, controlled and bore the risks and rewards associated with the option trading accounts.

(iii) Functioning as Prime Brokerage Trading Accounts

For all practical purposes, the COLT and MAPS accounts functioned like prime brokerage accounts actively traded by RenTec, rather than as proprietary accounts used by the banks to hedge the options.[321] Both of the banks recognized this fact and in internal communications frequently characterized the option accounts as "prime brokerage" accounts. Opening the COLT and MAPS accounts in the name of the banks and styling them as carrying out option agreements, rather than prime brokerage accounts intended to transact trading, were actions taken to achieve objectives related to lower taxes, increased leverage, and loss protection.

Barclays, in its initial approval documentation for the COLT basket option structure in 2002, described COLT as providing:

> "an after tax benefit to these investors [RenTec] through the conversion of their return from the fund from short term capital gains (taxed at 39.6%) to long term capital gains (taxed at 20%). This would be achieved by substituting the Fund's direct execution of its trading strategy with the cash settled call option over a Barclays proprietary account whose performance *substantially* replicates the Fund's trading strategy."[322]

This statement shows that Barclays acknowledged the tax objective of COLT and considered the "Barclays proprietary account" – which was a prime brokerage account opened in the name of a shell corporation, Palomino – to be a substitute for RenTec's own trading account.[323]

A 2003 Barclays memorandum approving a second COLT option with RenTec again described the option account as a prime brokerage account, while also making the point that the risks presented by the option account were "akin to the risks taken in a normal collateralised Prime Brokerage relationship":

> "The Second Renaissance Transaction would utilize the existing prime brokerage trading accounts held with both BCSL and BCI (collectively referred to as the 'PB Account'). … Palomino [the shell company used by Barclays in COLT] will not have any credit risk or market risk in the transaction, due to the fact that … its PB Account is hedged by the Synthetic Call Option and Prime Brokerage effectively has taken the downside risk. The risk borne by Prime Brokerage is akin to the risks taken in a normal collateralised Prime Brokerage relationship, where the risks generally are confined to catastrophic losses occurring over a short period of time."[324]

Barclays view of the option account as a prime brokerage account is further evidenced in a Barclays evaluation of the COLT structure in 2010:

> "The options reference the value of these PB [Prime Brokerage] accounts, which is equivalent to them referencing the assets directly, and therefore there is no leakage between the value of the assets … and the value of the options. Thus, the net effect is that Barclays is extending senior financing to RenTec."[325]

At Deutsche Bank, a 2009 email described the MAPS structure in similar terms, as a "PB" or Prime Brokerage facility used to carry out the trading strategy directed by RenTec:

> "The Renaissance MAPS trade is a synthetic, non-recourse PB-inspired facility. We [Deutsche Bank] carry the equity longs and shorts, as directed by Renaissance, on our BS [balance sheet] and pass the performance of [the] portfolio to Renaissance via swap."[326]

In fact, the so-called "option" accounts provided RenTec with more benefits than normal prime brokerage accounts. Prime brokerage accounts are subject to federal margin rules that limit the financing that can be provided by a broker-dealer to a client through the account for the purchase of securities, allowing no more than a 2:1 leverage ratio. The MAPs and COLT option accounts established in the name of the banks, which designated RenTec as the investment advisor rather than the owner of the assets, sidestepped those margin limits; any funds added to the account by the banks could be treated as the banks supplying money for their own trades. By engaging in that fiction, Deutsche Bank offered RenTec a leverage ratio of up to 18:1, while Barclays offered a leverage ratio of up to 20:1.[327]

In a true option account, the option holder would not be actively trading the securities that determine the value of the options. The option holder would not be seeking or using financing to make more trades. Instead, the option holder would be passively awaiting the financial return on a trading account under the control of the option seller. The accounts set up in connection with the so-called basket option structures, however, were designed and intended from their inception to be under the control of the option holder and to produce trading profits benefiting the option holder alone.

Here, RenTec served as both the controller and the beneficiary of the trading activity in the basket option accounts, and but for mischaracterizing this as option activity, RenTec would not have been permitted under law to receive the added leverage it sought. While those accounts were purportedly established to provide a reference account for the basket option as well as a hedge for the banks, and all trading assets were held in the name of the banks, in reality, the accounts functioned in substance as prime brokerage trading accounts used by RenTec to carry out its trading strategy, while claiming lower taxes and higher leverage than it could otherwise justify.

(b) Changing the Asset Pool

As previously noted, RenTec developed, employed, and continually adjusted a complex algorithm to implement its trading strategy. It initiated hundreds of thousands of short-term trades per day, resulting in rapid and significant turnover in the assets in the option accounts, creating an ever changing basket of securities in the referenced accounts. This activity, controlled by RenTec as the investment advisor, continually modified the portfolio of assets supposedly supporting the option contracts. The constant changes undermined the notion of an option whose value was linked to a specific set of assets, and could also be seen as having given rise to realization events for tax purposes.

(i) Constantly Changing Algorithm

During the period examined by the Subcommittee, RenTec indicated that it employed over 90 professionals with doctorates in mathematics, physics, and computer science, and directed them to constantly monitor, update, and improve its key trading algorithm, which encompassed many different strategies that RenTec used to trade.[328] RenTec explained to the Subcommittee that those employees constantly worked on and modified the algorithm, carefully modeling new factors and introducing them into the algorithm over time to alter how it decided what trading recommendations to make.[329]

In addition, according to Peter Brown, RenTec's Co-CEO, RenTec's investment strategy was not confined to application of its algorithm; at times, RenTec employees also personally intervened to suggest trading strategies. In a 2008 telephone call between Deutsche Bank and RenTec, Dr. Brown was asked the question: "[H]ow would we react when some extraordinary thing happened that can't be so easily measured in market statistics?"[330] Dr. Brown answered:

> "Well, the answer there is that we have a risk control department and we also have senior management, all of whom are quite tuned into what is going on in a qualitative sense in the market. . . . We then take that into account and it adjust the levels at which we run. So, for example … now is a perfect example. [O]ur models are functioning very well in this environment. Nonetheless, we are … running at reduced levels and the reason we are running at reduced levels is precisely the reasons that you bring up. It's … not clear –we're still in unchartered territory here. We don't know exactly – is government intervention going on. … [T]he models don't see the government intervention but we do and we are nervous that something could happen. … So we have actually intervened and we do that from time to time when things like this happen."[331]

In interviews with the Subcommittee, RenTec representatives explained that the algorithm executing its investment strategy was also managed by a separate "allocation function," that worked off of data manually entered by

RenTec employees and could be updated at any time by RenTec employees.[332] A RenTec email exchange provided an example of how this function worked, indicating that, during the Greek crisis in 2011, RenTec used the allocation function to alter the priorities of its accounts between Deutsche Bank and Barclays, directing trades away from Barclays and towards Deutsche Bank to reduce counterparty risk, which then altered the size of the respective option structures at the two bank by nearly $4 billion.[333] RenTec told the Subcommittee that the allocations between option accounts and its other prime brokerage accounts, which use the same algorithm strategy, are also updated regularly and manually by RenTec employees.[334]

Together, these facts indicate that RenTec's trading strategy relied on a complex, computer-based algorithm that was undergoing constant modifications and upgrades and whose results were further modified at times by trading suggestions and by manual allocation functions. The end result was that RenTec's trading strategy changed on a regular and ongoing basis.

(ii) Constantly Changing Asset Mix

RenTec's constantly changing trading strategy and high-volume trading approach produced continuous turnover in the assets attributed to the option accounts. Prior to 2012, the majority of RenTec's basket options were exercised more than one year after they were created. A 2010 SEC examination report found that the average length of the 42 options RenTec had exercised to that point was 385 days.[335] In addition, the SEC examination report found that, during the one-year period from April 1, 2008 to March 31, 2009, RenTec placed approximately 129 million trade orders, involving nearly 10,000 different financial instruments across 18 countries.[336] As previously noted, RenTec advised the Subcommittee that it "recommended" between 100,000 and 150,00 trades per day, each, through Deutsche Bank and Barclays' trading platforms.[337] Those estimates of the daily trading activities at each bank yield a combined estimated average of 26-39 million trades per year through the option accounts.

In addition to initiating a high volume of trades, the data indicates that RenTec generally held the assets it acquired for relatively short periods of time. As part of its 2010 examination, the SEC prepared a chart analyzing the length of time that RenTec held its positions.[338] An excerpt from that chart, reprinted below, showed that, during the two-year period examined, RenTec's Medallion funds held positions for less than three months 87% of the time. They held positions for over six months less than 1% of the time. As a result of this constant turnover, RenTec regularly altered the entire composition of the assets included in the option accounts several times a year. When asked about this turnover rate, RenTec told the Subcommittee that it viewed the rate of change as critical to the success of RenTec's investment strategy.[339]

Not an option. Options and other derivatives usually require the participants to make careful calculations about how specified financial assets will perform, but in the case of the basket options, the hedge funds and banks agreed to allow constant change in the option assets. The agreement to allow such extensive asset changes is evidence that the option accounts were intended to function as trading accounts rather than an option or other derivative.

A fundamental feature of a derivative is the presence of an underlying or referenced set of assets that can be identified, analyzed, and used to determine the derivative's price, performance, and ultimate resolution with respect to the participating parties.[340] To evaluate and price a derivative, including an option, the participants typically analyze the referenced assets; if those assets are not fixed or easily identified, and are instead permitted to undergo constant and fundamental change, the required analysis cannot be performed. Products like the basket options that cannot, as a practical matter, produce an identifiable set of referenced assets do not function as true options or even as derivatives.

The basket option contracts between RenTec, Deutsche Bank, and Barclays did not set up an arrangement that would produce an identifiable set of referenced assets. The contracts stated that the determinant of what the banks would owe RenTec upon exercise of the option would be the performance of a designated option account. The account, which was to be managed and controlled by RenTec, was permitted to include a broad array of assets, whose selection was at the discretion of RenTec, subject only to some basic guidelines to reduce trading risk.[341]

RenTec then used the basket option accounts to implement a proprietary investment strategy that employed as many as 300,000 securities trades at two banks per day, constantly changing the mix of assets in the option accounts. RenTec personnel were continually monitoring and adjusting the factors used by the complex computer model that RenTec developed and employed to execute its strategy. The volume of trades that RenTec conducted in the account was so large and the length of time that the assets were held was generally so short that the entire composition of tens of thousands of assets in the option accounts changed several times a year. In essence, the banks allowed RenTec to write an option on RenTec's own daily trading activity, whatever RenTec might decide that trading activity would be. The contracts did not further identify the referenced assets

Holding Period Medallion

From January 1, 2007 thru March 31, 2009		
Lots Relieved In*	**MED****	**Cumulative**
3 months	12.25%	86.97%
4 months	5.95%	92.91%
5 months	2.92%	95.84%
6 months	1.57%	97.41%
7 months	0.85%	98.26%
8 months	0.61%	98.87%
9 months	0.43%	99.30%
10 months	0.27%	99.58%
11 months	0.16%	99.74%
12 months	0.10%	99.84%
over 1 year	0.16%	100.00%

*Turnover time frame.

**Medallion holding time for its securities.

Source: Undated chart, "Holding Period Comparison RIEF vs. Medallion" January 1, 2007 through March 31, 2009," prepared by RenTec, SEC_RT13_010650-651 [Sealed Exhibit].

.

Material, fundamental changes to the option. RenTec's extensive, continual changes to the basket of assets in the referenced accounts had a second consequence. Even if the basket option structure were determined to be a derivative, the basket of assets was altered in such a fundamental and material way by the trading activity that the changes may be deemed to be an exchange of one property for another, resulting in an exchange of the existing option for a new one, triggering a "realization event" for RenTec under Section 1001 of the tax code.[342] Section 1001 determines the point at which gains should be recognized for tax purposes.

An IRS regulation states that a taxpayer must recognize gain "from the exchange of property for other property differing materially either in kind or in extent."[343] It has also determined that a realization event triggering the report of gain from an exchange of property may occur when there is a material change in an option contract:

> "A change in contractual terms effected through an option provided in the original contract is treated as an exchange under section 1001 if there is a sufficiently fundamental or material change that the substance of the original contract is altered through the exercise of the option.

> Under such circumstances, the old contract is treated as if it were actually exchange for a new one."[344]

Given how rapidly the assets in the option accounts turned over, any such gains would be short-term and not long-term, thus undercutting the option's objective of producing long-term capital gains subject to a lower tax rate.

(c) Ignoring Option Formalities

RenTec entered into 29 options with Deutsche Bank and 31 with Barclays for a total of 60 basket options that RenTec exercised after the one-year mark. George Weiss entered into 10 basket options with Deutsche Bank. One striking feature of how they operated is that neither the hedge funds nor the banks traded the option assets on an individualized, per option basis; instead, they pooled the assets from multiple options before trading them, transferred assets among different option accounts, and used a single trading strategy for all of them. By ignoring the option formalities and treating the assets as part of a single, large investment pool, the hedge funds and banks showed the option format was a pretext for enabling the hedge funds to conduct a complex trading strategy while claiming the strategy produced lower taxes and higher leverage than would otherwise be available through a normal prime brokerage account.

(i) Option Accounts as One Big Investment Pool

The banks and RenTec told the Subcommittee that, from 1999 to 2008, they did not keep track of assets on a per-option basis. Instead, the assets from multiple options were pooled together in a single proprietary trading account opened in the name of the bank. Once assets were added to the pool, they lost their identity as being associated with a particular option. Thereafter, to determine its profits, each individual option was viewed as having claim to a specified percentage of the overall portfolio of assets.

While Barclays has continued using that approach from 2002 to the present, in 2008, after Deutsche Bank restructured the MAPS option, it required each MAPS option to be tracked separately and the assets purchased through each option to be assigned to a separate subaccount within the larger proprietary trading account used for basket options. Even then, however, once separate subaccounts were established for each option, Deutsche Bank allowed RenTec to transfer assets between the subaccounts using book entries to transfer the assets without trading on the market, a practice called journaling.

Deutsche Bank's practice of allowing the free transfer of assets between option subaccounts offers further evidence that the parties did not view the option contracts as creating separate financial instruments referencing separate, distinct sets of assets, but instead viewed them as interrelated parts of a single trading strategy under RenTec's control.

Percentage Allocations. Because the assets purchased through multiple options were pooled, at Deutsche Bank until the end of the year 2008, and at Barclays through the present day, RenTec and George Weiss determined the value of an individual option using a rough-cut percentage allocation, meaning using a process to allocate a percentage of the pooled assets to a particular option.[345] In other words, neither the hedge funds nor the banks made any attempt to assign specific securities to specific options and track those specific securities on an ongoing basis. Instead, given the pooling of assets, RenTec told the Subcommittee that it was impossible to say at any given time that the gains from any given holding in the pooled securities applied or did not apply to a particular option.[346] One RenTec employee agreed that, during the time that the options were accounted for in this manner, it would have been impossible to walk it back and determine which assets from the pooled securities had belonged to which option.[347] Similarly, Barclays personnel told the Subcommittee that they accounted for RenTec trading and compliance with the bank's investment guidelines on a single, structure-wide basis.[348]

The evidence indicates that the method actually used for calculating the value of an option under the old Deutsche Bank structure and the Barclays structure required looking at each option in existence at the time that a new one was added and assigning a percentage of the total assets invested in the structure at that time to each existing option.[349] In other words, each time that a new option was added or an existing option was exercised, every other option was re- valued and assigned a new percentage of the total pooled assets.

This rough-cut percentage allocation method meant that every option affected the overall value of every other option that coexisted with it at any point in time. The value of each option was not individually tracked, but calculated as a percentage of the value of the overall pooled assets at each bank. This practice provides additional evidence that the assets in the individual options were pooled and treated as an integrated whole, rather than being associated with specific options. It is also far from clear that an "option" with an ever changing basket of securities with no identifiable assets of its own merits treatment as a true option, or even as a derivative.

(ii) Journaling Between Deutsche Bank Option Subaccounts

From 1998 to 2008, in the old MAPS system, Deutsche Bank pooled all of the assets purchased through multiple basket options and hired RenTec as the investment advisor for the account containing all of those assets. RenTec told the Subcommittee that the same account simultaneously served as the bank's hedge for all of the outstanding options.[350] In 2008, as part of Deutsche Bank's restructuring of the MAPS option, Deutsche Bank created a new system that purported to divide up the holdings for each separate option and assign the assets for each option to a separate subaccount. At the same time, the new system continued using a single proprietary trading account that contained all of the option assets. Despite continued use of that pooled account, RenTec told the Subcommittee that the new subaccounts ensured specific assets individually corresponded to and hedged each option separately.[351] Both Deutsche Bank and RenTec explained that the new system also "resolved ambiguity" relating to how an individual option could be liquidated in the event of the option breaching its barrier, because with subaccounts, it would be clear what assets to liquidate.[352]

At the same time, as part of the new system, Deutsche Bank allowed RenTec to "journal" assets between different subaccounts.[353] A "journal" in this context is the ability to transfer a stock position from one subaccount to another, using book entries for the two accounts to accomplish the transfer, without the need to sell the position to the market and then immediately buy it back.[354] According to both Thomas Kerns and Eamon McCooey, who managed operations for Deutsche Bank's updated MAPS system at different times, this kind of transfer would have been problematic if it had been conducted through the market, since selling and repurchasing identical securities could have been misinterpreted as "wash sales" or some other type of manipulative trading.[355]

RenTec completely controlled the journaling process through its authority to determine what assets could be included in a particular option account. According to RenTec, it used journaling for "Portfolio rebalancing due to Option Exercise," meaning to "reallocate the positions in the sub-account underlying the exercised option to the remaining options based on their relative cash settlement amounts."[356] Peter Brown, co-CEO of RenTec, explained to the Subcommittee that the journaling process was important, because it assisted RenTec with loss protection.[357] He explained that it also made sense to be able to journal from a business perspective because, under the new MAPS structure, Deutsche was charging RenTec an "upfront 20% of the premium as prepaid financing," incentivizing RenTec to start with high leverage because they were already paying for it.[358]

RenTec used the journal process frequently to transfer positions between Deutsche Bank subaccounts when a new option was opened or an older option was exercised.[359] At the Subcommittee's request, RenTec provided a listing of journal entries it had made in preparation for the exercise of an option or the initiation of a new option. The list shows that, after 2008, journaling was used to transfer assets at all but one European style option at Deutsche Bank.[360] The list also indicates that the journals were used to transfer between 14% and 100% of the assets in a particular option subaccount.[361] Of the ten journals RenTec identified for the Subcommittee as undertaken in anticipation of an option exercise, two transferred 100% of the assets in the option that was about to be exercised, and two more transferred 99% of the assets in the option about to be exercised.[362] The average value of each of those ten journal entries represented over $800 million in positions, and RenTec used those journals to transfer those positions to other option subaccounts it controlled, before exercising the options that referenced those positions.[363] The data indicates that RenTec also used journals at other points in the life of an option contract: many were done just prior to exercise, but a few journals transferred assets more than three months prior to the exercise of the option from which they were journaled.[364] In 2011, RenTec conducted a pair of journals after an option had already been exercised but prior to its final valuation.[365]

A 2008 RenTec email also noted that the process could be used to "reshuffle" assets among options at the end of a trading day. As James Rowen, RenTec's COO stated in an email to another RenTec executive: "[T]here is no prohibition against end-of-day transfers in our new MAPS documentation. We may reshuffle the constituents of the underlying options at the end of the day, at the current closing price."[366] Mr. Rowen also advised in the email that Mark Silber, RenTec's legal and compliance head, was involved in the planning to keep the reshuffling "manageable" and "below the radar of DB."[367] When asked about his email, Dr. Brown told the Subcommittee that RenTec did not actually make any journal entries simply to reshuffle assets among existing options at the end of a trading day, even though it was allowed under the terms of the management agreement.[368]

RenTec's frequent usage of journaling exposed several features of the new MAPS structure that may not have been immediately clear. First, it demonstrated that, although the new MAPS structure purported to set up separate option subaccounts to separate the assets assigned to each option, journaling allowed RenTec to continue to transfer assets among the options.

Second, exercising an option did not require RenTec to give up assets that it wanted to retain; instead, RenTec could use journaling to transfer the assets it wanted to keep from the option being exercised to a different option subaccount, thereby maintaining the underlying assets. Third, each option subaccount was not operated on an independent basis, but was used by RenTec to pursue trading strategies that reached across all of its options. Fourth, journaling allowed RenTec to transfer assets out of a particular option subaccount and then exercise that option to cash out only a percentage of what had been its overall portfolio, just as it had been able to do through the old MAPS structure.

RenTec's active journaling showed that the new MAPS structure did not stop the hedge fund from switching assets among options. To the contrary, it provided additional evidence of RenTec acting as if it were the owner of the option assets, as opposed to a passive option holder. RenTec's journaling again raised the issue of whether the basket options operated as true options, when their reference assets could be and were so easily altered.

(d) Withdrawing Cash at Regular Intervals

After Deutsche Bank restructured the MAPS options in 2008, and began using European style options that required option exercise on a specific date, RenTec set up the options it purchased so that it could regularly withdraw cash throughout the year from the option accounts and use that cash to support its business operations.

RenTec told the Subcommittee that it wanted to cash out its earnings from its basket option holdings on a regular basis in order to protect its gains from a significant market downturn.[369] RenTec also indicated that it wanted to regularly access the option earnings to cover employee salaries and bonuses, and to make distributions to shareholders in order to keep the Medallion funds at a specified size.[370] Peter Brown, RenTec's Co-CEO, told the Subcommittee that RenTec explicitly designed its 2008 option purchases to facilitate cash flow from the basket option structures on at least a semiannual basis to run its business operations, including paying salaries.[371]

The technique that RenTec used was to stagger the initiation of the options it purchased so that they reached the one-year mark at intervals that enabled RenTec to withdraw funds on a regular basis, either quarterly or semi-annually, past the one-year time frame.[372] When an option matured, RenTec typically cashed out the earnings it needed and rolled the remaining assets from the expired option's subaccount into the subaccount of an existing or newly initiated option. RenTec referred to this practice as the "Steady

State."[373] RenTec apparently communicated its desire to maintain that steady state to Deutsche Bank, since a 2008 email from Satish Ramakrishna, head of risk for the Global Prime Finance division at Deutsche Bank, indicated that he understood that RenTec "wish[ed] to stagger options once every 3 months."[374]

The fact that RenTec was able to orchestrate the timing of the options to guarantee itself regular access to the gains from short-term trades underscores how completely it controlled the transactions. In addition, RenTec's ability to make routine cash withdrawals from the basket option accounts to support its business operations is additional evidence that RenTec acted in the role of an owner of the underlying account assets, rather than as an option holder awaiting final resolution of an option under the control of another party.

(2) George Weiss Utilization of Basket Option Structure

The use of the basket option structure by George Weiss Associates – the second largest user of the basket option structures – further calls into question the legitimacy of this structure as a derivative, and whether resulting gains qualified for long-term capital gains treatment.

From 2003 to 2007, George Weiss bought ten MAPS basket options from Deutsche Bank, involving assets that at their inception had a notional value totaling about $2.8 billion.[375] Those basket options functioned in the same manner as the MAPS options purchased by RenTec. The option assets were held in the name of Deutsche Bank and kept in a proprietary trading account opened in the name of the bank. Like RenTec, George Weiss was named as the investment advisor for the option accounts, and it was George Weiss that determined the trading strategy and initiated the trading orders, which were then executed using Deutsche Bank's trading software. Like RenTec, the assets purchased through George Weiss' individual options were pooled, and the hedge fund traded them as part of an integrated trading strategy. Unlike RenTec, George Weiss did not trade as frequently nor did it rely on a trading algorithm.

(a) Crossing Trades between Accounts

On several occasions, George Weiss used basket option assets in ways that appeared to disregard which entity nominally owned the assets.

For example, in July 2008, prior to closing out several MAPS options, George Weiss moved some of the assets from the MAPS account it managed to a prime brokerage account opened in the name of OGI Associates LLC, a related entity.[376] The OGI prime brokerage account was also located at Deutsche Bank. In an email instructing the transfer – or journal – to occur,

George Weiss personnel requested movement of the assets "to [the] OGI account from the MAPS account."[377] Later, in the same year, crossing positions were suggested again by George Weiss personnel in order to correct a perceived imbalance between long and short exposure in the MAPS account.[378] On both occasions, George Weiss transferred assets that had been held in the name of the bank to a brokerage account where those same assets would be held in the name of a related entity. When asked about the trades, George Weiss COO Federick Doucette told the Subcommittee that "a handful" of these trades did occur, but that George Weiss viewed them as "a mistake" and that they involved "very small amounts."[379]

In addition to moving assets from MAPS accounts to the brokerage account of a related entity, OGI, George Weiss negotiated a "Master Netting Agreement" with Deutsche Bank, which allowed it to avoid financing charges when it had assets in MAPS accounts that left it economically neutral when combined with assets in the OGI prime brokerage account.[380] This 2003 agreement allowed George Weiss to offset assets from the two accounts, even though the assets in the OGI account were held in the name of a George Weiss entity and the assets in the MAPS account were held in the name of Deutsche Bank. That Deutsche Bank allowed this arrangement for some of the MAPS transactions conducted with George Weiss shows that the bank, as well as George Weiss, viewed the assets in the basket option accounts as belonging to the hedge fund rather than the bank.

When Deutsche Bank restructured the MAPS options in 2008, Deutsche Bank decided that it would no longer allow George Weiss to "cross sell positions" held in its MAPS accounts to its OGI prime brokerage account.[381]

(b) Using MAPS Assets as Collateral for Other Accounts

Despite the fact that the assets in the MAPS accounts – and the accounts themselves – were held in the name of Deutsche Bank, for several years, Deutsche Bank allowed George Weiss to use the options as collateral in other financial transactions. For example, Deutsche Bank permitted George Weiss to use "100% of the options market value to cross collateralize its OGI account," a prime brokerage account also located at Deutsche Bank.[382] When asked, George Weiss told the Subcommittee that the bank had agreed to the collateral arrangement, because of the long duration of its basket options and the relatively large amount of equity that had accrued in its MAPS option accounts.[383] George Weiss indicated that the bank had also permitted it to pledge the MAPS option accounts as collateral for a line of credit offered by Deutsche Bank, which the hedge fund then used to run its day-to-day business.[384] In both cases, the bank essentially allowed the hedge fund to treat the option account assets as if the hedge fund owned them.

In response to questions, George Weiss COO Frederick Doucette told the Subcommittee that neither George Weiss nor Deutsche Bank had fully considered what would happen if a margin call on the OGI account had required Deutsche Bank to draw upon the option equity as collateral.[385] Mr. Doucette noted that founder, George Weiss, had enough funds personally to cover the borrowed funds.[386]

When Deutsche Bank restructured the MAPS option in 2008, it indicated to George Weiss that it wanted to limit or remove the ability to use the options as collateral in other transactions.[387] During negotiations over a proposed term sheet for the restructured MAPS option, a George Weiss employee noted in an email: "As the draft is written, the failure to fund the collateral does not trigger our ability to terminate the IMA [Investment Management Agreement] and the option. In our view it should ...."[388] In another email to Deutsche Bank, George Weiss noted that the lack of cross-collateralization could reduce George Weiss' MAPS investments by as much as 60%, because the hedge fund would have to find additional liquidity structures elsewhere to finance its business operations.[389] When Deutsche Bank declined to allow the restructured MAPS option accounts to be used as collateral in other financial transactions, it contributed to the decision of George Weiss to discontinue its involvement with MAPS.[390]

Mr. Doucette told the Subcommittee that Deutsche Bank indicated that it was restructuring MAPS, in part, because of tax concerns.[391] He further noted that, because of the increased costs associated with the new structure, George Weiss declined to use it and, instead, decided to use its own prime brokerage accounts to execute the same trading strategies.[392]

(3) Claiming a Business Purpose

Deutsche Bank, Barclays, George Weiss, and RenTec all claimed that the motivation for using basket options was that it offered increased leverage to the option buyer as well as downside loss protection which was capped at the initial premium. They all claimed that tax avoidance was not a key motivator for the transactions.[393] Other evidence shows, however, that tax avoidance was a key aspect motivating the basket option structure. In addition, as indicated earlier, SEC examination reports determined that basket options appear to have enabled a handful of hedge funds, in less than five years, to avoid paying taxes totaling an estimated $915 million, while other data suggests that total tax avoidance could exceed $6 billion.

(a) Facilitating Tax Avoidance

Barclays, which dealt only with RenTec, was very direct about the tax-based motivation for their COLT transactions. In its original 2002 product approval memorandum for project COLT, Barclays' Structured Capital Markets (SCM) group wrote that COLT would provide "an after tax benefit to these investors through the conversion of their return from the fund from short term capital gains (taxed at 39.6%) to long term capital gains (taxed at 20%)."[394] In a 2004 product approval memorandum, SCM wrote the following about the "economic driver" for the COLT basket options being purchased by RenTec:

> "Fund Benefit
>
> US individual investors of the Fund would obtain a post-tax benefit if the Call Option is exercised after 12 months, because all the gain on the Call option would be treated as a long-term gain for US tax purposes and would therefore be taxed at 15%, as opposed to 35%."[395]

Barclays also conveyed this message to its regulator. In 2002, after it had underwritten its first basket option with RenTec, Barclays wrote to its U.K. regulator, the Financial Services Authority (FSA), explaining the COLT transaction and its tax benefits. Barclays wrote: "This transaction is designed to provide hedge funds with a tax effective means of undertaking the business and for Barclays it would generate both a structuring fee and additional volume for its prime brokerage business."[396] These documents show that, from its inception, Barclays understood tax to be a major component of the basket options structure and designed the product with that in mind.

Like Barclays, Deutsche Bank senior executives understood that tax avoidance was a key motivator for MAPS basket options. The following excerpt from a 2008 telephone conversation between Satish Ramakrishna, then Deutche Bank's Global Head of Risk, and William Broeksmit, then Co-Global Head of Finance, discussing RenTec's use of MAPS options illustrates the significance of the tax benefit:

> Satish Ramakrishna: "[S]o that's the way option is supposed to work. [N]ow what I've uh – now this is meant – this is structured as an option because – "
>
> William Broeksmit: "Yeah for tax reasons[.]"
>
> Satish Ramakrishna: "For tax reasons but the.... [T]he option makes it clear that the premium is the only ... commitment that the option holder has[.]"
>
> William Broeksmit: "Yeah umm hum[.]"

Satish Ramakrishna: "And so it's like a non-recourse strike[.]"
William Broeksmit: "Yes[.]"[397]

MAPS Restructuring. Information provided to the Subcommittee indicates that tax considerations also played a significant role in the restructuring of the MAPS option in 2008.

Mark Haas, a former Deutsche Bank employee who was in charge of the MAPS restructuring negotiations in the first half of 2008, told the Subcommittee that a tax attorney had informed him at the time that the MAPS restructuring had been undertaken as part of a broader review of structured transactions at the bank.[398] He told the Subcommittee that Deutsche Bank was concerned about whether the MAPS structure, as it was then configured, qualified as a derivative, and undertook the 2008 restructuring in an effort to obtain a favorable legal opinion that the basket options could, in fact, be characterized as derivatives.[399] Mr. Haas explained that he had learned that the changes were made, because the bank's legal and compliance department had viewed the structure as "not enough like an option."[400] He indicated that tax considerations were a "major driver" in making the changes to the structure at that time.[401]

Other Deutsche Bank representatives confirmed Mr. Haas's description of the 2008 changes. Deutsche Bank's counsel told the Subcommittee that the pre-2008 MAPS structure had been similar to the types of basket options described in the November 2010 IRS GLAM, and that tax considerations had been a factor in the changes made to the overall structure in 2008.[402] Deutsche Bank's counsel explained further that, in 2008, the bank placed McKee Nelson, Deutsche Bank's counsel for tax and transaction matters, in charge of determining the necessary changes to the MAPS structure in order for the bank to obtain a favorable tax opinion on MAPS' compliance with the tax code and for it to be respected as an option.[403]

Mr. Haas' description of the 2008 restructuring effort is also supported by Deutsche Bank documents. In 2008, the Global Prime Finance Division initiated a division-wide effort called "Change the Bank Programs" to revise systems and products throughout the division. A September 2008 presentation describing the ongoing and planned projects provided the following description of the program's focus: "Due to recent market conditions, we have focused some efforts on research and tactical developments to circumvent regulatory and reputational risks." [404]

One of the projects was the MAPS re-structuring. The project objectives were described as follows:

> "The object of this initiative is to provide a New Multiple MAPS structure that will more closely resemble a traditional options structure – premium risk. This new structure will require a major overhaul of our existing MAPS product …."[405]

The expected benefits of the project were also identified:

> "Will enable us to more actively market this structure to new clients as well as protect existing revenue streams of the existing MAPS clients."[406]

Deutsche Bank developed the new MAPS structure by the end of 2008. As already detailed above, the changes included subdividing each option's referenced assets into separate subaccounts; creating separate investment guidelines for each subaccount as well as guidelines for the overall structure; switching to European style options from American style options; paying the investment advisor – the hedge fund – a performance fee rather than a fixed fee; and changing the formula used to calculate the premium paid by the hedge fund, to make it appear more like conventional pricing mechanisms used in options.[407]

George Weiss told the Subcommittee that Deutsche Bank personnel also told its representatives that tax considerations drove a number of the 2008 changes to the MAPS structure.[408] George Weiss CEO Frederick Doucette stated that, when the hedge fund entered into negotiations with Deutsche Bank over the MAPS restructuring, Deutsche Bank had explained that most of the new provisions in the option were necessary "for tax purposes."[409] At another point during the negotiations, George Weiss raised concerns that a 2009 codification of the economic substance doctrine by Congress could pose a problem for the structure, noting in an email that the codification "could have serious implications with respect to the DB option transaction."[410]

During the negotiations on the MAPS restructuring, RenTec also appeared to insist on certain features for tax reasons. For example, on a telephone call with Deutsche Bank personnel who were discussing the possibility of lowering the available leverage offered by the MAPS options, RenTec's counsel Jonathan Mayers explained that a high initial leverage was a requirement for the structure by RenTec counsel.[411] Presumably, RenTec viewed the provision of high leverage levels as a defensible business justification for MAPS and wanted to be able to point to that feature aside from the option's tax benefits.

Together, the statements made by Barclays, Deutche Bank, George Weiss, and RenTec personnel provide strong evidence that tax considerations were a key driver in the original development and later restructuring of the basket options.

Delayed Disclosure of the Basket Options to DOJ. In 2010, as described above, after being caught participating in a number of abusive tax shelters, Deustche Bank entered into a Non-Prosecution Agreement (NPA) with the Department of Justice (DOJ) promising to stop "participat[ing] in and implement[ing] fraudulent tax shelters."[412] In addition, as part of the NPA, Deutsche Bank agreed to bring to the attention of DOJ: "products or transactions that may run afoul of U.S. federal income tax laws, rules, and regulations."[413] Despite negotiations on the NPA that lasted several years and the affirmative disclosure requirement in the final agreement, Deutsche Bank apparently did not, during the negotiations, notify federal prosecutors about the basket options product the bank had been selling to hedge fund clients for years.[414]

During the negotiations and while the NPA was in force, Deutsche Bank issued dozens of new basket options.[415] Deutsche Bank told the Subcommittee that, because it had obtained a legal opinion from outside counsel that the basket option structure, as revised in 2008, "should" withstand IRS scrutiny and the restructured options were different from those described in the 2010 IRS GLAM, the bank had not found it necessary to report the transactions to DOJ.[416] Deutsche Bank also indicated that, after the 2010 GLAM was issued, the bank had placed a moratorium on underwriting any new options, because of reputational concerns for the bank.[417] Deutsche Bank advised the Subcommittee that it was being conservative by staying away from anything that could be viewed as a listed transaction.[418]

In 2012, the Federal Reserve Bank of New York (FRBNY) examiners learned of the basket options being sold by Deutsche Bank to RenTec.[419] The FRBNY examiners raised concerns about the tax implications of the basket option transactions and, at the Federal Reserve's insistence, Deutsche Bank reported the transactions in connection with the NPA to the U.S. Attorney's Office for the Southern District of New York in January 2013, two years after signing the NPA.[420] The Subcommittee is unaware of what actions, if any, were taken by federal prosecutors in response to the bank's disclosure.

(b) Circumventing Leverage Requirements

The hedge funds told the Subcommittee that, rather than tax, a major motivating factor behind their participation in the basket options was the opportunity to obtain high levels of leverage, beyond the federal leverage limit of 2:1 normally applicable to brokerage accounts, an assertion supported by the banks. Deutsche Bank used its MAP accounts to provide a leverage level of up to 18:1,[421] while Barclays used its COLT accounts to provide a leverage level of up to 20:1.[422]

As explained earlier, federal securities laws and financial regulations impose restrictions on the use of credit to purchase securities.[423] Those restrictions were developed after highly leveraged securities transactions led to the stock crash of 1929, which imposed losses, not only on stock speculators, but also on the banks and broker-dealers that had lent them funds to buy securities, and led to the years of the Great Depression, the country's worst economic period.[424] To prevent future stock market shocks of a similar nature, Section 7 of the Securities Exchange Act of 1934 required federal financial regulators to issue "margin rules" to limit the amount of credit that a broker-dealer or other party may lend to a customer to buy securities, using those securities as collateral for the loan. One analyst summarized the policy reasons for imposing the margin rules as follows:

> "(1) to 'prevent[ ] the excessive use of credit for the purchase or carrying of securities'; (2) 'to protect the margin purchaser by making it impossible for him to buy securities on too thin a margin'; and (3) to 'prevent undue market fluctuations and help stabilize the economy generally ….' In short, margin rules were created to protect individual investors, the market, and the economy as a whole."[425]

A number of representatives indicated that Deutsche Bank, Barclays, RenTec, and George Weiss viewed achieving leverage beyond the limits of Regulation T as a major business objective for entering into the basket options.[426] In a 2012 letter to the IRS, for example, RenTec described its past use of leverage and how the basket options provided more leverage than it had achieved in any other setting:

> "Leverage … is restricted by the U.S. Federal Reserve's Regulations T, U, and X, commonly referred to as the 'margin rules.' The margin rules limit the extent to which brokerage customers can borrow against the stock positions that they own. …
>
> A brokerage account in which an investor can trade stocks utilizing money borrowed from the broker is referred to as a 'margin account.' A margin account can be opened in connection with a prime brokerage arrangement. Under the relevant Federal Reserve Regulations, if a Renaissance fund were to seek to obtain leverage by trading long and short positions in such a prime brokerage margin account held at a U.S.

> broker-dealer, it would be able to achieve leverage of no more than 2:1. That is, in order to hold $100 of long positions and $100 of short positions, the Renaissance fund would have to have invested $100 in the account.
>
> To achieve greater leverage, Renaissance made use of a 'joint back office' or 'JBO' arrangement. This involved qualifying one of Renaissance's investment funds as a registered broker-dealer in its own right, trading for its own account. As a result, the fund was exempt from the margin rules and was instead subject to the SEC 'net capital' rules .... This amounted to a leverage ratio limit of approximately 7.6:1[427] (*i.e.*, with $100 of equity the fund could hold approximately $335 of long positions and $335 of short positions.) Renaissance's fund that had a JBO arrangement during 2005 and 2006 had an average leverage ratio of 4.6:1 during those years, with a peak leverage ratio of 6.4:1.
>
> In the late 1990s, Renaissance began discussions with DB [Deutsche Bank] regarding the possibility of purchasing options from DB that would give Renaissance funds highly leveraged exposure .... DB was initially prepared to make leverage of up to 16:1 available to Renaissance pursuant to each option – a level that it later increased to 18:1. That is, if the premium paid by the Renaissance fund for the option was $100, the notional portfolio referenced by the option could consist of as much as $900 of long positions and $900 of short positions. This represented a dramatic increase over the leverage that Renaissance had been able to achieve through the JBO arrangement and substantially enhanced the opportunity to profit from the Algorithm. ...
>
> During 2005 and 2006, the average leverage in the DB Options was 11.7:1 and the maximum leverage utilized in those Options was 15.9:1. During the same period, the average leverage in the Barclays Options was 12.9:1, with the maximum leverage being 16.8:1."[428]

This letter indicates that, if RenTec had utilized a normal prime brokerage trading account at Deutsche Bank or Barclays, it would have been subject to the margin limits in Regulation T. But by using the basket option structure, which RenTec used to trade securities in virtually the same manner as normal prime brokerage trading accounts, the hedge fund claimed it could operate free of the federal margin rules imposing leverage limits. Because the basket option accounts were opened in the name of the banks and the account assets were also held in the name of the banks, the banks treated funds deposited into those accounts as supplying money to themselves rather than lending money to the hedge funds, which meant the federal leverage limits did not apply. The banks took the position that they were not lending money to the hedge funds, even though the hedge funds paid financing fees for use of the bank funds;[429] the hedge funds' premiums provided collateral to secure the financing;[430] and the banks described the options as a way to provide financing to their hedge-fund clients.[431] RenTec used the billions of dollars deposited into its option accounts by the banks to conduct millions of trades per year, and reported to the IRS that Deutsche Bank made "available to Renaissance" leverage as high as 17:1, secured only by the assets purchased with the borrowed money. At its peak, with bank financing, RenTec's basket option securities portfolio reached an outstanding notional value of more than $50 billion.[432]

The banks and hedge funds claimed the option accounts could operate entirely outside of the federal margin rules, even though those accounts operated in the same way as prime brokerage accounts subject to margin rules. Circumventing margin rules by relabeling a prime brokerage account as an "option" account is not, however, a legitimate business purpose. Moreover, bypassing the leverage limits did not displace tax avoidance as a key motivating factor for the basket option activity, as detailed above. Using the basket option structure as a way to circumvent federal leverage limits is another example of how the attempt to classify this transaction as a derivative was used to skirt laws and regulations in addition to tax.

(4) Restructuring the Basket Option Products

The final part of the basket options story involves the response of the banks and hedge funds to IRS efforts to stop the basket options from being misused to avoid federal taxes.

Deutsche Bank has offered basket options to a shrinking number of clients since around 1998; Barclays has offered them to a single large client, RenTec, since 2002. From 1998 to 2013, Deutsche Bank issued a total of 156 MAPS options to 13 hedge funds, including 36 to RenTec and 10 to George Weiss.[433] Barclays issued a total of 43 COLT options, all to RenTec. The hedge funds used those basket options to conduct more than $100 billion in securities transactions, presumably claiming that virtually all of the trading profits from options that lasted more than one year could be treated as long-term capital gains subject to the lower tax rate.

In November 2010, the IRS issued the Generic Legal Advice Memorandum (GLAM) advising that basket options cannot be used to turn short-term trading profits into long-term capital gains. Both Deutsche Bank and Barclays acknowledged to the Subcommittee that the banks were aware of the GLAM when it was issued, and that the IRS had determined that the basket option structure did not function as an option and should not be respected as such for tax purposes. Despite knowing of the GLAM, Barclays personnel continued issuing the same types of basket options to RenTec for another two years. Deutsche Bank responded to the GLAM by suspending its issuance of new basket options, while continuing to administer multiple basket options already in existence. In 2012 for Deutsche Bank and 2013 for Barclays, the banks issued revised basket option products, with terms lasting less than one year, so that the structures could no longer be used to characterize short-term trading profits as long-term capital gains.

For years, Deutsche Bank and Barclays spent a great deal of time, energy, and money to secure legal advice and opinions reaffirming the basket options as derivatives, in order to maintain the benefits that such a characterization provided. While the banks have not changed their position that the basket options are derivatives – a position which benefits the banks as well as their hedge fund clients – they have abandoned their longstanding efforts to facilitate their clients' claims that the option earnings should be classified as long-term capital gains.

(a) Barclays' Restructuring

Despite learning of the IRS GLAM in November 2010, Barclays continued issuing basket options to RenTec for another two years. Barclays internal communications justified its actions by noting that RenTec had provided the bank with a tax indemnity agreement and the bank had already participated in so many COLT transactions that its reputational risk would not be affected by participating in additional transactions.

Learning of the GLAM. The IRS GLAM was issued on November 12, 2010. That same day, Graham Wade, an SCM employee, sent an email to his colleagues, including Jonathan Zenios and Nizam Siddiq, notifying them of the GLAM and describing it as a "detailed write up" of the COLT basket options product. He reported that he planned to discuss the GLAM with RenTec and other bank personnel, and suggested that the GLAM did not affect the bank:

> "This [the GLAM] is a detailed write up of Colt concluding it doesn't work. We can discuss on MDs [managing directors'] call but I intend to reach out to RenTec and Ed Cohen this morning to make sure they are aware. We will also confirm it does not impact Barclays. The only issue for Barclays I could see is some deemed wht [withholding] agent issue as the memo concludes that RenTec are the legal owner of the stocks.
>
> To me this would signal that IRS is inevitably going to litigate Colt."[434]

At that point, Barclays recognized that the IRS had concluded that its basket option structure "doesn't work." Yet, that realization did not dissuade Barclays from continuing with the transaction. Over the next two years, Barclays entered into another nine basket option transactions with RenTec.[435]

Approving Additional COLT Options. One of those COLT transactions was presented to the Barclays SCM Approvals Committee in October 2012, which decided to approve it. Meeting attendees included Gerard LaRocca, Barclays' Chief Administrative Officer (CAO) and the most senior bank executive in the United States, as well as executives Graham Wade, Nizam Siddiq, and Marty Malloy, among others.

According to a memorandum summarizing the meeting, some of the key points made during the discussion that led to approval of the new COLT option were as follows:

- "The tax risk is assumed by the Client.
- The New Option Transaction does not meaningfully increase Barclays' reputation risk in relation to the Option Transactions, because writing a new option (or exercising an existing one) should be viewed as the maintenance of a longstanding structure."[436]

The memorandum also stated: "[S]enior management may desire to be informed of Option Transactions in the context of the current internal and external reviews at Barclays (Project Mango and the Salz Review)."[437] As explained earlier, because the bank was then under criticism for engaging in questionable conduct in a variety of settings, including participating in abusive tax shelters, Barclays leadership had initiated the Salz Review to get an independent review of Barclays' business practices and determine "what went wrong."[438]

On October 3, 2012, the SCM Group sent a memo to Barclays' Tax Risk Committee, informing it of the Group's decision to approve the new COLT transaction and explaining the controversy surrounding basket options.[439] The memorandum noted: "Barclays is entitled to a contractual tax indemnity from the client."[440]

On October 4, 2012, Gerard LaRocca, Barclays CAO, also sent an email alerting the Chair of Barclays' CIB Reputational Risk Committee to the COLT situation: "The SCM US Approvals Committee recently approved an option transaction in which US tax reputation risk is an issue."[441]

The new option was actually issued on October 9, 2012.[442]

On October 12, 2012, SCM sent a second memo to the Barclays Tax Risk Committee about the COLT transaction, even though the option had already been issued.[443] In it, SCM advocated approving the new COLT transaction, because while Barclays faced "reputation risk," the risk of litigation fell to the client.[444] SCM concluded that "we believe it remains an appropriate transaction for Barclays to be a party to."[445]

The memorandum acknowledged that, "[i]n 2010, the IRS issued a memo … arguing that options like the ones in the Option Transactions should not be treated as options for tax purposes."[446] In a section entitled, "Why the Option Transaction Remains Appropriate Notwithstanding the IRS Challenge," the SCM memorandum made the following points:

> "There is a reputation risk for Barclays, especially if the matter proceeds to court and the IRS's challenge and Barclays' role become publicly disclosed. However, continuing with the Option Transactions should not meaningfully increase Barclays' reputation risk, insofar as any court litigation would relate to the entire structure. Barclays' role will be that of a witness (alongside Deutsche Bank) and, provided Barclays fully cooperates with the process, there is no reason to expect damaging accusations from the IRS or the court. In particular, Barclays could not be considered to have sold a risky investment structure to an unsophisticated investor that did not understand the risk."[447]

Essentially, the memorandum contended that since Barclays was already at risk, due to previous basket option transactions, it would not "meaningfully increase" its reputational risk by participating in additional transactions, so there was no reason to stop offering the COLT options at that point in time. It also attempted to characterize Barclays' role as a "witness," even though the bank had designed, sold, and administered multiple COLT options for a decade. The memorandum also noted that Barclays had collected £322.7 million in revenue since the inception of the tax product, which, in 2012, was equivalent to about $415 million.[448]

The next month, in November 2012, the SCM Approvals Committee met to discuss RenTec's request to purchase yet another COLT option.[449] A memorandum summarizing the meeting again referred to the IRS investigation into the COLT product: "In AM 2010-005, the IRS concluded the call option does not function as an option and should not be treated as one for US tax purposes." Nevertheless, the memorandum again advocated approving the new option. It noted that many Barclays committees had already expressed approval of the product:

> "SCM has notified and received approval from the following in relation to proceeding with the proposed transaction: Tax, Finance, Credit Risk, Market Risk, Regulatory, Legal, Compliance, and Operations."[450]

The Barclays Tax Committee concurred. On November 23, two COLT options were issued to RenTec.[451] That same day, an email from one of the SCM employees noted that if the COLT structure were later found not to be in compliance with the U.S. tax code, the bank could terminate any open option in 60 days and also had a tax indemnification from RenTec which would protect the bank from the payment of any tax penalties.[452]

These documents indicate that multiple departments within Barclays were notified of and approved use of the COLT product, despite the IRS memorandum advising that those types of options were being used to violate U.S. tax law. Barclays continued issuing the suspect options even though the bank was then under public criticism for its involvement with abusive tax shelters.

Revising the COLT Options. During 2012, Barclays issued five COLT options to RenTec, all of which had terms longer than one year. In contrast, during 2013, Barclays did not issue any until the end of the year when it offered RenTec a revised option designed to prevent it from being used to claim that it produced long-term capital gains. During 2013, the Salz Review had intensified and produced a report.[453] In addition, in early 2013, Barclays initiated a bank- wide effort, described above, called Project Transform, to ensure the bank no longer offered or participated in abusive tax shelter products.[454] As part of that effort, during 2013, the COLT option was revised so that the term of the option was less than twelve months.[455]

In December 2013, a newly established Barclays Transaction Review Committee met to discuss the revised COLT structure.[456] In that meeting, the committee reviewed the proposed COLT transaction, along with a document entitled, "Background and Commercial Drivers."[457] That document described the new features of the COLT transaction as follows:

> "On 25 March 2013, following the conclusion of Barclays' strategic review (TRANSFORM), the Tax Risk Committee agreed that Renaissance be permitted to enter the New COLT Transaction with the maturity of the options no greater than 11 months. US individual investors of Renaissance would no longer claim the Rate Differential Benefit."[458]

In late 2013, Barclays offered the new, short-duration COLT option to RenTec.[459] RenTec purchased one of the new COLT options in early 2014.[460]

(b) Deutsche Bank's Restructuring

Deutsche Bank took a different approach than Barclays in reacting to the IRS GLAM. Instead of essentially ignoring or disputing the GLAM's findings and continuing to issue basket options, Deutsche Bank stopped issuing new MAPS options for more than a year.

Prior to the release of the GLAM, Deutsche Bank had been under investigation by the U.S. Department of Justice for its involvement with abusive tax shelters and, over several years ending in 2010, was negotiating with federal prosecutors over a Non-Prosecution Agreement (NPA).[461] After release of the GLAM in November 2010, Deutsche Bank chose to suspend writing any new options for the rest of that year and all of 2011, while it re-evaluated the MAPS structure.[462]

Within the bank, some executives expressed reluctance to accept the IRS' analysis and stop offering the product. One Deutsche Bank official wrote in an email: "GLAM is not of precedential value [and] merely represents the current view of the IRS chief counsel office of a particular set of facts."[463] Deutsche Bank representatives explained to the Subcommittee that some in the bank viewed the MAPS option, which had been significantly restructured in 2008, as sufficiently different from the option described in the GLAM to allow it to continue, but others were "sensitive" to any issues related to tax, given the NPA, which was why the bank chose to suspend offering the options.[464]

In 2012, Deutsche Bank resumed issuing MAPS options, but with a new requirement that the option term be less than 12 months and the option agreement include a provision requiring the option buyer to treat the option proceeds as short-term capital gains.[465]

The NPA. As discussed above, Deutsche Bank had been under investigation by DOJ for its involvement with abusive tax shelters and had been in the process of negotiating the Non- Prosecution Agreement (NPA) for several years. The NPA was finally issued on December 21, 2010, a month after the GLAM was released. Among other measures, the NPA imposed an affirmative disclosure obligation on the bank, requiring Deutsche Bank to bring to the attention of DOJ: "products or transactions that may run afoul of U.S. federal income tax laws, rules, and regulations."[466] Failure to comply with that requirement, among other terms of the NPA, could have subjected the bank to criminal prosecution.[467] In addition, Deutsche Bank was required to engage an independent expert to review the bank's compliance systems and ensure its compliance with the NPA, including steering clear of abusive tax transactions.[468]

About six weeks later, on February 3, 2011, the bank met with the independent expert, Bart Schwartz, who had been hired by the bank to oversee the bank's compliance with the NPA.[469] The Subcommittee has received conflicting accounts about whether Deutsche Bank informed the independent examiner, as required by the NPA, about its involvement with the MAPS options. According to Mr. Schwartz, neither he nor anyone on his team recalled Deutsche Bank ever informing them about the MAPS transactions, in 2011 or later.[470] Mr. Schwartz told the Subcommittee that MAPS was the "kind of transaction that he expected to know about" and he was surprised that the Bank had not informed him of it.[471] In contrast, Deutsche Bank representatives told the Subcommittee that the bank had, in fact, discussed the MAPS transaction with Mr. Schwartz and team members working directly for him, after a member of Mr. Schwartz's team raised the issue.[472] According to Deutsche Bank, Mr. Schwartz's team was aware of the GLAM, was informed of the MAPS structure in one of the initial meetings with Deutsche Bank, and did not request any further information, despite the concerns expressed by the IRS.[473]

In the spring of 2012, the Federal Reserve Bank of New York began examining the MAPS transactions and instructed Deutsche Bank to alert the U.S. Attorney's Office for the Southern District of New York, which was overseeing the NPA, about the options. According to Deutsche Bank's counsel, in August 2012, Deutsche Bank contacted the U.S. Attorney's Office and then had followup conversations and meetings with the office in September and December 2012 and February 2013.[474] The Subcommittee is unaware of what actions, if any, were taken by the U.S. Attorney's Office on the matter.

Reaction to the GLAM. Due to the NPA and reputational concerns, after the issuance of the GLAM in 2010, Deutsche Bank determined not to issue any further MAPS options without evaluating the transaction.[475] However, when the GLAM came out, Deutsche Bank had coincidentally nearly finished issuing another option to RenTec and chose to finish that process, completing the option just two days after the GLAM was released.[476] In addition to the new option, at that time, Deutsche Bank had several other outstanding MAPS options with RenTec.[477]

In connection with evaluating the GLAM, Deutsche Bank personnel noted that there was a "30d [day] right of termination for DB [Deutsche Bank] embedded in all these contracts" that did not require cause for termination.[478] That provision would have allowed Deutsche Bank to terminate the contracts, using a method that would have required it to terminate one account at a time with a gap of twenty exchange business days between each account.[479] Deutsche Bank declined to terminate the options, however, for several reasons. According to the bank, it declined to terminate the options, because the post-2008 MAPS structure differed from the options described in the GLAM; it had acquired a legal opinion stating the new MAPS complied with the tax law; liquidation of multiple options could have suppressed the option asset values; it was concerned about its client relationship; and it wanted to protect its reputation as a reliable counterparty.[480] However, the bank stopped issuing additional MAPS options pending a re- evaluation of the product.

Attempts to Develop New Structures. In 2010 and 2011, Deutsche Bank conducted a review of the MAPS options product. It also worked to develop a new product that would not raise the same tax problems. In October 2011, Deutsche Bank reviewed a product developed under what was called Project Dawn, involving the writing of call options to Mosel, a Delaware partnership in which RenTec served as the general partner.[481] Under the proposal, each Project Dawn call option would be an outperformance option which, at expiration, would result in payment to the option holder of the difference in the performance of RenTec's strategy and the performance of the S&P 500.[482] Each option would be a European style option with a 13-month term.[483] These outperformance options were intended to isolate the portion of RenTec's trading strategy that performed above the S&P 500 and provide a payoff "attributable to [that] portion only of the Strategy."[484]

In November 2011, Deutsche Bank drafted preliminary terms and conditions of another proposed transaction.[485] This transaction involved a call option "outright on [RenTec's] fund rather than the relative performance version."[486]

An email exchange concerning those proposals at the time indicates that senior Deutsche Bank officials recognized that it was difficult to characterize the MAPS transaction as a true derivative. In a discussion between Satish Ramakrishna, then Deutsche Bank's risk management head, and Anthony Tuths, a former member of the Tax Structuring and Planning Division at Deutsche Bank, Mr. Ramakrishna raised the concern that under the new proposal, RenTec would not receive back any portion of its premium.[487] Mr. Tuths responded: "That's the result of having a real option," in contrast to the previous transactions between the parties.[488] In an interview with the Subcommittee, Mr. Ramakrishna said that RenTec had indicated that it was not interested in Deutsche Bank's proposed transactions because they did not closely track the performance of the trading recommended by RenTec's algorithm.[489] Ultimately, RenTec rejected both proposed transactions.[490]

Resumption of MAPS in 2012. After RenTec rejected the proposed new structures in 2011, Deutsche Bank considered resuming MAPS. Ultimately, two years after issuance of the GLAM, Deutsche Bank decided to offer MAPS to RenTec on modified terms with a shorter duration that would not risk the misreporting of trading profits as long-term capital gains.[491] As part of the new terms, all post-2012 MAPS options had terms that lasted less than one year (generally around 11 months), and all included a new rider in the option confirmation contract stating: "Buyer represents that for tax purposes, it will report the Transaction as a derivative financial instrument generating short-term capital gains at exercise or maturity."[492] The new option confirmation contract also stated in part: "Seller represents that for tax purposes, it and any Affiliate thereof will report the Transaction as a derivative financial instrument."[493] In the end, Deutsche Bank, like Barclays, took years to stop offering a product that it knew was being used to dodge the payment of U.S. taxes.

IV. SYSTEMIC CONCERNS

In its Generic Legal Advice Memorandum of November 2010, the IRS rejected the attempt to use basket option structures to try to convert short-term trading profits into long-term capital gains with lower tax rates. It also initiated a review of the largest basket options user to evaluate its tax liability. While those actions have begun to address some of the specific conduct examined in this investigation, they are incomplete and unresolved. The basket option case studies also raise four larger, systemic concerns.

Invalidating Derivative Tax Schemes. First, the basket option case studies are emblematic of a larger effort by some tax practitioners and sophisticated financial firms to claim that derivatives can be used to lower tax liability even when those derivatives mimic economic activity giving rise to taxable income. Treasury, the IRS, and Congress need to make it clear that derivatives alone cannot magically eliminate or lower tax liability. As part of that effort, tax regulations providing special benefits to derivatives, such as the U.S. source rule for swaps, should be revised or eliminated, and the message driven home that financial engineering using derivatives is insufficient to avoid income taxation.

Analyzing Circumvention of Leverage Limits. Second, basket options are just one example of derivatives and other arrangements being used to circumvent federal limits on the use of borrowed funds to purchase securities. In the case of RenTec, basket options were used to provide it with leverage levels as high as 20:1, which the hedge fund said it had been unable to achieve in other settings under federal rules.

In recent years, a few studies have examined how financial institutions, using derivatives, structured financial products, and other arrangements, have weakened or circumvented federal leverage limits.[494] One recent study by the Office of Financial Research in the Treasury Department noted that "data [is] currently insufficient to understand the exposures and the extent of leverage" being used in the U.S. financial system.[495]

The Financial Stability Oversight Council, working with the Office of Financial Research and other federal agencies, should establish new reporting and data collection mechanisms to gather the data needed for an indepth analysis of the extent of leverage in the U.S. financial system, the many ways in which financial firms are bypassing federal margin rules and leverage limits, and the extent to which highly leveraged financial instruments and arrangements may be contributing to overextensions of credit by lenders, asset bubbles, and systemic risks. Federal margin rules, which are a direct response to the stock market crash of 1929, represent a vital financial safeguard whose circumvention is too important to be disregarded by federal regulators charged with detecting and evaluating systemic risk.

More generally, the financial sector and the corporate community are using derivatives to try to achieve a variety of favorable outcomes in accounting, tax, financial, and other regulatory contexts, even when the derivative instruments mimic economic activities that by themselves yield different results. Two examples have been highlighted in this report. Congress and the appropriate agencies should closely examine the growing use of derivatives to circumvent accounting, tax, or regulatory rules, and what steps should be taken to prevent disparate outcomes, particularly when they may pose a threat to the transparency, safety, soundness of our financial system or the economy as a whole.

Auditing Large Partnerships. Third, despite ongoing IRS audits of RenTec's basket options activities, the IRS' overall audit coverage of large partnerships similar to RenTec is poor. Large partnerships – which include hedge funds, private equity funds, and publicly traded partnerships – are some of the most profitable entities in the United States. According to a 2013 preliminary report issued by the U.S. Government Accountability Office (GAO), "[i]n tax year 2011, nearly 3.3 million partnerships accounted for $20.6 trillion in assets and $580.9 billion in total net income."[496]

That GAO report also found that the IRS was failing to audit 99% of the tax returns filed by large partnerships with assets exceeding $100 million.[497] The GAO report showed that while the number of those large partnerships had increased significantly in recent years, IRS audits had not kept pace. According to the GAO after examining a ten-year time frame, between tax years 2002 and 2011, the number of businesses organized as "large partnerships (with 100 or more direct partners and $100 million or more in assets) increased more than 200 percent, accounting for $2.3 trillion in total assets and $69.1 billion in total net income by tax year 2011." [498] The IRS' audit efforts worsened yet again in 2012. According to the preliminary report, IRS field audits reviewed the books and records of only 0.8% of large partnership returns.[499]

In response to a Subcommittee inquiry about low audit coverage of large partnerships, the IRS Large Business and International Division and Office of Chief Counsel explained that one of the reasons for the low audit performance was because of the procedural hurdles erected by the Tax Equity and Fiscal Responsibility Act (TEFRA).[500] The IRS pointed out that a TEFRA notification provision requires the IRS to notify all partners holding more than a 1% interest in a partnership prior to initiating an audit.[501] The IRS explained that some large partnerships, such as publicly traded partnerships, may have more than 100,000 partners at a time, some of whom hold a partnership interest for only a few trading days in a given year, making identifying and notifying all partners difficult, if not impossible. In addition, at the end of an audit, TEFRA requires the IRS to notify each partner of any tax assessment for the deficiencies attributable to the partnership, failure of which may cause the assessment to become invalid.[502] That notification burden is equally difficult, time consuming, and expensive to implement. A possible solution is amending TEFRA to allow the IRS, in the case of large partnerships, to notify the partnership itself when initiating or concluding an audit, and to rely on that partnership to notify the individual partners it deems appropriate.

Ending Bank Participation in Abusive Tax Structures. Finally, this investigation is not the first by the Subcommittee to examine bank participation in transactions involving substantial tax avoidance.[503] Past investigations have exposed highly suspect transactions involving major financial institutions, major law firms, sophisticated counterparties, and hundreds of millions or billions of dollars. Because banks employ personnel and systems capable of designing, implementing, and administering complex transactions involving structured financial products and other derivatives, too many have too often become facilitators of financially engineered tax avoidance and even tax evasion schemes. In some cases, federal prosecutors and regulators have imposed civil or criminal penalties against banks for aiding or abetting tax misconduct. But more is needed. To end bank involvement with abusive tax structures, federal financial regulators, as well as Treasury and the IRS, need to intensify their warnings against, scrutiny of, and legal actions to penalize bank participation in tax-motivated transactions.

End Notes

[1] See, e.g., U.S. Senate Permanent Subcommittee on Investigations reports and hearings, "Fishtail, Bacchus, Sundance, and Slapshot: Four Enron Transactions Funded and Facilitated by U.S. Financial Institutions," S. Prt. 107-82 (1/2/2003); "U.S. Tax Shelter Industry: The Role of Accountants, Lawyers, and Financial Professionals," S. Hrg. 108-473 (11/18 and 20/2003); "Tax Haven Abuses: The Enablers, The Tools and Secrecy," S. Hrg 109-797 (8/1/2006); "Repatriating Offshore Funds: 2004 Tax Windfall for Select Multinationals," S. Prt. 112-27 (10/11/2011); "Offshore Profit Shifting and the U.S. Tax Code – Part 1 (Microsoft and Hewlett-Packard)," S. Hrg. 112-781 (9/20/2012); and "Offshore Profit Shifting and the U.S. Tax Code - Part 2 (Apple Inc.)," S. Hrg. 113-90 (5/13/2013).

[2] 4/2008 "Examination Report for Deutsche Bank," prepared by New York Regional Office of the Securities and Exchange Commission, SEC_RT13_002020-074, at 074 [Sealed Exhibit].

[3] 9/2007 "Examination Report for Barclays," prepared by New York Regional Office of the Securities and Exchange Commission, SEC_RT13_001994-2019, at 2013 [Sealed Exhibit].

[4] 12/2/2011 "Present Law and Issues Related to the Taxation of Financial Instruments and Products," prepared by the Joint Committee on Taxation, JCX-56-11, at 7, https://www.jct.gov/publications.html?func=startdown&id=4372.

[5] 1/1/1997 "Risk Management of Financial Derivatives," Comptroller's Handbook, at 1, http://www.occ.gov/publications/publications-by-type/comptrollers-handbook/deriv.pdf.

[6] Id.

[7] 12/2/2011 "Present Law and Issues Related to the Taxation of Financial Instruments and Products," prepared by the Joint Committee on Taxation, JCX-56-11, at 7-8, https://www.jct.gov/publications.html?func=startdown&id=4372.

[8] 1/1/1997 "Risk Management of Financial Derivatives," Comptroller's Handbook, at 1, http://www.occ.gov/publications/publications-by-type/comptrollers-handbook/deriv.pdf.

[9] 12/2/2011 "Present Law and Issues Related to the Taxation of Financial Instruments and Products," prepared by the Joint Committee on Taxation, JCX-56-11, at 44, https://www.jct.gov/publications.html?func=startdown&id=4372.

[10] Id. at 46.

[11] Id. at 47.

[12] Id.

[13] See, e.g., 26 U.S.C. § 865 (IRS source rule which treats derivative income as non-U.S. source income if it is paid to a recipient outside of the United States). The derivatives source rule

means that, even if a U.S. bank makes the derivative payment from the United States, so long as the payment is sent to an offshore recipient, it would not be treated as U.S. source income and any taxes on that income could be deferred until the funds were returned to the United States.

[14] David M. Schizer, "Stick and Snakes: Derivatives and Curtailing Aggressive Tax Planning," 73 S. Cal. L. Rev. 1339, 1341 n.4 (2000).

[15] See "Dividend Tax Abuse: How Offshore Entities Dodge Taxes on U.S. Stock Dividends," U.S. Senate Permanent Subcommittee on Investigations, S. Hrg. 110-778 (Sept. 11, 2008).

[16] Leverage involves "the use of credit to enhance one's ability to speculate financially." See definition of leverage, Merriam Webster Dictionary, http://www.merriam-webster.com/dictionary/leverage.

[17] See, e.g., 15 U.S.C. § 78(g) (Section 7 of the Securities Exchange Act of 1934); Regulations T, U, and X, which are commonly referred to as the "margin rules." 12 C.F.R. § 220 (Regulation T); 12 C.F.R. § 221 (Regulation U); 12 C.F.R. § 224 (Regulation X).

[18] See 9/2000 "Margin Requirements, Margin Loans, and Margin Rates: Practice and Principles," New England Economic Review, Peter Fortune, at 25.

[19] 3/4/2008 "Present-Law and Analysis Relating to the Tax Treatment of Derivatives" prepared by the Joint Committee on Taxation, JCX-21-08, at 4, https://www.jct.gov/publications.html?func=startdown&id=1319.

[20] Credit by Brokers and Dealers (Regulation T), 12 C.F.R. § 220.1(a).

[21] See "Purchasing on Margin, Risks Involved With Trading in a Margin Account," prepared by Financial Industry Regulatory Authority (FINRA) http://www.finra.org/Investors/SmartInvesting/AdvancedInvesting/MarginInformation/P005927.

[22] Id.

[23] A "prime broker" is a large financial institution that offers a set of services to hedge funds and large institutional clients. The services are typically bundled together and include execution of trades, settlement, financing, and custody services. Money managers typically use the services to trade with multiple brokerage houses while maintaining cash and assets in a master account at the prime broker, referred to as a "prime brokerage account." See "Financial Glossary: Prime Broker," prepared by NASDAQ, http://www.nasdaq.com/investing/ glossary/p/prime- broker; Wikipedia definition of "prime brokerage," http://en.wikipedia.org/wiki/Prime_brokerage.

[24] Credit by Brokers and Dealers (Regulation T), 12 C.F.R. § 220.12(a). The leverage limit may also be set by the regulatory authority where the trade occurs. Id. "Joint Back Office" (JBO) and international prime brokerage accounts offer two alternatives for hedge funds seeking higher leverage. JBO arrangements have been given an exemption from Regulation T and are permitted leverage of 7.6 times. JBO arrangements require the margin lender and margin borrower to form a joint venture, creating a closer association than is typical for a prime brokerage relationship. The SEC also requires JBO accounts to be placed with a registered prime broker. See "Information Memo 00-8," prepared by the New York Stock Exchange, http://www.nyse.com/nysenotices/nyse/rule-changes/detail;jsessionid=074AD9FCCC9CA438C8130FB91BE50B48?memo_id=00-8; Subcommittee interview of Mark Silber, RenTec (6/10/2014). In addition, after 1998, much higher margins could be "arranged" by U.S. banks and broker-dealers between a borrower and a lender based outside of the United States in a jurisdiction allowing higher leverage. See Credit by Brokers and Dealers (Regulation T), 12 C.F.R. § 220.1(a).

[25] See "Purchasing on Margin, Risks Involved With Trading in a Margin Account," prepared by Financial Industry Regulatory Authority, http://www.finra.org/Investors/SmartInvesting/AdvancedInvesting/MarginInformation/ P005927.

[26] "Schedule 13D," U.S. Securities and Exchange Commission, https://www.sec.gov/answers/sched13.htm, (last visited June 26, 2014).

[27] 7/1/2006 "What Every Investor Should Know Before Acquiring a Large Stake in a Public Company," prepared by Davis Polk & Wardwell, at 2, http://www.davispolk.com/

files/07_13_06_PrivateEquityNews_jul_06.pdf ("[I]t is broadly accepted on [Wall] Street that an investor may increase its economic interest in an issuer's securities beyond 4.9 percent without the need to make a 13D ... filing if it does so via a derivative contract that is both by its terms and in fact cash-settled."). In a 2013 Guidance Update, the SEC addressed concerns that funds inadequately disclose derivative interests. The SEC has encouraged mutual funds, through Form N-1A, and closed-end funds, through Form N-2, to provide specifically tailored disclosures for any principal investment strategies related to derivatives. To combat the transparency issue, the SEC has called on funds to continually assess the completeness and accuracy of their derivatives-related disclosures in their registration statements to ensure they are consistent with actual operations. 8/1/2013, "Guidance Update Disclosure and Compliance Matters for Investment Company Registrants That Invest in Commodity Interests," prepared by the SEC Division of Investment Management, No. 2013-05, at 2-3, http://www.sec.gov/divisions/investment/guidance/im-guidance-2013-05.pdf.

[28] 12/2/2011 "Present Law and Issues Related to the Taxation of Financial Instruments and Products," prepared by the Joint Committee on Taxation, JCX-56-11, at 1, https://www.jct.gov/publications.html?func=startdown&id=4372.

[29] 3/4/2008 "Present Law and Analysis Relating to the Tax Treatment of Derivatives," prepared by the Joint Committee on Taxation, JCX-21-08, at 32, https://www.jct.gov/publications.html?func=startdown&id=1319.

[30] 5/1973 "The Pricing of Options and Corporate Liabilities," Journal of Political Economy, volume 81, No. 3, Fischer Black and Myron Scholes, at 637, http://www.jstor.org/stable/1831029.

[31] 3/4/2008 "Present Law and Analysis Relating to the Tax Treatment of Derivatives," prepared by the Joint Committee on Taxation, JCX-21-08, at 5, https://www.jct.gov/publications.html?func=startdown&id=1319.

[32] Id.

[33] Id.

[34] "The Pricing of Options and Corporate Liabilities," *Journal of Political Economy*, volume 81, No. 3, (May-June 1973), at 637, http://www.jstor.org/stable/1831029.

[35] Id.

[36] 12/2/2011 "Present Law and Issues Related to the Taxation of Financial Instruments and Products," prepared by the Joint Committee on Taxation, JCX-56-11, at 7, https://www.jct.gov/publications.html?func=startdown&id=4372.

[37] Id. at 8.

[38] A "managed account" is "an investment portfolio one or more clients entrusted to a manager who decides how to invest it." "Financial Glossary: Managed Account," prepared by NASDAQ, http://www.nasdaq.com/investing/glossary/m/managed-account. In this case, the managed account opened to carry out the basket option contract is called a "proprietary" account, because it is formally set up in the name of the bank, rather than in the name of a client, such as the option holder.

[39] For example, the Investment Advisory Agreement between Deutsche Bank and RenTec gave RenTec "discretion and without prior consultation" to execute trades in the managed account. It also contained certain limits and guidelines on what assets could be selected for the account. For example, RenTec agreed with Deutsche Bank not to own more than 4% of the shares of any one issuer, not to acquire more than 5% or more of any class of voting security, and not to trade equities on the bank's restricted list. 12/15/2008, "Master Investment Advisory Agreement: Execution Copy," Deutsche Bank and RenTec, DB-PSI 00000001-047, at 022-025. Otherwise, RenTec had complete discretion to identify assets to be acquired for the managed account. "[T]he Advisor shall ... have full power, authority and right to ... supervise and direct the investment and reinvestment of all assets in the Accounts, and engage in such transactions on behalf of the Client's Account, in the

Advisor's discretion and without prior consultation with the Client, subject only to the terms of this agreement." Id. at DB-PSI 00000001-002.

[40] For example, to ensure that the investment advisor had complete control over the account, the Investment Advisory Agreement between Deutsche Bank and RenTec specified that, if an order placed by RenTec was not executed, or was subsequently undone without orders from RenTec, the assets that were supposed to have been purchased would still be considered to be part of the reference account for purposes of calculating the option's gain or loss. See, e.g., 10/8/2009 "Barrier Option Transaction No. 941-50310 Pursuant to the 1992 ISDA Master Agreement as supplemented in December 15, 2008," DB-PSI 001130213-241 at 222 (defining the basket as consisting of "positions that (i) actually result from transactions specified by the Investment Advisor ... or (ii) are Designated Positions (as such term is defined in the Master Investment Advisory Agreement ...)"; 12/15/2008 "Master Investment Advisory Agreement: Execution Copy," signed by Deutsche Bank and RenTec, DB-PSI 00000001-047, at 002 (defining a designated position as any position "rejected," "unwound," or "liquidated" by the Client "without the direction of the Advisor").

[41] In interviews with the Subcommittee and in some documents presented to the IRS, copies of which were provided by RenTec to the Subcommittee, RenTec insisted that, rather than one account with dual roles, the basket option structure actually created two distinct accounts: a reference account and a hedge account. Subcommittee interviews of Jonathan Mayers, RenTec (5/28/2014), Peter Brown, RenTec (6/3/2014); and Mark Silber, RenTec (6/10/2014). RenTec told the Subcommittee that the hedge account consisted of physical stocks that the bank actually held, and claimed that RenTec had no idea what physical assets were actually in that hedge account. RenTec claimed it was familiar with and had control over only the reference account, which was a "synthetic" account with no actual assets.

Despite RenTec's insistence on the existence of two accounts, the legal documents governing the basket option structures used by RenTec and the banks make no mention of two accounts. All of the investment advisory agreements mention only a single account made up of a combination of effected (actually held) and designated (hypothetical) positions. See, e.g., 12/15/2008, "Master Investment Advisory Agreement," signed by Deutsche Bank and RenTec, DB-PSI 00000001-047; 12/6/2006 "Amended and Restated Investment Management Agreement," signed by Barclays and RenTec, RT-PSI-00134963. In addition, as a practical matter, in each of the basket option trades examined by the Subcommittee, all trades were accounted for and executed through a single, designated account which was managed at the direction of the investment advisor. The basket option participants provided no documentation or paperwork suggesting the existence of two distinct accounts operating in tandem.

Deutsche Bank also informed the Subcommittee that in the entire course of over a decade of MAPS transactions, it had never created even a single synthetic "designated position." See Deutsche Bank responses to Subcommittee supplemental questions (6/20/2014). In other words, all trades ordered by the hedge funds in conformance with the investment guidelines in the Investment Management Advisory Agreement had been executed and the resulting assets held in the trading accounts. Barclays documents similarly indicated that, as a matter of standard practice, all of the referenced trades had been fully hedged through physical trades in the designated option account, with "no leakage." 5/19/2010 email from Edward Sherwood to Brett Beldner of Barclays, "COLT XIX – Draft SCM Approvals Notification," BARCLAYS-PSI-010082. In a presentation on the restructuring of MAPS transactions, Deutsche Bank stated that it had "rejected [designated positions'] execution or liquidated the holding for various business (i.e., hedging) reasons." See "Renaissance Technologies: MAPS Restructuring Highlights," prepared by Deutsche Bank, RT-PSI-00068592-599, at 594. When asked about the trades, RenTec Co-CEO Peter Brown told the Subcommittee that, "as a first order" he assumed that "they [the banks] hedged every single transaction." Subcommittee interview of Peter Brown, RenTec (6/3/2014).

[42] According to RenTec Co-CEO Peter Brown, the option was a "delta 1" option, meaning that its value perfectly tracked the value of the underlying assets. Subcommittee interview of Peter Brown, RenTec (6/3/2014). Barclays risk management personnel also confirmed that this was a "delta 1 option" and explained to the Subcommittee that basket options did not pose either "market risk" or "credit risk" for the bank. Subcommittee interview of Lansford Dyer, Barclays (4/3/2014). In addition, Barclays represented to its regulator, the Financial Services Authority, that the COLT structure "does not give rise to market risk within Palomino Limited. As such it is equivalent to a forward sale." 9/5/2002 letter from Barclays to the Financial Services Authority, "Project COLT," BARCLAYS- PSI-005260-261.

[43] See "Renaissance Technologies: MAPS Restructuring Highlights," prepared by Deutsche Bank, RT-PSI-00068592-599, at 594; Subcommittee interviews of Eamon McCooey, Deutsche Bank (5/2/2014) and Martin Malloy, Barclays (5/1/2014). See also Subcommittee interview of Jonathan Mayers, RenTec (5/28/2014).

[44] See Credit by Brokers and Dealers (Regulation T), 12 C.F.R. § 220.1(a).

[45] The Deutsche Bank MAPS options authorized the bank to take over the account and liquidate the assets when the losses hit a threshold level equal to a specified portion of the premium, while the Barclays COLT options authorized the bank to take over the account and liquidate the assets when the losses extinguished the entire premium. Subcommittee interview of Satish Ramakrishna, Deutsche Bank (5/16/2014); 12/6/2006 "Amended and Restated Investment Management Agreement," signed by Barclays and RenTec, RT-PSI-00134963-5013, at 4973.

[46] The seller of the option used part of the premium to fund the initial purchase of the referenced assets that were held in the basket portfolio. The remainder of the premium – generally 20% - 25% of the total premium – was taken by the option seller as a financing fee for the leverage that it was providing to the hedge fund.

[47] 2/27/2014 "Topic 409-Capital Gains and Losses," prepared by IRS, http://www.irs.gov/taxtopics/tc409.html.

[48] Id.

[49] Id.

[50] Id.

[51] Id.

[52] Id.

[53] 4/11/2007 "Individual Capital Gains Income: Legislative History," prepared by Congressional Research Service, http://congressionalresearch.com/98-473/document.php?study=Individual+Capital+Gains+Income+Legislative+History.

[54] 6/13/2013 "Federal Capital Gains Tax Rates, 1988-2013," prepared by the Tax Foundation, http://taxfoundation.org/article/federal-capital-gains-tax-rates-1988-2013.

[55] *Comm'r of Internal Revenue v. Glenshaw Glass Co.*, 348 U.S. 426, 431 (1955).

[56] 12/2/2011 "Present Law and Issues Related to the Taxation of Financial Instruments and Products," prepared by the Joint Committee on Taxation, JCX-56-11, at 16, https://www.jct.gov/publications.html?func=startdown&id=4372; see 26 U.S.C. § 1001.

[57] Id. at 34.

[58] Id. at 17.

[59] See 26 U.S.C. § 1001.

[60] Id.

[61] See 26 U.S.C. §§ 871(a)(1)(A) and 881(a)(1); 3/27/2014 "United States Income Tax Treaties - A to Z," prepared by IRS, http://www.irs.gov/Businesses/International-Businesses/United-States-Income-Tax-Treaties---A-to-Z.

[62] 26 U.S.C. §§§ 1441(a), 1441(b), and 1442(a).

[63] See id.

[64] The first federal withholding statute was enacted in 1913; the first comprehensive set of IRS withholding regulations for nonresident aliens was issued in 1956. See 12/1/2007, "Tax Compliance: Qualified Intermediary Program Provides Some Assurance That Taxes on

Foreign Investors are Withheld and Reported, but Can Be Improved," prepared by Government Accountability Office, GAO-08-99, at 6, http://www.gao.gov/new.items/d0899.pdf.

[65] See, e.g., "Tax-Advantaged Hedge Fund Returns Under Code Sec. 1260," 3 J. Taxation of Financial Products 19, David M. Schizer (2002), http://heinonline.org/HOL/Page?handle=hein.journals/jrlfin3&div=18&g_sent=1&collection=journals#68.

[66] Id.

[67] Id. at 19.

[68] Id. at 20.

[69] Id.

[70] Id. at 19.

[71] 26 U.S.C. §1260 (a).

[72] H.R. Rep. No. 106-478, at 159 (1999) (Conf. Rep.).

[73] Id.

[74] 26 U.S.C. § 1260 (d)(1)(A-D). No regulations have been promulgated under section D.

[75] See, e.g., "Tax-Advantaged Hedge Fund Returns Under Code Sec. 1260," 3 J. Taxation of Financial Products 19, David M. Schizer (2002), http://heinonline.org/HOL/Page?handle=hein.journals/jrlfin3&div=18&g_sent=1&collection=journals#68.

[76] See, e.g., *Comm'r of Internal Revenue v. Court Holding Co.*, 324 U.S. 331, 334 (1945); *Gregory v. Helvering*, 293 U.S. 465, 470 (1935).

[77] *Weiss v. Stearn*, 265 U.S. 242, 254 (1924); "When Substance-over-Form Argument is Available to the Taxpayer," 48 Marq. L. Rev. 41, 42, J. Bruce Donaldson (1964).

[78] 11/10/1999 "Description and Analysis of Present-Law Tax Rules and Recent Proposals Relating to Corporate Tax Shelters," prepared by the Joint Committee on Taxation, JCX-84-99, at 7, https://www.jct.gov/publications.html?func=showdown&id=2846 (citing *Gregory v. Helvering*, 293 U.S. 465, 469 (1935)).

[79] Id. at 7.

[80] Id. at 18.

[81] Id. at 19.

[82] J. Bruce Donaldson, "When Substance-over-Form Argument is Available to the Taxpayer," 48 Marq. L. Rev. 41, 41 (1964).

[83] See *Comm'r of Internal Revenue v. Court Holding Co.*, 324 U.S. 331, 334 (1945).

[84] 3/4/2008 "Present Law and Analysis Relating to the Tax Treatment of Derivatives," prepared by the Joint Committee on Taxation, JCX-21-08, at 13-14, https://www.jct.gov/publications.html?func=startdown&id=1319.

[85] 11/10/1999 "Description and Analysis of Present-Law Tax Rules and Recent Proposals Relating to Corporate Tax Shelters," prepared by the Joint Committee on Taxation, JCX-84-99, at 19-20, https://www.jct.gov/publications.html?func=showdown&id=2846 (citing *Penrod v. Comm'r*, 88 T.C. 1415, 1428 (1987)).

[86] Id. at 20.

[87] Id. (citing *McDonalds Restaurants of Ill. v. Comm'r*, 688 F.2d 520 (7th Cir. 1982)).

[88] *AeroQuip-Vickers, Inc. v. Comm'r*, 347 F.3d 173 (6th Cir. 2003) (citing *Associated Wholesale Grocers, Inc. v. U.S.*, 927 F.2d 1517, 1526 (10th Cir. 1991) and quoting *Kuper v. Comm'r*, 533 F.2d 152, 158 (5th Cir. 1976)). See also *Jacobs Eng'g Grp., Inc. v. U.S.*, No. CV 96-2662, 1997 WL 314167 (C.D. Cal. Mar. 5, 1997) (*aff'd,* without public opinion, No. 97-55647, 1999 WL 89057 (9th Cir. 1999) (ruling against the taxpayer, the court found that twelve short-term loans from CFC really functioned as a long-term loan lasting over two years)).

[89] 11/12/10 "Hedge Fund Basket Option Contracts," prepared by IRS Office of Chief Counsel Memorandum, at 2, http://www.irs.gov/pub/irs-utl/am2010005.pdf.

[90] See 6/13/2014, "Legal Advice Issued by Associate Chief Counsel," prepared by IRS, http://www.irs.gov/uac/Legal-Advice-Issued-by-Associate-Chief-Counsel (GLAMs "are legal advice, signed by executives in the National Office of the Office of Chief Counsel and

issued to Internal Revenue Service personnel who are national program executives and managers. They are issued to assist Service personnel in administering their programs by providing authoritative legal opinions on certain matters, such as industry-wide issues.").

[91] 11/12/2010 "Hedge Fund Basket Option Contracts," prepared by IRS Office of Chief Counsel Memorandum, at 2, http://www.irs.gov/pub/irs-utl/am2010005.pdf.

[92] Id. at 1.

[93] Id. at 9.

[94] Id. at 8. See also two 2010 Tax Court opinions consistent with this method of analysis. *Anschutz v. Comm'r*, 135 T.C. No. 5 (July 22, 2010); *Calloway v. Comm'r*, 135 T.C. No. 3 (July 8, 2010). The Court of Appeals for the Eighth Circuit has focused on the same factors in determining the ownership of mutual fund shares. See *Christoffersen v. U.S.*, 749 F.2d 513 (8th Cir. 1984).

[95] 11/12/2010 "Hedge Fund Basket Option Contracts," prepared by IRS Office of Chief Counsel Memorandum, at 9, http://www.irs.gov/pub/irs-utl/am2010005.pdf.

[96] Id.

[97] Id. at 10.

[98] "Chronicle - from 1870 until today," prepared by Deutsche Bank, at 2, 8, https://www.db.com/en/media/Deutsche-Bank-History-Chronicle-from-1870-until-today.pdf. See also "Addresses," prepared by Deutsche Bank, https://www.db.com/en/content/Addresses.htm.

[99] "Annual Financial Statements and Management Report of Deutsche Bank AG 2012," prepared by Deutsche Bank, at 2, https://agm.db.com/en/docs/Annual_Financial_Statements_and_Management_Report_Deutsche_Bank_ AG_2012.pdf.

[100] "Deutsche Bank AG (DB) Balance Sheet," Yahoo Finance, http://finance.yahoo.com/q/bs?s=DB&annual.

[101] 5/2013 "Deutsche Bank at a Glance," prepared by Deutsche Bank, at 9, 12, https://www.db.com/medien/en/downloads/Deutsche_Bank_at_a_glance.pdf.

[102] 10/31/2013 "Deutsche Bank Resolution Plan," prepared by Deutsche Bank, at 20, http://www.fdic.gov/regulations/reform/resplans/plans/deutschebank-165-1310.pdf.

[103] Id. at 5-9.

[104] Id.

[105] Id. at 5-6.

[106] 5/2013 "Deutsche Bank at a Glance," prepared by Deutsche Bank, at 4, 8, https://www.db.com/medien/en/downloads/Deutsche_Bank_at_a_glance.pdf.

[107] Id.

[108] "Deutsche Bank Names Co-C.E.O.'s to Succeed Ackermann," *The New York Times*, Jack Ewing (7/25/2011), http://dealbook.nytimes.com/2011/07/25/deutsche-bank-taps-co-ceos-to-replace-ackermann/.

[109] Id.

[110] 11/1/2012 "Deutsche Bank appoints Jacques Brand and Bill Woodley as CEO and Deputy CEO of North America," prepared by Deutsche Bank, https://www.db.com/medien/en/content/3862_4221.htm.

[111] Id.

[112] 12/21/2010 letter from Preet Bharara, United States Attorney for the Southern District of New York, to Deutsche Bank's counsel, "Deutsche Bank AG – Non-Prosecution Agreement," at 1, http://lib.law.virginia.edu/Garrett/ prosecution_ agreements/sites/default/files/pdf/deutschebank.pdf. See also "U.S Tax Shelter Industry: The Role of Accountants, Lawyers, and Financial Professionals," U.S. Senate Permanent Subcommittee on Investigations, S. Hrg. 108-473 (Nov. 18 and 20, 2003).

[113] 12/21/2010 letter from Preet Bharara, United States Attorney for the Southern District of New York, to Deutsche Bank's counsel, "Deutsche Bank AG – Non-Prosecution Agreement," at 1, http://lib.law.virginia.edu/Garrett/prosecution_agreements/sites/default/files/pdf/deutschebank.pdf.

[114] The $553,633,153 payment represented the fees Deutsche Bank earned from its participation in the tax shelter activity, the amount of taxes and interest the IRS was unable to collect from the taxpayers because of Deutsche Bank's activity, and a civil penalty of more than $149 million. 12/21/2010 "Deutsche Bank to Pay More Than $550 Million to Resolve Federal Tax Shelter Fraud Investigation," U.S. Attorney for the Southern District of New York Press Release, at 1, http://www.justice.gov/tax/usaopress/2010/deutschebankpr.pdf.

[115] 12/21/2010 letter from Preet Bharara, United States Attorney for the Southern District of New York, to Deutsche Bank's counsel, "Deutsche Bank AG – Non-Prosecution Agreement," at 1-6, http://lib.law.virginia.edu/Garrett/ prosecution_agreements/sites/default/files/ pdf/ deutschebank.pdf.

[116] 12/21/2010 "Deutsche Bank to Pay More Than $550 Million to Resolve Federal Tax Shelter Fraud Investigation," U.S. Attorney for the Southern District of New York Press Release, at 1, http://www.justice.gov/tax/usaopress/2010/deutschebankpr.pdf.

[117] Id.

[118] Id. at 2.

[119] Id.

[120] 12/21/2010 letter from Preet Bharara, United States Attorney for the Southern District of New York, to Deutsche Bank's counsel, "Deutsche Bank AG – Non-Prosecution Agreement," at 2-3, Exhibit B 8, http://lib.law.virginia.edu/Garrett/prosecution_agreements/sites/default/ files/pdf/ deutschebank.pdf.

[121] Information provided by the Federal Reserve Bank of New York, (6/17 and 6/18/2014).

[122] Subcommittee briefing by Deutsche Bank counsel (6/2/2014 and 6/30/2014).

[123] A 12/21/2010 letter from Preet Bharara, United States Attorney for the Southern District of New York ("SDNY"), to Deutsche Bank's counsel, entitled "Deutsche Bank AG – Non-Prosecution Agreement," contained the following language: "*Unless otherwise stated in this Agreement*, Deutsche Bank's obligations under this Agreement will continue until the later of (1) a period of two years from the date of the signing of this Agreement, or (2) the expiration of the tenure of the Independent Expert, as that term is defined in here." [Emphasis added.] However, under the following section of the letter (entitled "Continuing Obligation to Cooperate"), detailing Deutsche Bank's obligations to cooperate on an ongoing basis with the SDNY, the IRS, the civil branch of the Department of Justice ("DOJ") tax and any other law enforcement agency designated by the SDNY, the SDNY writes that: "Deutsche Bank's obligations under this paragraph will continue until the later of (1) a period of two years from the date of the signing of this Agreement, or (2) the date upon which all prosecutions and appeals arising out of, or relating in any way to, the conduct described in the Statement of Facts are finally concluded, or (3) the date when all IRS and DOJ Tax civil proceedings and appeals relating to the tax shelter activity described in the Agreement are finally concluded." 12/21/2010 letter from Preet Bharara, United States Attorney for the Southern District of New York, to Deutsche Bank's counsel, "Deutsche Bank AG – Non-Prosecution Agreement," at 2-3, http://lib.law.virginia.edu/ Garrett/prosecution_agreements/sites/default/files/pdf/deutschebank.pdf. According to the Department of Justice, the NPA is still in effect because IRS and DOJ Tax civil proceedings relating to the tax shelter activity described in the NPA are not yet finally concluded. Report on the status of Deutsche Bank's Non-Prosecution Agreement, provided by the Department of Justice to the Subcommittee on 2/19/2014 and 9/27/2014.

[124] "Barclays Timeline," prepared by Barclays, http://www.timeline.barclays.com/timeline.html; "Lombard Street," prepared by Barclays, http://www.barclays.com/about-barclays/history/ lombard-street.html; 7/2012 "Resolution Plan Section 1: Public Section," prepared by Barclays, at 2, http://www.fdic.gov/regulations/reform/resplans/ plans/barclays-1207.pdf.

[125] 3/3/2014, Barclays "Annual Report 2013," at 277, http://reports.barclays.com/ar13/# highlights.

[126] 10/2013 "Barclays Resolution Plan: Public Section, October 2013," prepared by Barclays, at 17, http://www.fdic.gov/regulations/reform/resplans/plans/barclays-165-1310.pdf.

[127] See "UK financial regulation overhauled," *BBC*, (3/31/13), http://www.bbc.com/news/business-21987829.

[128] 10/2013 "Barclays Resolution Plan: Public Section, October 2013," prepared by Barclays, at 3, 6, http://www.fdic.gov/regulations/reform/resplans/plans/barclays-165-1310.pdf.

[129] Id. at 9.

[130] Id. at 14.

[131] Id.

[132] Id.

[133] Id.

[134] "Leadership: Sir David Walker," prepared by Barclays, http://www.barclays.com/about-barclays/leadership- team/sir-david-walker.html.

[135] Id.

[136] See "Barclays to close 'tax avoidance' unit," *BBC*, (2/10/2013), http://www.bbc.com/news/business-21397844.

[137] Id.

[138] "Barclays £500m tax loophole closed by Treasury in rare retrospective action," *The Guardian*, Jill Treanor (2/27/2012), http://www.theguardian.com/business/2012/feb/28/treasury-closes-barclays-tax- schemes?guni=Article:in%20body%20link.

[139] See 4/2013 "Salz Review: An Independent Review of Barclays' Business Practices," prepared by Anthony Salz et al., at 2, http://online.wsj.com/public/resources/documents/SalzReview04032013.pdf.

[140] See id. at opening letter from Anthony Salz.

[141] Id. at Disclaimer.

[142] Id. at 82.

[143] Id. at 70.

[144] Id. at 74.

[145] Id. at 82.

[146] See 11/2002 "Project COLT Renaissance Technologies Corp User Guide," prepared by Barclays, BARCLAYS- PSI-213567-585.

[147] See 2/11/14 "2013 Transform Highlights," prepared by Barclays, http://www.barclays.com/content/dam/barclayspublic/docs/Microsites/Transform/TransformUpdates/full-year-results-Transform-110213.pdf.

[148] See "Barclays' response to the Salz Review," prepared by Barclays, at 2, 3, http://www.barclays.com/content/dam/barclayspublic/documents/news/471-392-250413-salz-response.pdf; 2/11/14 "2013 Transform Highlights," prepared by Barclays, at 5, 8 http://www.barclays.com/content/dam/barclayspublic/docs/Microsites/Transform/TransformUpdates/full-year-results-Transform-110213.pdf.

[149] See 2/12/2013 "Barclays Strategic Review," Barclays Press Release, http://www.newsroom.barclays.com/Press- releases/Barclays-Strategic-Review-9db.aspx; "Barclays to close 'tax avoidance' unit," *BBC*, (2/10/2013), http://www.bbc.com/news/business-21397844.

[150] "Barclays to close 'tax avoidance' unit," *BBC*, (2/10/2013), http://www.bbc.com/news/business-21397844.

[151] 5/26/2010 letter from SEC to RenTec, "Examination of Renaissance Technologies LLC ('RenTec')," SEC_RT13_001965-993, at 989 [Sealed Exhibit]; Subcommittee interview of Mark Silber, RenTec (6/10/2014).

[152] "Renaissance Locations," prepared by RenTec, https://www.rentec.com/vm/locations.vm; Subcommittee interview of Peter Brown, RenTec (6/3/2014).

[153] 3/31/14 "Form 13F," prepared by RenTec, http://www.sec.gov/Archives/edgar/data/1037389/000103738914000071/xslForm13F_X01/primary_doc.xml.

[154] See "The World's Billionaires #94 James Simons," *Forbes*, (7/11/2014), http://www.forbes.com/profile/james- simons/.

[155] Subcommittee interview of Peter Brown, RenTec (6/3/2014).

[156] Subcommittee interview of Mark Silber, RenTec (6/10/2014).

[157] Subcommittee briefing by RenTec counsel (6/20/2014). RenTec was initially formed as an S-Corporation owned directly by a number of employee stockholders and their related trusts. On June 30, 2007, RenTec was reorganized and converted into a limited liability company called Renaissance Technologies Corporation LLC (RTC). At that time stockholders of the S-Corporation received shares in a new entity known as Renaissance Technology Holdings Corporation (RTHC). RTHC then acquired the same number of class A member interests in RTC. In addition, another entity was created at that time called RCT II Holdings LLC (RCT II), which became the sole holder of Class B interests in RTC. Class A and B interests are identical and have the same voting and economic rights. RTC II was created to permit newer employees to hold an ownership interest in Renaissance Technologies LLC. Current ownership of RTC is split, with 85.7% held by RTHC and the remaining 14.3% held by RTC II. Id.

[158] Id. The five members of the RenTec's Executive Committee are James Simons, Mark Silber, Henry Laufer, Peter Brown, and Robert Mercer. Id.

[159] Subcommittee interview of Peter Brown, RenTec (6/3/2014).

[160] StatArb analyzes historical relationships between related securities and trades when those relationships are determined to be unbalanced. See 7/11/2008 "Statistical Arbitrage in the U.S. Equities Market," prepared by Marco Avellaneda and Jeong-Hyun Lee, at 1-2, http://math.nyu.edu/faculty/avellane/AvellanedaLeeStatArb071108.pdf.

[161] See, e.g., "Schneiderman (and Einstein) Pressure High-Speed Trading," *Bloomberg*, Michael P. Regan and Sam Mamudi, (3/21/2014), http://www.bloomberg.com/news/2014-03-21/schneiderman-joins-einstein-in-pressuring- high-frequency-trading.html.

[162] "Renaissance suffers rare disappointment," *Financial Times*, Sam Jones (2/17/2010), http://www.ft.com/intl/cms/s/0/66970a64-1b2e-11df-953f-00144feab49a.html#axzz31Fw LINs5; 7/23/2013 "Quants: the math geniuses running Wall Street," *The Telegraph*, Sarfraz Manzoor, http://www.telegraph.co.uk/finance/10188335/Quants-the-maths-geniuses-running-Wall-Street.html. RenTec alumni include several prominent mathematicians and statisticians who directly contributed to developing what is known as the "Medallion Algorithm." Mr. Ax worked on "model theory," which is the study of classes of mathematical structures and founded Axcom Trading Solutions, which was purchased by RenTec in the early 1990s. See 1965 "Diophantine problems over local fields," American Journal of Mathematics, vol. 87, James B. Ax and Simon B. Kochen, 605-630; "Business and Finance Biography," prepared by Elwyn Berlekamp, http://math.berkeley.edu/~berlek/bus.html; "The Code Breaker," *Bloomberg*, http://www.bloomberg.com/apps/news?pid=nw&pname=mm_0108_story1.html. Elwyn Berlekamp is another mathematician who worked for RenTec and was known for his work on coding theory and combinational game theory, including the study of sequential games with perfect information. See "Faculty Publications-Elwyn R. Berlekamp," prepared by UC Berkeley College of Engineering, http://www.eecs.berkeley.edu/Pubs/Faculty/berlekamp.html. See also Elwyn Berlekamp's Home page, prepared by Elwyn Berlekamp, http://math.berkeley.edu/~berlek/; "Business and Finance Biography," prepared by Elwyn Berlekamp, http://math.berkeley.edu/~berlek/bus.html. From 1988 to 1989, Mr. Berlekamp purchased the largest interest in a trading company named Axcom Trading Advisors. "Financial Engineering," prepared by Elwyn Berlekamp, http://math.berkeley.edu/~berlek/fineng.html.

[163] The Medallion Fund is discussed further below. The RIEF fund was started in 2005, with the objective to achieve superior rates of return with low volatility. The minimum initial investment in RIEF was $20 million. 4/7/2008 Confidential Private Placement Memorandum, prepared by RenTec, "Renaissance Institutional Equities Fund LLC," RT-PSI-00386514-741, at 522, 531 [Sealed Exhibit]. At the end of 2013, RIEF had $7.9 billion of assets under management; 50% of those assets were from RenTec employees. Subcommittee interview of James Rowen, RenTec (5/20/2014). The RIFF fund was started in 2007, with the objective of receiving target returns of 15% per annum. 2/6/2008 Confidential Private Placement Memorandum, prepared by RenTec, "Renaissance

Institutional Equities Fund LLC," RT-PSI-00385993-6124, at 6001 [Sealed Exhibit]. The minimum initial investment in RIFF was $20 million. 4/15/2008 Confidential Private Placement Memorandum, prepared by RenTec, "Renaissance Institutional Futures Fund SICAV P.L.C.," RT-PSI-00386466-513, at 470 [Sealed Exhibit]. At the end of 2013, RIFF had $645 million of assets under management; 75% of those assets were from RenTec employees. Subcommittee interview of James Rowen, RenTec (5/20/2014). The RIDA fund was started in 2012, with the objective to maximize long-term return while attempting to meet a standard deviation selected by the company. The minimum initial investment in RIDA was $5 million. 12/31/2012 Confidential Private Placement Memorandum, prepared by RenTec, "Renaissance Institutional Diversified Alpha Fund SICAV P.L.C.," RT-PSI-00387786-921, at 791, 793 [Sealed Exhibit]. At the end of 2013, the RIDA fund had $4.2 billion in assets under management. 4/1/2014 "Renaissance Institutional Diversified Alpha Fund SICAV P.L.C.," RT-PSI-00384778 [Sealed Exhibit]. Between 50% and 75% of those assets under management were from RenTec employees. Subcommittee interview of James Rowen, RenTec (5/20/2014).

164 Subcommittee interview of Mark Silber, RenTec (6/10/2014). According to RenTec, "master and feeder funds" refer to two tiers of related entities, in which the master funds invest directly in a financial product and then pass the earnings to feeder funds which, in turn, distribute them to individual investors. Subcommittee briefing by RenTec counsel (6/20/2014).

165 See 2/26/2013 Power Point Presentation, "Renaissance Technologies LLC," PSI-Renaissance-06-000004.

166 The five domestic feeder funds were established in Delaware: Medallion Associates LP, Medallion Fund LP, Medallion USA LP, Medallion RF LP, and Medallion RMP Fund LP. The two foreign feeder funds, Medallion International LTD and Medallion Capital Investment LTD, were incorporated in Bermuda. See 5/21/2008 email from Thomas Kerns to Mark Silber of RenTec, "Legal Entity Org Chart Powerpoint," RT-PSI-00363679-717, at 681. See also undated spreadsheet, "Confidential Treatment Requested by Renaissance Technologies LLC," prepared by RenTec, RT-PSI-00390362 [Sealed Exhibit].

167 See 5/21/2008 email from Thomas Kerns to Mark Silber of RenTec, "Legal Entity Org Chart Powerpoint," RT- PSI-00363679-717, at 682.

168 The six Medallion feeder fund subsidiaries are [Redacted] Trading Ltd (Bermuda), [Redacted] Trading S.A. (Uruguay), [Redacted] Holdings LLC (Delaware), [Redacted] Trading Ltd (Bermuda), [Redacted] Trading LLC (Delaware), and [Redacted] LLC (Delaware). See id. at 691.

169 The five Medallion master funds are Mosel Equities LP (Delaware), Badger Holdings LP (Delaware), Medallion Holdings LTD (Bermuda), Medallion Trading (Bermuda), and Nova Fund LP (Delaware). See id. at 694.

170 The nine trading subsidiaries include seven formed in Bermuda: Baden Equities Ltd, Bass Equities Ltd, Franconia Equities Ltd., [Redacted] Equities Ltd., [Redacted] Trading Ltd., St. Veran Equities Ltd., and [Redacted] Equities Ltd. One trading subsidiary, [Redacted] Trading LLC, was formed in Delaware. The final trading subsidiary, [Redacted] Investment Ltd., was formed in Mauritius. See id. at 696.

171 Id. at 697.

172 The three subsidiaries no longer active are Bass Equities Ltd., [Redacted] Trading Ltd., and [Redacted] Equities Ltd. Id.

173 Subcommittee interview of Peter Brown, RenTec (6/3/2014). See also "Simons Strategy to Shield Profit From Taxes Draws IRS Ire," *Bloomberg*, Zachary R. Mider and Jesse Drucker, (7/1/2013), http://www.bloomberg.com/news/2013-07-01/simons-strategy-to-shield-profit-from-taxes-draws-irs-ire.html.

174 See 5/26/2010 letter from SEC to RenTec, "Re: Examination of Renaissance Technologies LLC ('RenTec')," SEC_RT13_001965-993, at 979, n.6 [Sealed Exhibit].

[175] 5/23/2012 "Weiss Enterprise Audit Organizational Overview," prepared by George Weiss, GWALLC-PSI-0002164, at 167.

[176] Id. at 172.

[177] Id. at 177.

[178] Id. at 178.

[179] Id.

[180] Id. at 183.

[181] Subcommittee interview of Frederick Doucette, GWA (5/23/2014).

[182] Id.

[183] Id.

[184] See Table, "MAPS Transaction," produced by Deutsche Bank, 6/27/2014, DB-PSI 00052577-582, at 579.

[185] Subcommittee interview of Frederick Doucette, GWA (5/23/2014).

[186] Id.

[187] Subcommittee interview of James Rowen, RenTec (5/20/2014). Morgan Stanley was also developing a similar product around the same time, with the goal of selling an option that would allow a hedge fund to engage in its own trading activity by managing a proprietary account held at an investment bank. Id.

[188] Id.

[189] Subcommittee interviews of Mark Silber, RenTec (6/10/2014) and Satish Ramakrishna, Deutsche Bank (5/16/2014).

[190] Subcommittee interview of Frederick Doucette, GWA (5/23/2014).

[191] Id.

[192] Id.

[193] Id.

[194] Id.

[195] Id.

[196] Id.

[197] Id.

[198] Id.

[199] Id.

[200] See George Weiss response to an IRS Information Document Request, (8/8/2012), GWALLC-PSI-0000745-844, at 745 [Sealed Exhibit].

[201] Subcommittee interview of Frederick Doucette, GWA (5/23/2014).

[202] George Weiss response to an IRS Information Document Request, (8/8/2012), GWALLC-PSI-0000745-844, at 745 [Sealed Exhibit]; Table, "MAPS Transaction," produced by Deutsche Bank, 6/27/2014, DB-PSI 00052577-582, at 579.

[203] See Table, "MAPS Transaction," produced by Deutsche Bank, 6/27/2014, DB-PSI 00052577-582, at 579.

[204] Subcommittee interview of Peter Brown, RenTec (6/3/2014).

[205] Subcommittee interview of Mark Silber, RenTec (6/10/2014).

[206] Id.

[207] Subcommittee interview of Peter Brown, RenTec (6/3/2014).

[208] Chart produced by Deutsche Bank, 6/27/2014, DB-PSI 00052583-585.

[209] The Deutsche Bank personnel who moved to RenTec included Peter Brophy who worked with Deutsche Bank clients and later handled fund accounting at RenTec; Thomas Kerns, who became head of Fund Accounting and Operations at RenTec and is now retired; James Rowen who became RenTec's Chief Operations Officer; and Jonathan Mayers who became RenTec's Counsel. Subcommittee interviews of James Rowen, RenTec (5/20/2014), Thomas Kerns, RenTec (5/6/2014), Peter Brophy, Deutsche Bank (5/13/2014 and 5/19/2014), and Jonathan Mayers, RenTec (5/28/2014).

[210] See Table, "MAPS Transaction," produced by Deutsche Bank, 6/27/2014, DB-PSI 00052577-582, at 577-578; Untitled chart produced by Deutsche Bank, 7/17/2014, DB-PSI 00052588-590. Profit calculated by subtracting premium from settlement mount.

[211] 7/31/2002 "Confidential: Project COLT," new product proposal, product sponsors Jonathan Zenios, Jerry Smith, Martin Malloy, and Mark D'Andrea, BARCLAYS-PSI-212559-566.

[212] The counterparty credit risk in this circumstance was the risk that the bank would be unable to pay its obligation to the hedge fund.

[213] Subcommittee interview of Mark Silber, RenTec (6/10/2014).

[214] See, e.g., 7/31/2002 "Confidential: Project COLT," prepared by Barclays product sponsors Jonathan Zenios, Jerry Smith, Martin Malloy, and Mark D'Andrea, BARCLAYS-PSI-212559-566, at 561.

[215] As detailed below, the options involved three Barclays entities, Palomino, BBPLC, and the New York branch of Barclays PLC, as well as a RenTec subsidiary, Bass Equities Ltd. Later, Bass was replaced with another RenTec entity called Badger Holding LP. Subcommittee interview of Martin Malloy, Barclays (5/1/2014).

[216] See undated chart, "History of COLT Options," prepared by Barclays, BARCLAYS-PSI-748604. These figures do not include eight options that were exercised within a year or four options that have not been exercised to date. Notional value for the Barclays accounts was derived by multiplying the premiums by 10 as the premiums represented 10% of the notional value based on Barclays Investment Management Account.

[217] 10/15/2010 memo, "Hedge Fund Basket Option Contracts," Internal Revenue Service, BARCLAYS-PSI-748148-158.

[218] 6/30/2014 briefing by Deutsche Bank counsel to the Subcommittee. See also 7/22/2014 "Post-GLAM Basket Option Contracts," Memorandum to File prepared by the Subcommittee (summarizing Deutsche Bank, Barclays, and RenTec involvement with basket options after the November 2010 issuance of the IRS advisory memorandum on basket options).

[219] 12/2013 "Barclays Powerpoint," prepared by Barclays, BARCLAYS-PSI-748589. See also 7/22/2014 "Post- GLAM Basket Option Contracts," Memorandum to File prepared by the Subcommittee (summarizing Deutsche Bank, Barclays, and RenTec involvement with basket options after the November 2010 issuance of the IRS advisory memorandum on basket options).

[220] Subcommittee interview of Peter Brown, RenTec (6/3/2014). 4/13/2012 "Protest of 60 Day Letters by Renaissance Technologies LLC et al.," RT-PSI-00000001-402 [Sealed Exhibit].

[221] Table, "MAPS Transaction," produced by Deutsche Bank, 6/27/2014, DB-PSI 00052577-582. The hedge funds that purchased MAPS options included: RenTec, GWA LLC, Ballentine Capital Management, Deephaven Capital Management, SAC Capital Advisors, Talon Capital LLC, Provident Advisors LLC, MFT Limited, MWN Limited, Analytic Investors Inc., Riverside Asset Management LLC, 646 Advisors LLC, and Northern Asset Management, Inc.

[222] 8/11/2008 referral letter from SEC to IRS, "Portfolio Option Strategies," prepared by SEC, SEC_RT13_002078 [Sealed Exhibit]. See also Table, "MAPS Transaction," produced by Deutsche Bank, 6/27/2014, DB-PSI 00052577-582.

[223] Table, "MAPS Transaction," produced by Deutsche Bank, 6/27/2014, DB-PSI 00052577-582, at 577-578.

[224] Id. at 577-582; Subcommittee interview of Frederick Doucette, GWA (5/23/2014); 6/2/2014 briefing by Deutsche Bank counsel to the Subcommittee.

[225] Subcommittee interview of Martin Malloy, Barclays (5/1/2014).

[226] See 2/12/2013 "Barclays Strategic Review," Barclays Press Release, http://www.newsroom.barclays.com/Press- releases/Barclays-Strategic-Review-9db.aspx (announcing closure of SCM group); "Barclays to Close 'Tax Avoidance' Unit," *BBC*, (2/10/2013), http://www.bbc.com/news/business-21397844.

[227] 5/28/2002 "Confidential: Project COLT," Barclays new product proposal, product sponsors: Jonathan Zenios, Jerry Smith, Martin Malloy, and Mark D'Andrea, BARCLAYS-PSI-212544-557, at 548.

[228] Subcommittee interview of Sadat Mannan, Barclays (5/15/2014).

[229] Id.

[230] 5/28/2002 "Confidential: Project COLT," Barclays new product proposal, product sponsors: Jonathan Zenios, Jerry Smith, Martin Malloy, and Mark D'Andrea, BARCLAYS-PSI-212544-557, at 545-546.

[231] See, e.g., 12/6/2006 "Amended and Restated Investment Management Agreement," signed by Barclays and RenTec, RT-PSI-00134963. The Investment Management Agreement contained certain limits and guidelines on what could be selected for the account. For example, RenTec could invest only in stocks from a limited set of countries, and no single position could constitute more than 1.5% of the outstanding shares of a company or more than 55% of the total equity in the account. Otherwise, RenTec had complete discretion to identify assets to be acquired for the portfolio. If an order placed by RenTec was not executed, or subsequently undone without orders from RenTec, the assets were still considered part of the reference account for purposes of considering the gain or the loss to Badger. Id. at 964.

[232] Subcommittee interviews of Peter Brown, RenTec (6/3/2014) and Jonathan Mayers, RenTec (5/28/2014).

[233] See 8/5/2004 "Certification of Limited Partnership of Badger L.P.," prepared by the Delaware Secretary of State, RT-PSI-00396317.

[234] 8/13/2002 "Certification of Incorporation," prepared by the Registrar of Companies of Bermuda for Bass Equities Ltd., RT-PSI-00396344.

[235] 8/5/2004 "Certification of Limited Partnership of Badger L.P.," prepared by the Delaware Secretary of State, RT- PSI-00396317

[236] See, e.g., 6/13/2008 Barclays Bank PLC letter agreement with Badger Holdings L.P., "Option RR," BARCLAYS-PSI-000345-363, at 45.

[237] See chart, "History of COLT Options," prepared by Barclays, BARCLAYS-PSI-748604.

[238] Subcommittee interviews of James Rowen, RenTec (5/20/2014) and Jonathan Mayers, RenTec (5/28/2014).

[239] Subcommittee interview of Sadat Mannan, Barclays (5/515/2014). For more information about this pooling arrangement, see below.

[240] See, e.g., 1/5/2010 letter from Barclays to SEC, "Follow-up to meeting regarding Colt Transaction Summary," BARCLAYS-PSI-287767-770, at 767, 769 (explaining to the SEC that it offered accounts in which "[c]lients enter orders electronically via … proprietary trading engines [and] [t]he desk then routes those orders to exchanges, Alternating Trading Systems (ATSs) and Electronic Communications Networks (ECNS)," and that the RenTec "Flip Account" was "RenTec's execution account that 'flips' executions … for clearing purposes," while Palomino's account acted as "RenTec's clearing account … to facilitate settlement").

[241] Subcommittee interview of Peter Brown, RenTec (6/3/2014). See also 1/5/2010 letter from Barclays to SEC, "Follow-up to meeting regarding Colt Transaction Summary," BARCLAYS-PSI-287767-770, at 767 (explaining to the SEC that some of its accounts, including RenTec and Palomino accounts, offered "sub-millisecond internal latency for execution").

[242] According to RenTec, its trading algorithms were dynamic and had to be updated and adjusted on a regular basis by its programmers. RenTec explained that the algorithm was frequently modified manually by programmers through what was described as an "objective function." For example, the objective function could be modified to direct trades to particular options to reduce or increase its portfolio size, or to reduce or increase exposure at a particular bank. Subcommittee Interview of Peter Brown, RenTec (6/3/2014).

[243] Subcommittee interview of Lansford Dyer, Barclays (4/3/2014).

[244] Id. In response to Subcommittee inquiries, Barclays indicated that it did not use its legal authority to create any synthetic positions in the COLT option accounts as a result of rejecting a RenTec trading instruction. Subcommittee briefing by Barclays counsel (7/16/2014).

[245] The trading executions by RenTec were required to be in compliance with the investment guidelines for the account in order to be included in the valuation of the account. See e.g., 12/21/2005 Barclays Bank PLC letter agreement with Badger Holdings L.P., "Option HH," BARCLAYS-PSI-002879-896.

[246] 12/6/2006 "Amended and Restated Investment Management Agreement," signed by Barclays and RenTec, RT- PSI-00134963-5013, at 983-984.

[247] Id. at 4973.

[248] In memoranda presented to its own bank executives and to its U.K. regulator at the time, the Financial Services Authority (FSA), Barclays personnel described the actual risk of catastrophic loss as minimal and comparable to risks undertaken by the bank on a routine basis. See, e.g., 9/13/2002 letter from FSA to Barclays, "PROJECT COLT," BARCLAYS-PSI-005258-259 (indicating Barclays had told its U.K. regulator that basket options carried low risks that were comparable to standard brokerage accounts, in part because "[c]redit and operation controls around this transaction are equivalent to those that are in place for a standard prime brokerage transaction"); 7/4/2002 letter from Barclays to FSA, "PROJECT COLT," BARCLAYS-PSI-005241-243, at 241 ("Controls exist within the prime [brokerage account] to ensure that the risk of loss is minimized."); 8/12/2002 letter from Barclays to FSA, "PROJECT COLT." BARCLAYS-PSI-005246-250, at 249; 9/2/2004 Barclays memorandum from Jonathan Zenios to Barclays' SCM Approvals Committee, "Approvals paper – COLT V: Renaissance Restructuring," BARCLAYS-PSI-004161-165, at 164 (describing the risk to the bank from the COLT options as "akin to the risks taken in a normal collateralized Prime Brokerage relationship, where the risks generally are confined to catastrophic losses occurring over a short period of time"); 4/4/2003 Barclays memorandum from SCM to SCM Approvals Committee, "SCM Approvals paper – Project COLT (Renaissance II)," BARCLAYS-PSI-213947-953, at 949. See also Subcommittee interview of Lansford Dyer, Barclays (4/3/2014)(indicating that Mr. Dyer had calculated the risk of RenTec's options suffering sudden catastrophic losses and breaching an option limit as insignificant, in that it was thought to be less than .0001).

[249] Id. In addition, the COLT options imposed "limits on liquidity, sector exposure, size and leverage in order to substantially reduce the risk that any gap risk loss is greater than the call option premiums." 6/24/2009 memorandum from Barclays to PricewaterhouseCoopers, "Palomino Limited ('Palomino')," BARCLAYS-PSI-139757-166, at 764. See also 9/3/2004 Barclays memorandum from Jonathan Zenios to SCM Approvals Committee, "Approvals paper – COLT V: Renaissance Restructuring," BARCLAYS-PSI-004161-165.

[250] See, e.g., 6/13/2008 Barclays letter agreement with Badger Holdings L.P., "Option RR," BARCLAYS-PSI-000345-363, at 350-351.

[251] See 6/27/2014 RenTec counsel's letter to Subcommittee, PSI-Renaissance-37-000001, at 003. This fee was consistently imposed after 2004. Id.

[252] See, e.g., 6/13/2008 Barclays letter agreement with Badger Holdings L.P., "Option RR," BARCLAYS-PSI-000345-363, at 355.

[253] See, e.g., 10/1/2004 "Indemnity Agreement," signed by Barclay's Bank PLC, Palomino Limited, Badger Holdings L.P., Medallion International Limited, Medallion Capital Investments Ltd., Medallion Associates L.P., Medallion Fund L.P., Medallion USA L.P., and Medallion RMP Fund L.P., BARCLAYS-PSI-632877-904.

[254] Id at 880.

[255] Subcommittee interview of Lansford Dyer, Barclays (4/3/2014); 7/15/2014 letter from Barclays counsel to the Subcommittee, PSI-Barclays-22-000005-014, at 007.

[256] For example, under the Investment Advisory Agreement between Deutsche Bank and RenTec, RenTec agreed not to acquire more than 4% of the shares of any one issuer, not to acquire

more than 5% or more of any class of voting security, and not to trade equities on the bank's restricted list. See 12/15/2008 "Master Investment Advisory Agreement: Execution Copy," signed by Deutsche Bank and RenTec, DB-PSI 00000001-047, at 022-025. Otherwise, the hedge fund had complete discretion to select assets for the portfolio.

[257] Chart produced by Deutsche Bank, 6/27/2014, DB-PSI 00052583-585.

[258] Subcommittee interview of Thomas Kerns, RenTec (5/6/2014).

[259] Subcommittee briefing by Deutsche Bank counsel (6/30/2014).

[260] Subcommittee interview of Thomas Kerns, RenTec (5/6/2014). For more information on this pooling arrangement, see below.

[261] RenTec obtained Deutsche Bank's agreement to provide financing up to a maximum leverage level of 18:1; other hedge funds may have reached other agreements, although all sought high leverage. See 12/16/2007 Deutsche Bank letter agreement with Mosel Equities L.P., 'OUTPERFORMANCE' BARRIER OPTION TRANSACTION—Cash Settled, Linear Amortizing Premium—DB Reference No. 941-50053," DB-PSI 00000320-337 at 328; 8/24/2009 email from William Broeksmit to Satish Ramakrishna of Deutsche Bank, "Renaissance Technologies," DB-PSI 00005713-715, at 714.

[262] See 6/27/2014 letter from RenTec counsel to the Subcommittee, PSI-Renaissance-37-000001-007, at 003. Those payments were far below market rates. In comparison, many hedge funds acting as investment advisor to funds during the same period charged a management fee equal to 2% of the assets under management plus a performance fee equal to 20% of the gains.

[263] 12/16/2007 Deutsche Bank letter agreement to Mosel Equities L.P., 'OUTPERFORMANCE' BARRIER OPTION TRANSACTION—Cash Settled, Linear Amortizing Premium—DB Reference No. 941-50053," DB-PSI 00000320-337 at 328.

[264] 11/16/2007 "Amended & Restated Investment Advisory Agreement: Execution Copy," signed by Deutsche Bank and RenTec, RT-PSI-00000914-931. See also Subcommittee interviews of Peter Brown, RenTec (6/2/2014), Satish Ramakrishna, Deutsche Bank (5/16/2014); and Jonathan Mayers, RenTec (5/28/2014).

[265] 11/16/2007 "Amended & Restated Investment Advisory Agreement: Execution Copy," signed by Deutsche Bank and RenTec, RT-PSI-00000914-931; Subcommittee interview of Satish Ramakrishna, Deutsche Bank (5/16/2014).

[266] Id.

[267] Id.

[268] Subcommittee interviews of Satish Ramakrishna, Deutsche Bank (5/16/2014) and Jonathan Mayers, RenTec (5/28/2014).

[269] Subcommittee interviews of Peter Brown, RenTec (6/3/2014) and Satish Ramakrishna, Deutsche Bank (5/16/2014).

[270] See, e.g., "Quant Quake Shakes Hedge-fund Giants," *Market Watch*, Alistair Barr, (8/13/2007), http://www.marketwatch.com/story/quant-quake-shakes-hedge-fund-giants.

[271] Subcommittee interview of Lansford Dyer, Barclays (4/13/2014).

[272] Subcommittee interview of Thomas Kerns, RenTec (5/6/2014).

[273] 6/27/2014 letter from RenTec counsel to the Subcommittee, PSI-Renaissance-37-000001-007, at 003.

[274] 7/30/2008 e-mail from Eamon McCooey of Deutsche Bank to Tom Kerns of RenTec, "RE: Optionality Value" RT-PSI-00046119

[275] See, e.g., 12/15/2008 "Master Investment Advisory Agreement," between Deutsche Bank AG London and RenTec, DB-PSI 00000001-047, at 010.

[276] Subcommittee interview of Frederick Doucette, GWA (5/23/2014).

[277] Id.

[278] Id.

[279] 2/26/2009 email from Frederick Doucette, GWA, to Frank Nelson, Deutsche Bank, "MAPS comments," DB-PSI-00033762, at 763-764 (listing out George Weiss concerns with new MAPS structure).

[280] Subcommittee interview of Frederick Doucette, GWA (5/23/2014).

[281] See 10/1/2004 "Indemnity Agreement," signed by Barclays Bank PLC, Palomino Limited, Badger Holdings L.P., Medallion International Limited, Medallion Capital Investments Ltd., Medallion Associates L.P., Medallion Fund L.P., Medallion USA L.P., and Medallion RMP Fund L.P., BARCLAYS-PSI-632877-904, at 880.

[282] Chart produced by Deutsche Bank, 6/27/2014, DB-PSI 00052583-585.

[283] See, e.g., 6/7/2012 Deutsche Bank letter agreement with Mosel Equities L.P., "BARRIER OPTION TRANSACTION—Cash Settled, DBSI Reference No. 941-50340," DB-PSI 00047768-796, at 786.

[284] See "History of COLT Options," prepared by Barclays, BARCLAYS-PSI-748604.

[285] See chart, "History of COLT Options," prepared by Barclays, BARCLAYS-PSI-748604. See also chart produced by Deutsche Bank, 6/27/2014, DB-PSI 00052583-585. Six of those options remain outstanding.

[286] 6/27/2014 letter from RenTec's counsel to the Subcommittee, "Response to Renaissance Follow Up Questions," PSI-Renaissance-37-000001-007, at 004.

[287] Subcommittee estimate based on the daily trading estimates supplied by RenTec. 6/27/2014 letter from RenTec's counsel to the Subcommittee, "Response to Renaissance Follow Up Questions," PSI-Renaissance-37-000001-007, at 004. These large figures appear to be corroborated by an SEC examination report that calculated, for the one-year period from April 1, 2008 to March 31, 2009, that RenTec executed approximately 129 million orders. "Examination Report for: Renaissance Technologies LLC (801-53609)," prepared by the SEC, SEC_RT13_001971-993, at 972 [Sealed Exhibit].

[288] 11/18/2008 memorandum prepared by Barclays, "Renaissance Technologies Corp Prime Services Brief on existing BarCap relationship and legacy Lehman relationship," BARCLAYS-PSI-018701-704.

[289] Subcommittee interviews of Jonathan Mayers, RenTec (5/28/2014) and Mark Silber, RenTec (6/10/2014).

[290] Email from Daniel Koranyi, RenTec, replicated in 11/19/2008 email from Colin Masson, RenTec, to Daniel Koranyi, "DB counteroffer," RT-PSI-00368695-697.

[291] For the Barclays confirmations, see, e.g., 12/21/2005 Barclays letter agreement with Badger Holdings L.P., "Option HH," BARCLAYS-PSI-002879-896, at 887-888. For the Deutsche Bank confirmations, see, e.g., 12/16/2007 Deutsche Bank letter agreement to Mosel Equities L.P., "'OUTPERFORMANCE' BARRIER OPTION TRANSACTION—Cash Settled, Linear Amortizing Premium—DB Reference No. 941-50053," DB-PSI 00000320-337, at 327.

[292] These costs were enumerated in the Barclays confirmations and in the Deutsche Bank investment advisory agreements. See, e.g., 12/21/2005 Barclays letter agreement with Badger Holdings L.P., "Option HH," BARCLAYS-PSI-002879-896, at 887-888; 3/14/2002 "Investment Advisory Agreement" between Deutsche Bank, London Branch, and RenTec, DB-PSI 00123209-221, at 210.

[293] See 5/21/2008 email from Thomas Kerns to Mark Silber of RenTec, "Legal Entity Org Chart Powerpoint," RT- PSI-00363679-717, at 681 and 695; Subcommittee interview of Jonathan Mayers, RenTec (5/28/2014).

[294] *Sun Capital Partners III, LP v. New England Teamsters & Trucking Indus. Pension Fund*, 724 F.3d 129, 146-47 (1st Cir. 2013) (citing Del. Code. Ann. tit. 6 § 15-301 (West 2000)). Additionally, the option confirmations included "any investment advisor fees accrued during such period, whether or not actually paid by Seller" as a component of the "Basket Expenses" that had to be paid from the account profits. 10/8/2009 Deutsche Bank letter agreement with Mosel Equities L.P., "BARRIER OPTION TRANSACTION—Cash Settled—DBSI Reference No. 941-50310," DB-PSI 00000181-209, at 191.

[295] 12/15/2008 "Master Investment Advisory Agreement," between Deutsche Bank London and RenTec, DB-PSI 00000001-047, at 001-002.

[296] 10/8/2009 Deutsche Bank letter agreement with Mosel Equities L.P., "BARRIER OPTION TRANSACTION— Cash Settled—DBSI Reference No. 941-50310," DB-PSI 00000181-209, at 201.

[297] Franconia Equities Ltd. made a similar representation in earlier MAPS options, stating that "the Buyer [of the option, Franconia] agrees that it shall not contact directly the Investment Advisor regarding the terms or subject matter of this Transaction." 3/14/2002 "OUTPERFORMANCE' BARRIER OPTION TRANSACTION – Cash Settled, Linear Amortizing Premium – DBSI Reference No. 1244131," DB_PSI 00123196-208, at 206. Since Franconia was a shell corporation under RenTec's control, its statement that it would not contact the Investment Advisor – RenTec – does not seem possible. Like the Mosel representation, it was a fiction disguising RenTec's control over the option holder as well as the option's trading activity.

[298] 2/5/2008 email from Adrienne Browning, Deutsche Bank, to Steven Purvis, Deutsche Bank, "do you remember.......," RT-PSI-00062957-959, at 959.

[299] Id.

[300] 2/5/2008 email from Steven Purvis, Deutsche Bank, to Adrienne Browning, Deutsche Bank, "do you remember.......," RT-PSI-00062957-959, at 958.

[301] 5/2011 email exchange among Marty Malloy, John Feraca, Lansford Dyer, and others of Barclays, "Palomino deconsolidates from Barclays Group," BARCLAYS-PSI-036091-102.

[302] See 6/24/2009 Barclays memorandum from "SCM" to "PwC," meaning PricewaterhouseCoopers, Barclay's auditor, "Palomino Limited ('Palomino')," BARCLAYS-PSI-139757-766, at 764.

[303] Id. at 765.

[304] 7/2/2008 email from Rafal Medak, Barclays, to Nidhi Bajaj, PricewaterhouseCoopers, "Palomino's PB accounts," BARCLAYS-PSI-632060-063, at 061.

[305] 6/19/2009 email from Simon Constant to Paolo Mammola of Barclays, "Project COLT – articles amendment," BARCLAYS-PSI-577747.

[306] 6/26/2009 letter from RenTec to Barclays, New York Branch, "Palomino Limited," signed by Mark Silber on behalf of both RenTec and Badger Holdings, RT-PSI-00236651-655, at 652.

[307] 5/29/2009 email exchange among Abhinav Shah, Rob Konowalchuk, Louise McSweeney, and others of Barclays, "Palamino to PwC 20/5/09," BARCLAYS-PSI-328074-077.

[308] 5/29/2009 email from Rob Konowalchuk, PWC, to Louise McSweeney, Barclays l, "Palamino to PwC 20/5/09," BARCLAYS-PSI-328074-077, at 074-075.

[309] See April-May 2009 email exchange among Abhinav Shah and Louise McSweeney of Barclays, Rob Konowalchuk, PWC, and others, "Palamino to PwC 20/5/09," BARCLAYS-PSI-328074-077, at 074.

[310] 6/24/2009 Barclays memorandum from "SCM" to "PwC," "Palomino Limited ('Palomino')," BARCLAYS-PSI-139757-766, at 762; 6/30/2009 "Amended and Restated Memorandum and Articles of Association of Palomino Limited (Adopted Pursuant to Special Resolution Dated 26 June 2009)," RT-PSI-00234974-998; 6/26/2009 letter from Mark Silber, RenTec, to Martin Malloy, Barclays, "Palomino Limited," signed by Mark Silber on behalf of both RenTec and Badger Holdings, RT-PSI-00236651-655.

[311] 6/24/2009 Barclays memorandum from "SCM" to "PwC," "Palomino Limited ('Palomino')," BARCLAYS-PSI-139757-766, at 762; 6/26/2009 letter from Mark Silber, RenTec, to Martin Malloy, Barclays, "Palomino Limited," signed by Mark Silber on behalf of both RenTec and Badger Holdings, RT-PSI-00236651-655.

[312] 6/24/2009 Barclays l memorandum from "SCM" to "PwC," "Palomino Limited ('Palomino')," BARCLAYS- PSI-139757-766.

[313] Id. at 763-764.

[314] Barclays told the Subcommittee that it distinguished its accounting deconsolidation from regulatory deconsolidation, and that it continued to report to the Financial Services Authority (FSA), its U.K. financial regulator, that Palomino was consolidated for regulatory purposes under an FSA requirement to consolidate any entity in which it owned more than

20% of the shares, even if it did not control that entity. See 5/18/2011 email from Marty Malloy to John Feraca of Barclays, "Palomino deconsolidates from Barclays Group," BARCLAYS-PSI-036091.

[315] Subcommittee interview of Mark Silber, RenTec (6/10/2014).

[316] 5/27/2014 email from Barclays counsel to the Subcommittee, "My response to your e-mailed questions," PSI- Barclays-20-000001-006 at 003.

[317] Id. at 004.

[318] Id.

[319] 2009 "Barclays PLC Annual Report 2009, Notes to the Accounts," prepared by Barclays, at 256, http://files.the- group.net/library/barclays/annualreport2009/pdfs/barcar09_ financialstatements.pdf. This disclosure was also made in other SEC filings in subsequent years. See Form 20-F for year ending 12/31/2009, prepared by Barclays for the SEC (3/19/2010), http://www.sec.gov/Archives/edgar/data/312069/000119312510061597/d20f. htm; Form 20-F (for year ending 12/31/2010), prepared by Barclays for the SEC (3/21/2011), http://www.sec.gov/Archives/edgar/data/312069/000119312511072441/d20f. htm; Form 20-F (for year ending 12/31/2011), prepared by Barclays for the SEC (3/30/2012), http://www.sec.gov/Archives/edgar/data/312069/000119312512142026/d27 8890d20f.htm; Form 20-F (for year ending 12/31/2012, prepared by Barclays for the SEC (3/13/2013), http://www.sec.gov/Archives/edgar/data/312069/000119312513105055/ d497934d20f.htm; The language in Barclay's SEC filings from 2009 through 2012 was virtually identical to that described above. In its most recent filings, however, Barclays modified this language substantially. This change occurred while Barclay's activities were being investigated by the Subcommittee. See Form 20-F (for year ending 12/31/2013), prepared by Barclays for SEC (3/14/2014), http://www.sec.gov/Archives/edgar/data/ 312069/000119312514099379/d686589d20f.htm.

[320] 6/24/2009 Barclays memorandum from SCM to PwC, "Palomino Limited ('Palomino')," BARCLAYS-PSI-139757-766, at 763-764.

[321] As indicated earlier, a "prime brokerage account" is a trading account at a large financial institution which provides the account holder with a bundled set of services, including execution of trades, settlement, financing, and custody services, that the account holder uses to trade with multiple brokerage houses while maintaining cash and assets in the master account. See, e.g., "Financial Glossary: Prime Broker," prepared by NASDAQ, http://www.nasdaq.com/investing/glossary/p/prime-broker; Wikipedia definition of "prime brokerage," http://en.wikipedia.org/wiki/Prime_brokerage.

[322] 8/22/2002 Barclays memorandum from Jonathan Zenios et al. to Iain Abrahams et al., "SCM Approvals paper – Project COLT," BARCLAYS-PSI-212590-598, at 590.

[323] Id. See also 9/13/2002 letter from Financial Services Authority to Barclays, "Project COLT," BARCLAYS-PSI-005258-259 ("Credit and operational controls around this [COLT] transaction are equivalent to those that are in place for a standard prime brokerage transaction.").

[324] 4/4/2003 Barclays memorandum from SCM to SCM Approvals Committee, "SCM Approvals paper – Project COLT (Renaissance II)," BARCLAYS-PSI-213947-953, at 949.

[325] 5/19/2010 email from Edward Sherwood to Brett Beldner of Barclays, "COLT XIX – Draft SCM Approvals Notification," BARCLAYS-PSI-010082. "Senior financing" refers to very secure financing, senior debt that has a position of priority relative to other lenders in the event of bankruptcy. See, e.g., 12 C.F.R. § 327 app. C. ("Senior debt includes any portion of total debt that has a priority claim on any of the borrower's assets. A priority claim is a claim that entitles the holder to priority of payment over other debt holders in bankruptcy.")

[326] 8/25/2009 email from William Broeksmit to Anshu Jain of Deutsche Bank, "RenTech MAPS," DB-PSI 00006983-084, at 083.

[327] 12/6/2006 "Amended and Restated Investment Management Agreement," signed by Barclays and RenTec, RT- PSI-00134963-5013, at 983-984. Barclays provided an upper leverage limit of 20:1, 8/15/2007 memorandum from Hamish McPherson to Iain Abrahams of

Barclays, "Project Colt X (Renaissance Technologies)," BARCLAYS-PSI-003792; while DB provided an upper leverage limit of 18:1. 8/24/2009 email from William Broeksmit to Satish Ramakrishna of DB, "Renaissance Technologies," DB-PSI 00005713-715, at 714.

[328] 2/26/2013 RenTec briefing of the Subcommittee.

[329] Id.

[330] Audio recording of 11/6/2008 telephone call among James Rowen, RenTec, and Satish Ramakrishnan, and Deepak Agrawal of Deutsche Bank, DB-PSI 00122457.

[331] Id.

[332] Subcommittee interview of Peter Brown, RenTec (6/3/2014).

[333] 8/23/2011 email from Peter Brown to Daniel Koranyi of RenTec, "US portfolio shift – overrides?" RT-PSI-00364418; Subcommittee interview of Peter Brown, RenTec (6/3/2014).

[334] Subcommittee interview of Peter Brown, RenTec (6/3/2014).

[335] May 2010 Examination Report for RenTec, prepared by SEC New York Regional Office, SEC_RT13_001965-993 [Sealed Exhibit].

[336] Id. at 972 [Sealed Exhibit].

[337] 6/27/2014 letter from RenTec counsel to the Subcommittee, PSI-Renaissance-37-000001-000007, at 004. In an internal memorandum, Barclays described the trading activity of the Medallion Fund, the entity Renaissance used to implement the basket option transactions, as "very high frequency trading." 11/18/2008 memorandum prepared by Barclays, "Renaissance Technologies Corp Prime Services Brief on existing BarCap relationship and legacy Lehman relationship," BARCLAYS-PSI-018701-704, at 701.

[338] Undated chart, "Holding Period Comparison RIEF vs. Medallion, From January 1, 2007 thru March 31, 2009," prepared by RenTec, SEC_RT13_010650-651, at 651 [Sealed Exhibit].

[339] Subcommittee interview of Peter Brown, RenTec (6/3/2014).

[340] 12/2/2011 "Present Law and Issues Related to the Taxation of Financial Instruments and Products," prepared by the Joint Committee on Taxation, JCX-56-11, at 7, https://www.jct.gov/publications.html?func=startdown&id=4372.

[341] Multiple documents describe RenTec's absolute control over the trading accounts. In a letter to the IRS, a copy of which was provided by RenTec to the Subcommittee, RenTec stated that the option was on a "notional stock portfolio that changed in accordance with recommendations of the Algorithm." 4/13/2012 "Protest of 60 Day Letters by Renaissance Technologies LLC et al.," RT-PSI-00000001-402, at 016 [Sealed Exhibit]. In option confirmations with the banks, the basket of assets was defined as "positions that (i) actually result from transactions specified by the Investment Advisor … or (ii) are Designated Positions (as such term is defined in the Master Investment Advisory Agreement.)" 10/8/2009 Deutsche Bank letter agreement with Mosel Equities L.P., "BARRIER OPTION TRANSACTION—Cash Settled—DBSI Reference No. 941-50310," DB-PSI 00000181-209, at 190. Pursuant to the 1992 ISDA Master Agreement as supplemented in December 15, 2008, a designated position was any position "reject[ed]," "unwound," or "liquidated" by the Client "without the direction of the Advisor." 12/15/2008 "Master Investment Advisory Agreement: Execution Copy," signed by Deutsche Bank and RenTec, DB- PSI 00000001-047, at 002-003. The investment advisory agreement also stated: "[T]he Advisor shall … have full power, authority and right to … supervise and direct the investment and reinvestment of all assets in the Accounts, and engage in such transactions on behalf of the Client's Account, in the Advisor's discretion and without prior consultation with the Client, subject only to the terms of this Agreement …." Id. at 001-002.

[342] Analysis of the IRS GLAM suggests that the combination of direct control over the option account by the option buyer or its agent combined with changes in the referenced securities presents a good argument for a § 1001 "exchange every time there is a change to the referenced securities." "Options Over a Managed Account: The IRS Weighs in," *What's News in Tax*, KPMG, Daniel Mayo and Sam Chen, (12/17/2010), at 12, http://www.us.kpmg.com/microsite/taxnewsflash/2010/Dec/Options.pdf.

[343] Treas. Reg. § 1.1001-1(a).

[344] Rev. Rul. 90-109, 1990-2 C.B. 191.

[345] See, e.g., 12/16/2007 Deutsche Bank letter agreement with Mosel Equities L.P., "'OUTPERFORMANCE' BARRIER OPTION TRANSACTION—Cash Settled, Linear Amortizing Premium—DB Reference No. 941-50053," DB-PSI 00000320-337; 12/21/2005 Barclays letter agreement with Badger Holdings L.P., "Option HH," BARCLAYS-PSI-002879-896. See also Subcommittee interview of Frederick Doucette, George Weiss (5/23/2014); 12/17/2007 Deutsche Bank letter agreement to RenTec, "First Amendment to the Amended & Restated Investment Advisory Agreement," RT-PSI-00000932-933.

[346] Subcommittee interview of Thomas Kerns, RenTec (5/6/2014) (stating it would it be very difficult or even impossible to determine what stocks were assigned to a particular option during or after an unwind).

[347] Subcommittee interview of Thomas Kerns, RenTec (5/6/2014).

[348] Subcommitte interview of Lansford Dyer, Barclays (4/3/2014).

[349] See, e.g., 12/16/2007 Deutsche Bank letter agreement with Mosel Equities L.P., "'OUTPERFORMANCE' BARRIER OPTION TRANSACTION—Cash Settled, Linear Amortizing Premium—DB Reference No. 941-50053," DB-PSI 00000320-337; 12/21/2005 Barclays letter agreement with Badger Holdings L.P., "Option HH," BARCLAYS-PSI-002879-896. See also Subcommittee interview of Thomas Kerns, RenTec (5/6/2014).

[350] 7/31/13 letter from RenTec to the Subcommittee describing journaling between basket option sub-accounts, RT- PSI-00384749-761.

[351] Id.

[352] Subcommittee interviews of Satish Ramakrishna, Deutsche Bank (5/16/2014) and Jonathan Mayers, RenTec (5/28/2014).

[353] For a list of all journaling between subaccounts, see 7/31/13 letter from RenTec to the Subcommittee describing journaling between subaccounts, RT-PSI-00384749-761.

[354] Id. See also Subcommittee interview of Eamon McCooey, Deutsche Bank (5/2/2014).

[355] Subcommittee interviews of Eamon McCooey, Deutsche Bank (5/2/2014), Thomas Kerns, RenTec (5/6/2014), and Peter Brophy, Deutsche Bank and RenTec (5/13/2014 and 5/19/2014). Hoever, RenTec counsel told the Subcommittee that it was irrelevant whether its "recommendation" to remove a position from a subaccount resulted in a journal or a sale to the market. "There does not need to be, and there is not, any provision in the Deutsche Bank option confirmations relating to Renaissance's ability to recommend that securities positions be journaled from one sub-account to another. This is because, as previously discussed, each option references the notional portfolio resulting from Renaissance's recommendations for an individual Deutsche Bank sub-account, and it is irrelevant, from the standpoint of the option, whether Renaissance recommends that a position be removed from the sub- account by means of a journal to another sub-account or by means of a sale into the market." 8/30/2013 email from RenTec's counsel to the Subcommittee, "per our discussion," PSI-RenaissanceTech-20-000001-002, at 002. This position appears to be inconsistent, however, with RenTec's explanation for why it preferred journaling over asset sales when moving assets from one MAPS account to another.

[356] 5/15/2008 "Deutsche Bank Maps New Process/Procedures," prepared by RenTec, RT-PSI-00002319-322 at 321.

[357] Subcommittee interview of Peter Brown, RenTec (6/4/2014).

[358] Id.

[359] See 7/31/13 letter from RenTec to the Subcommittee listing journaling transfers between subaccounts, RT-PSI-00384749-761.

[360] See 8/30/2013 chart, "Journal Entry Dates," prepared by RenTec for the Subcommittee, RT-PSI-00384762.

[361] 7/31/2013 letter from RenTec to the Subcommittee describing journaling between sub-accounts, RT-PSI-00384749.

[362] Id.

[363] Statistics prepared by Subcommittee from data taken from 8/30/2013 chart, "Journal Entry Dates," prepared by RenTec for the Subcommittee, RT-PSI-00384762.

[364] Id.

[365] Id.

[366] 9/10/2008 email from James Rowen to Peter Brown of RenTec, "Re-shuffle- Follow-up," RT-PSI-00068362. See also "Deutsche Bank Maps: New Process/Procedures As of May 15, 2008," prepared by RenTec, RT-PSI-00002319-322, at 321.

[367] 9/10/2008 email from James Rowen to Peter Brown of RenTec, "Re-shuffle- Follow-up," RT-PSI-00068362.

[368] Subcommittee interview of Peter Brown, RenTec (6/4/2014). See also 12/15/2008 "Master Investment Advisory Agreement: Execution Copy," signed by Deutsche Bank London and RenTec, DB-PSI 00000001-047, at 001-002 (explaining that the advisor had discretion to conduct trades for all subaccounts without consulting the client).

[369] Subcommittee interview of Peter Brown, RenTec (6/3/2014).

[370] Subcommittee interviews of Peter Brown, RenTec (6/3/2014), James Rowen, RenTec (5/20/2014), and Mark Silber, RenTec (6/10/2014). But RenTec's counsel told the Subcommittee that the cash withdrawals were not used for employee salaries or bonuses, but only for returns to investors. Subcommittee briefing by RenTec counsel (6/16/2014).

[371] Subcommittee interview of Peter Brown, RenTec (6/3/2014).

[372] In addition to allowing cash withdrawals to support its business operations, RenTec described other benefits from using options with staggered start dates. A 2008 email suggested they could be helpful in preventing a large loss during a crisis by ensuring that no two options had the same starting values or maturing dates, preventing cascading effects. See 6/16/2008 email from Satish Ramakrishna of Deutsche Bank to James Rowen of RenTec, "Language," RT-PSI-00054256; Subcommittee interview of James Rowen, RenTec (5/20/2014). In addition, by rolling assets from exercised options into new options, RenTec could ensure that it took only the funds it needed and avoid large changes in the overall leverage or other parameters of its investment pool at Deutsche Bank and Barclays. See, e.g., 12/8/2011 email exchange among Noor Islam, Jordan Friedman, Devasish Majumdar and others of Barclays, "COLT Option XXIV – GFRM," BARCLAYS-PSI-013658 (explaining that as long as RenTec put on a new option in the right order, it could exercise three others without violating leverage guidelines).

[373] See, e.g., 9/10/2008 email from Peter Brown to James Rowen, "Re-shuffle- Follow-up," RT-PSI-00068362.

[374] 6/16/2008 email from Satish Ramakrishna of Deutsche Bank to James Rowen of RenTec, "Language," RT-PSI-00054256.

[375] See Table, "MAPS Transaction," produced by Deutsche Bank, 6/27/2014, DB-PSI 00052577-582, at 579.

[376] 7/10/2008 email from Apollo Wong to David Betten, "George Weiss MAPS Investment Guidelines – PLEASE READ," GWALLC-PSI-0002504. See also "Connecticut Companies" profile of OGI Associates LLC, http://www.connecticutcompaniesindex.com/ogi-associates-llc-5ahy/ (indicating the company's business address was care of George Weiss Associates Inc. and its "principal" was "George A. Weiss Manager").

[377] 7/9/2008 email from Apollo Wong to Susan Sevigny of GWA, "FW: George Weiss MAPS Investment Guidelines– PLEASE READ," GWALLC-PSI-0002492-494, at 493. See also Subcommittee interview of Frederick Doucette, GWA (5/23/2014) (confirming assets were moved from MAPS to OGI).

[378] 10/10/2008 email from Apollo Wong to Federick Doucette, "db maps account imbalance," GWALLC-PSI-0002328.

[379] Subcommittee interview of Frederick Doucette, GWA (5/23/2014).

[380] 6/16/2003 "Master Netting Agreement," GWA, LLC, OGI Associates, and Deutsche Bank, GWALLC-PSI-0003427.

[381] See, e.g., 10/26/2009 email from Jeffrey Dillabough, GWA, to Frank Nelson, Deutsche Bank, "DB/Weiss MAPS option," DB-PSI 00036700 (noting the restructured MAPS option would no longer allow George Weiss to "cross sell" assets from a MAPS account to a prime brokerage account as part of George Weiss' "routine rebalancing activities"); Subcommittee interview of Frederick Doucette, GWA (5/23/2014).

[382] See id. (noting that George Weiss had been allowed to use 100% of the option market value to "cross collateralize" its prime brokerage account at OGI).

[383] Subcommittee interview of Frederick Doucette, GWA (5/23/2014).

[384] Id.

[385] Id.

[386] Id.

[387] See, e.g., 10/26/2009 email from Jeffrey Dillabough, GWA, to Frank Nelson, Deutsche Bank, "DB/Weiss MAPS option," DB-PSI-00036700 (indicating that under the new structure, cross-collateralization would be limited to 25% of the option value).

[388] 8/16/2010 email from Jeffrey Dillabough, GWA, to Peter Brophy and Frank Nelson, Deutsche Bank, "RE: New MAPs Term Sheet," GWALLC-PSI-0009484.

[389] 2/26/2009 email from Federick Doucette, GWA, to Frank Nelson, Deutsche Bank, "MAPS comments," DB-PSI-00033762, at 763-764 (listing George Weiss concerns with proposed new MAPS structure).

[390] 2/25/2009 email from Federick Doucette, GWA, to Frank Nelson, Deutsche Bank, "MAPs comments," DB-PSI-00033762-765, at 763.

[391] Subcommittee interview of Frederick Doucette, GWA (5/23/2014).

[392] Id.

[393] Subcommittee interviews of Peter Brown, RenTec (6/3/2014), Mark Silber, RenTec (6/10/2014); and James Rowen, RenTec (5/20/2014); 6/30/2014 briefing by Deutsche Bank counsel to the Subcommittee; Subcommittee interview of Frederick Doucette, GWA (5/23/2014).

[394] 5/28/2002 "Confidential: Project COLT," Barclays new product proposal, product sponsors: Jonathan Zenios, Jerry Smith, Marty Malloy, and Mark D'Andrea, BARCLAYS-PSI-212544-557, at 547; 8/22/2002 Barclays memorandum from Jonathan Zenios and Jerry Smith to Iain Abrahams and others, "SCM Approvals paper – Project COLT," BARCLAYS-PSI-212590-598, at 593. See also 4/4/2003 Barclays memorandum from SCM to SCM Approvals Committee, "SCM Approvals paper – Project COLT (Renaissance II)," BARCLAYS-PSI-213947-953, at 950-951.

[395] 9/3/2004 Barclays memorandum from Jonathan Zenios to SCM Approvals Committee, "Approvals paper – Colt V: Renaissance Restructuring," BARCLAYS-PSI-004159-172, at 163.

[396] 6/4/2002 letter from Barclays to Financial Services Authority, "Project Colt," BARCLAYS-PSI-005241.

[397] Audio recording of 11/7/2008 telephone call between William Broeksmit and Satish Ramakrishna of Deutsche Bank, DB-PSI 00122458.

[398] Subcommittee interview of Mark Haas, Deutsche Bank (5/30/2014). Mr. Hass served as the global head of Deutsche Bank's Prime Brokerage division from 2005 to 2007, and as head of its Global Business Development Relations for Prime Finance from 2007 to 2009. Id. According to Deutsche Bank personnel, the Global Prime Finance Division was engaged in a division-wide effort (called "Change the Bank Programs") to revise and restructure systems and products throughout the division. A September 2008 presentation that described ongoing and planned projects provided this explanation of the program: "Due to recent market conditions, we have focused some efforts on research and tactical developments to circumvent regulatory and reputational risks." 9/2008 "GPF Business Development - CTB Program Portfolio," prepared by Deutsche Bank Global Prime Finance Division, DB- PSI-00116157-185, at 158.

[399] Subcommittee interview of Mark Haas, Deutsche Bank (5/30/2014).

400 Id.

401 Id.

402 6/30/2014 briefing by Deutsche Bank counsel to the Subcommittee.

403 Id. See also undated email from Joshua Goldstein and McKee Nelson of Deutsche Bank, to Michael O'Brien, Winston and Strawn, "DB/Rentec – Responses to Issues Discussed on 10/16," DB-PSI 00079017; 8/13/2008 email from James Rowen, RenTec, to Jonathan Hitchon and Richard Carson of Deutsche Bank, DB-PSI-00028006.

404 September 2008 "GPF Business Development CTB Program Portfolio," prepared by Deutsche Bank Global Prime Finance, DB-PSI-00116157-185, at 158.

405 Id. at 177.

406 Id.

407 Previously, there were two components of the premium. The first was a fixed fee, which served as the collateral for the initial acquisition of assets for the account. All purchases for the account drew first on that fee. The second component was the "amortization amount," which was a finance charge anticipated to be paid by the hedge fund over the life of the option. Any part of the finance charge (amortization amount) that was unused when the option was exercised or expired was returned to the option holder. See 5/15/2008 "Deutsche Bank MAPS New Process/Procedures As of May 15, 2008," prepared by RenTec, RT-PSI-00002319 - 322; undated "MAPS Restructuring Highlights," prepared by Deutsche Bank, RT-PSI-00068592-599.

Under the restructured MAPS, the premium included two similar components. The first was a "fixed amount," which served the same purpose as the fixed fee in the old structure. The second component which reflected a financing charge and was called the "amortization amount" in the original MAPS structure, was called the "optionality value" in the new MAPS. It was an up-front, non-refundable fee, based on the cost of financing the transaction over the life of the option. Ostensibly, the "optionality value" was based on a formula deriving from the anticipated debt balance over the life of the option, called the "Anticipated Leverage Amount." The anticipated leverage amount was adjusted, however, to ensure that the fee (the "optionality value") would be between 20% and 25% of the initial premium amount. In an email to colleagues, Satish Ramakrishna, the Deutsche Bank Global Head of Risk for Global Prime Finance, wrote: "The anticipated leverage am[oun]t is not randomly chosen. It is chosen so that the funding cost (which we will call the 'optionality value') on the long side ... is between 20%-25% of the initial premium …." 6/17/2008 email from Satish Ramakrishna to Axel Niemann of Deutsche Bank, "What we need coded on PEAS apart from guidelines," DB-PSI 00010767-769 at 768. In other words, the formula had been designed to ensure the bank received a financing fee equal to 20%-25% of the premium, instead of calculating a premium that reflected the value of the so-called "option."

408 Subcommittee interview of Frederick Doucette, GWA (5/23/2014).

409 Id.

410 10/6/2009 email from Steve Kleinman to Federick Doucette of GWA, "DB Option – possible new development," DB-PSI 00036241, at 242.

411 Audio recording of 12/1/2008 telephone call among Satish Ramakrishna, Deutsche Bank, and Jonathan Mayers, and Thomas Kerns of RenTec, DB-PSI 00122467.

412 12/21/2010 letter from Preet Bharara, United States Attorney for the Southern District of New York, to Deutsche Bank's counsel, "Deutsche Bank AG – Non-Prosecution Agreement," at 1, http://lib.law.virginia.edu/Garrett/prosecution_agreements/sites/default/files/pdf/deutschebank.pdf.

413 Id. at 2.

414 6/2/2014 and 6/30/2104 briefings by Deutsche Bank counsel to the Subcommittee.

415 Table, "MAPS Transaction," produced by Deutsche Bank, 6/27/2014, DB-PSI 00052577-582.

416 6/2/2014 Deutsche Bank briefing to the Subcommittee.

417 Id.

418 1/24/2013 Deutsche Bank briefing to the Subcommittee.

[419] 8/2/2012 meetings notes, "MAPS Meetings Highlights," prepared by the Federal Reserve Bank of New York, FRBNY to PSI (MAPs) 000238 [Sealed Exhibit].

[420] Information provided by the Federal Reserve Bank of New York (6/17 and 18/2014). See also 1/24/2013 Deutsche Bank briefing to the Subcommittee.

[421] See, e.g., 12/15/2008 "Master Investment Advisory Agreement: Execution Copy," signed by Deutsche Bank and RenTec, DB-PSI 00000001-047, at 021.

[422] See, e.g., 12/6/2006 "Amended and Restated Investment Management Agreement," signed by Barclays and RenTec, RT-PSI-00134963-5013, at 4983.

[423] See, e.g., Section 7 of the Securities Exchange Act of 1934 (codified at 15 U.S.C. § 78a); Regulations T, U, and X, commonly referred to as the "margin rules," 12 CFR 220.1(Regulation T); 12 CFR 221.1 (Regulation U); 12 CFR 224.1 (Regulation X).

[424] See, e.g., 9/2000 "Margin Requirements, Margin Loans, and Margin Rates: Practice and Principles," *New England Economic Review*, Peter Fortune, at 25.

[425] "Leveraged ETFs: The Trojan Horse has Passed the Margin-Rule Gates," 34 Seattle U.L. Rev. 299, 310, William M. Humphries (Fall 2010) (omitting citations).

[426] Subcommittee interviews of Frederick Doucette, GWA (5/23/2014), Peter Brown, RenTec (6/3/2014), Satish Ramakrishna, Deutsche Bank (5/16/2014) and Martin Malloy, Barclays (5/1/2014).

[427] RenTec informed the Subcommittee that in its original submission to the IRS, it transposed the numbers describing the permissible leverage of a JBO arrangement and incorrectly listed it as 6.7:1, but is providing corrected information to the IRS.

[428] 4/13/2012, "Protest of 60 Day Letters by Renaissance Technologies LLC et al.," RT-PSI-00000001-402, at 012-015 [Sealed Exhibit].

[429] See, e.g., financing fees listed in 12/21/2005 Barclays Bank PLC letter agreement to Badger Holdings L.P., "Option HH," BARCLAYS-PSI-002879-896, at 887-888; 12/16/2007 Deutsche Bank letter agreement to Mosel Equities L.P., "'OUTPERFORMANCE' BARRIER OPTION TRANSACTION—Cash Settled, Linear Amortizing Premium—DB Reference No. 941-50053," DB-PSI 00000320-337, at 327.

[430] See, e.g., 4/4/2003 Barclays memorandum from SCM to SCM Approvals Committee, "SCM Approvals paper – Project COLT (Renaissance II)," BARCLAYS-PSI-213947-953, at 949 (explaining, in a memorandum seeking approval of a second basket option transaction for RenTec, that the hedge fund "would pay a premium ... of [$136m[illion]] comprising: [$130m] representing the collateral for the Trading Strategy; and an amount representing SCM's fee from the transaction ($6m in the diagram)").

[431] See, e.g., 5/19/2010 email from Edward Sherwood to Brett Beldner of Barclays, "COLT XIX – Draft SCM Approvals Notification," BARCLAYS-PSI-010082 (describing the "net effect" of the COLT option "is that Barclays is extending senior financing to RenTec"); 2/17/2012 email from Satish Ramakrishna to Eamon McCooey and others of Deutsche Bank, "Two Sigma Follow-up," DB-PSI 00045265 ("Non-recourse financing is one option (MAPS is just a name for that)").

[432] See 6/25/2008 email exchange between Eamon McCooey and Michael Ginelli of Deutsche Bank, "Tentative: MAPS Working Group – Wednesday Sessions @ 3PM – June Meetings," DB-PSI 00025040-041. See also 6/25/2008 email from Michael Ginelli to Eamon McCooey of Deutsche Bank, "Re: Tentative: MAPS Working Group-Wednesday Sessions @3 PM-JuneMeetings," DB-PSI 0025040-041; 6/24/2009 memorandum, "Palomino Limited ("Palomino")," prepared by Barclays, BARCLAYS-PSI-139757-766, at 764.

[433] Table, "MAPS Transaction," produced by Deutsche Bank, 6/27/2014, DB-PSI 00052577-582.

[434] 11/12/2010 email from Graham Wade to Nizam Sidiq and Jonathan Zenios of Barclays, "Privileged Colt," BARCLAYS-PSI-748506.

[435] See undated spreadsheet, "History of COLT Options," BARCLAYS-PSI-748604.

[436] 10/3/2012 memorandum from Graham Wade to SCM, "COLT XXVII," BARCLAYS-PSI-016946-947.

[437] Id. at 947.

[438] See 4/2013 "Salz Review: An Independent Review of Barclays' Business Practices," prepared by Anthony Salz et al., at opening letter from Anthony Salz, http://online.wsj.com/public/resources/documents/SalzReview04032013.pdf.

[439] 10/3/2012 memorandum from SCM US Approvals Committee to Tax Risk Committee, "COLT," BARCLAYS- PSI-016951.

[440] Id.

[441] 10/4/2012 email from Gerard LaRocca to Larry Wiesene of Barclays, "COLT SCM Transaction/Important," BARCLAYS-PSI-748590.

[442] 10/12/2012 memorandum from SCM to Tax Risk Committee, "COLT," BARCLAYS-PSI-018114-116.

[443] Id.

[444] Id. at 116.

[445] Id. at 114.

[446] Id. at 115.

[447] Id. at 116.

[448] Id. at 114.

[449] 11/2012 memorandum from Maxim Kulikov and Rama Subramaniam to SCM US Approvals Committee, "Project COLT XXVIII (Renaissance Technologies) – Approvals Notification," BARCLAYS-PSI-017091-093, at 091.

[450] Id. at 093.

[451] 11/23/2012 email from Noor Islam to Eugene Kim of Barclays, "Colt – Market Risk/Credit Risk," BARCLAYS- PSI-293251-254, at 251.

[452] 11/23/2012 email from James Saxton to Marty Malloy of Barclays, "Palomino options," BARCLAYS-PSI-322103.

[453] 4/2013 "Salz Review: An Independent Review of Barclays' Business Practices," prepared by Anthony Salz et al., http://online.wsj.com/public/resources/documents/SalzReview04032013.pdf.

[454] See 2/12/2013 "Barclays Strategic Review," Barclays Press Release, http://www.newsroom.barclays.com/Press- releases/Barclays-Strategic-Review-9db.aspx .

[455] See undated spreadsheet, "History of COLT Options," BARCLAYS-PSI-748604.

[456] See December 2013 "The New COLT Transaction: Transaction Review Committee," PowerPoint prepared by Barclays, Barclays-PSI-748587-589.

[457] Id. at 588.

[458] Id.

[459] See undated spreadsheet, "History of COLT Options," BARCLAYS-PSI-748604.

[460] Id. See also 7/22/2014 "Post-GLAM Basket Option Contracts," Memorandum to File prepared by the Subcommittee (summarizing Deutsche Bank, Barclays, and RenTec involvement with basket options after the November 2010 issuance of the IRS advisory memorandum on basket options).

[461] 6/30/2014 briefing by Deutsche Bank counsel to the Subcommittee.

[462] Id.

[463] 10/26/2011 email from Mark Meachen to Anthony Tuths of Deutsche Bank, "Rentec [I],"DB-PSI 00019248-250, at 249.

[464] 6/2/2014 briefing by Deutsche Bank counsel to the Subcommittee.

[465] See, e.g., undated letter from Deutsche Bank to Mosel Equities LP, "Barrier Option Transaction – Cash Settled- DBSI Reference No. 941-50340," DB-PSI 00047768.

[466] 12/21/2010 letter from Preet Bharara, United States Attorney for the Southern District of New York, to Deutsche Bank's counsel, "Deutsche Bank AG – Non-Prosecution Agreement," at 2, http://lib.law.virginia.edu/Garrett/prosecution_agreements/sites/default/files/pdf/deutschebank.pdf.

[467] Id. at 4.

[468] Id. at 5.

[469] Subcommittee briefing by Bart Schwartz, independent expert for Deutsche Bank (10/8/2013).

[470] Id.
[471] Subcommittee briefing by Bart Schwartz, independent expert for Deutsche Bank (7/16/2014).
[472] 6/2/2014 and 6/30/2014 briefings by Deutsche Bank counsel to the Subcommittee.
[473] Id. Officials of the Federal Reserve Bank of New York reviewing the MAPS structure questioned Deutsche Bank about whether the bank had disclosed MAPS to Bart Schwartz's team. Deutsche Bank advised the examiners that it had informed Mr. Schwartz's team that Deutsche Bank had on its books a transaction like the one reported in the GLAM, but noted that the conversation was "very short." 8/2/2012 meetings notes, "MAPS Meetings Highlights," prepared by the Federal Reserve Bank of New York, FRBNY to PSI (MAPs) 000238 [Sealed Exhibit].
[474] 6/30/2014 briefing by Deutsche Bank counsel to the Subcommittee.
[475] Id.
[476] 6/2/2014 briefing by Deutsche Bank counsel to the Subcommittee.
[477] See chart produced by Deutsche Bank, 6/27/2014, DB-PSI 00052583-585. See also 7/22/2014 "Post-GLAM Basket Option Contracts," Memorandum to File prepared by the Subcommittee (summarizing Deutsche Bank, Barclays, and RenTec involvement with basket options after the November 2010 issuance of the IRS advisory memorandum on basket options).
[478] 1/6/2010 email from Axel Niemann to Giovanni Favretti of Deutsche Bank, "MAPS," DB-PSI-00006875.
[479] See 12/15/2008 "Master Investment Advisory Agreement: Execution Copy," signed by Deutsche Bank and RenTec, DB-PSI 00000001-047, at 006.
[480] 6/27/2014 letter from Deutsche Bank counsel to the Subcommittee, PSI-DeutscheBank-23-000001 [Sealed Exhibit].
[481] 10/27/2011 Approval Paper, "Project Dawn," prepared by Deutsche Bank, DB-PSI 00020110-117, at 110. Mosel had served as the option holder for the MAPS basket options since 2007.
[482] Id.
[483] Id.
[484] Id. at 112.
[485] 11/29/2011 Indicative Terms and Conditions, "[TBD] c/o Renaissance Technologies," prepared by Deutsche Bank, DB-PSI 00009727-730, at 728.
[486] 9/19/2011 email from Greg Bunn to Satish Ramakrishna of Deutsche Bank, "Fund Option," DB-PSI 00018723.
[487] 11/13/2011 email from Satish Ramakrishna to Anthony Tuths of Deutsche Bank, "Rentec," DB-PSI 00112522.
[488] Id.
[489] Subcommittee interview of Satish Ramakrishna, Deutsche Bank (5/16/2014) and James Rowen, RenTec (5/20/2014). In his interview, Mr. Rowen, Chief Operating Officer of RenTec, echoed Mr. Ramakrishna's description of why RenTec rejected both proposals.
[490] Subcommittee interview of Satish Ramakrishna, Deutsche Bank (5/16/2014) and James Rowen, RenTec (5/20/2014).
[491] 6/30/2014 briefing by Deutsche Bank counsel to the Subcommittee.
[492] 12/16/2011 email from Anthony Tuths to Satish Ramakrishna and Vincent Capone of Deutsche Bank, "Rentec confirm and IMAs [I]," DB-PSI-00020740-748, at 746. See also undated letter from Deutsche Bank to Mosel Equities LP, "Barrier Option Transaction – Cash Settled-DBSI Reference No. 941-50340," DB-PSI 00047768.
[493] Id. at 745.
[494] See, e.g., 9/2013 "Asset Management and Financial Stability," prepared by the Office of Financial Research of the U.S. Department of the Treasury, at 1, 17-18 http://www.treasury.gov/initiatives/ofr/research/Documents/OFR_AMFS_FINAL.pdf (examining in part asset management industry use of leverage); Concept Release on Use of Derivatives by Investment Companies, prepared by the SEC, 76 Fed. Reg. 55238 (Sept. 7, 2 011) (examining in part investment company use of derivatives to create leverage); 7/6/2010 "

Report of the Task Force on Investment Company Use of Derivatives and Leverage," prepared by the American Bar Association Business Law Section, Committee on Federal Regulation of Securities, Task Force on Investment Company Use of Derivatives and Leverage, https://apps.americanbar.org/buslaw/blt/content/ibl/2010/08/0002.pdf; 2012 "SEC Concept Release Tackles Investment Company Use of Derivatives," The Review of Securities & Commodities Regulation, vol. 45, Jay G. Baris and Andrew J. Donohue, http://media.mofo.com/files/Uploads/Images/120308-Securities-Commodities-Regulation.pdf.

[495] 9/2013 "Asset Management and Financial Stability," prepared by the Office of Financial Research of the U.S. Department of the Treasury, at 18, http: //www.trea sury.gov/ini tiatives/ofr/research/Documents/OFR_AMFS_FINAL.pdf.

[496] 3/19/2014 "Large Partnerships: Characteristics of Population and IRS Audits," prepared by the Government Accountability Office, GAO-14-379R, at 1, http://www.gao.gov/assets/670/661772.pdf.

[497] Id. at 4, 6.

[498] Id. at 1.

[499] Id. at 20.

[500] Tax Equity and Fiscal Responsibility Act of 1982, Pub. L. No. 97-248.

[501] 26 U.S.C. § 6223.

[502] 26 U.S.C. § 6225.

[503] See, e.g., U.S. Senate Permanent Subcommittee on Investigations reports and hearings, "Fishtail, Bacchus, Sundance, and Slapshot: Four Enron Transactions Funded and Facilitated by U.S. Financial Institutions," S. Prt.107-82 (1/2/2003); "U.S. Tax Shelter Industry: The Role of Accountants, Lawyers, and Financial Professionals," S. Hrg. 108-473 (11/18 and 20/2003); "Tax Haven Abuses: The Enablers, The Tools and Secrecy," S. Hrg 109-797 (8/1/2006); "Tax Haven Banks and U.S. Tax Compliance," S.Hrg. 110-614; "Dividend Tax Abuse: How Offshore Entities Dodge Taxes on U.S. Stock Dividends," S.Hrg. 110-778 (9/11/2008).

In: Structured Financial Products ...
Editor: Lenora Osborne

ISBN: 978-1-63463-785-5

Chapter 2

STATEMENT OF SENATOR CARL LEVIN, CHAIRMAN, SENATE PERMANENT SUBCOMMITTEE ON INVESTIGATIONS. HEARING ON "ABUSE OF STRUCTURED FINANCIAL PRODUCTS: MISUSING BASKET OPTIONS TO AVOID TAXES AND LEVERAGE LIMITS"*

In recent years, this Subcommittee has devoted significant time and effort to exposing complex financial arrangements that profitable corporations and wealthy individuals employ to avoid their obligations to pay all their U.S. taxes. We also have examined reckless behavior that has put the stability of the financial system – and by extension, the U.S. economy – at risk. Today's hearing brings those two themes together.

Our focus today is on how two banks and a handful of hedge funds developed a complex financial structure to engage in highly profitable trades while claiming an unjustified lower tax rate and avoiding limits on trading with borrowed money. This structure worked well for the banks, which earned hundreds of millions of dollars in fees. It worked well for the hedge funds, which made billions of dollars in profits. But it didn't work for average taxpayers, who had to shoulder the tax burden these hedge funds shrugged off

* This is an edited, reformatted and augmented version of an opening statement presented July 22, 2014 before the Senate Permanent Subcommittee on Investigations of the Homeland Security and Governmental Affairs Committee.

with the aid of the banks. And it didn't work for the financial system, which is still recovering from a devastating crisis brought on by excess risk, and remains ill-equipped to withstand another shock from over-leveraged financial institutions.

In essence, today's hearing is about a series of fictions, one piled on top of another, fictions that major banks and their hedge fund clients used to avoid taxes and federal leverage limits.

The key financial product involved in these fictions is called a "basket option." The basket options examined by the Subcommittee were developed and sold by two banks, Deutsche Bank AG and Barclays Bank PLC, to more than a dozen hedge funds. Together, the banks sold 199 basket options to hedge funds that used them to make over $100 billion in trades. Two of the largest basket option users were Renaissance Technologies LLC, known as RenTec, and George Weiss Associates.

Although there were minor differences in specifics, the basket option basics worked like this. The bank sold its hedge-fund client a structured financial product, labeled an "option," whose payoff equaled the profits generated by a "basket" of securities held in a designated account at the bank. The basket, here, is key. It was an open account with ever-changing contents. Technically, the account and the securities it contained were held in the name of the banks in its own trading account. The hedge fund put up 10% of the cash needed to buy the securities, and the bank lent the other 90%.

This arrangement included a number of fictions which defied reality, but resulted in big profits for the hedge funds and the banks.

First, though the structure was designed to create the appearance that the bank owned the assets in the basket option account, the hedge fund made all the trading decisions for those accounts – and in fact, used the bank's computerized trading system to execute trades in the account. RenTec estimates its trading through basket option accounts averaged more than 100,000 trades each day, or about 30 million trades a year. Also, the hedge fund reaped all of the trading profits, even though the financial structure created the illusion that the bank owned the assets. The beneficial owner, the real owner, was the hedge fund.

Second, the hedge fund's control of all the trading for the basket option account demolishes the fiction of a legitimate option. So the hedge funds set up new entities, which they controlled, to serve one function, and that was to act as the option holder. The hedge funds would then claim that their control of the option holder was totally independent of their role in making the trading decisions for the basket option account. Documents we will explore today show the extraordinary lengths to which RenTec and the banks went to perpetuate the illusion that the option holder and trader were somehow independent, when in fact the hedge fund, RenTec, played both roles.

The fictional option was structured so that it could be exercised more than one year after it was created. Under that structure, the hedge funds claimed that trading profits from the account were long-term capital gains and thereby qualified for the reduced long-term capital gains tax rate.

The tax code gives long-term capital gains a reduced rate on the theory that it provides an incentive for investors to risk their capital on the kind of long-term investments that grow the economy and create jobs. The high-volume trading that, for example, RenTec conducted through its basket options doesn't meet that test. When securities are held for weeks or days or even seconds, it's surreal to characterize those trading profits as long-term capital gains.

But that's what the hedge funds did. The banks and hedge funds used the fictional option structure to collapse millions of individual trades into one transaction, the execution of an option. As if by magic, the option structure transformed what would be short-term capital gains from an ordinary trading account into long-term capital gains subject to lower taxes. Subcommittee staff estimates, based on basket option profits that RenTec reported from 2000 to 2013, that RenTec avoided paying more than $6 billion in taxes.

That's a lot of money even by Washington standards. It would, for example, pay for almost two-thirds of the cost to replenish the Highway Trust Fund so that it doesn't run out of money next month and create havoc in road projects around the country.

This isn't the first time options have been abused to try to convert short-term trading profits into long-term capital gains. That's why, in 1999, Congress passed a law in part to stop that practice, Section 1260 of the tax code. The basket options at issue here were written to skirt Section 1260's prohibitions. In 2010, the IRS warned that the type of basket options used here could not claim the lower long-term capital gains tax rate. Despite that IRS warning, Barclays continued to sell basket options to RenTec for another two years, before finally revising its option product in 2013, so that the options expired in less than a year and couldn't be used to game the tax code. Deutsche Bank suspended its issuance of new basket options after the 2010 IRS warning, but continued to administer multiple basket option accounts already in existence.

It also resumed offering them in 2012, although with a term of less than one year and a requirement that the option holder treat the profits as short-term capital gains.

Tax avoidance through financial engineering is not the only problematic element here. These banks and hedge funds also used basket option accounts to circumvent regulations designed to limit systemic risks to the banking system posed by excessive leverage – that is, excessive lending to finance stock trading.

The stock market crash of 1929 devastated the U.S. economy, not just by the collapse of thousands of stock speculators, but also by the failure of thousands of banks that had lent them money and couldn't collect on the loans. In the aftermath of the Great Depression, Congress enacted laws limiting the use of borrowed money to trade securities. Those limits are included in a set of "margin rules" that essentially prohibit U.S. broker-dealers from lending more than $1 to brokerage clients for each $1 of the client's own money in the account – in other words, for every $2 in a brokerage account, only $1 of that $2 can be borrowed from the broker.

Had the hedge funds involved in these transactions been using normal brokerage accounts, they would have been subject to the 2-to-1 leverage limit. But because the basket option accounts were opened in the name of the banks in their own proprietary trading accounts, it looked as though the money placed into those accounts was the banks' own proprietary money rather than money they were loaning to a customer. This is another fiction. The banks and hedge funds pretended the bank funds were not loans, even though the hedge funds paid financing fees and posted collateral.

So instead of complying with the 2-to-1 leverage ratio, the banks offered their hedge-fund clients leverage as high as 20-to-1. RenTec used the increased leverage to borrow billions of dollars for its trading strategies, which produced huge profits for RenTec, while the lending generated huge additional fees for the banks.

But as we've learned over and over – in the Depression, in the 1990s collapse of the hedge fund Long Term Capital Management, and in the financial crisis from which we're still recovering – excessive leverage doesn't always produce profits. Sometimes it produces losses. And when huge losses happen, they can bring down not just a reckless borrower, but the financial institution that lent it money, and that failure can ripple throughout the entire financial system. While it appears the two banks the Subcommittee has examined have stopped selling basket options as a way to claim long-term capital gains rates, they are still selling these products as a way to avoid leverage limits – meaning our financial system and economy still face unnecessary risk.

RenTec, through its Medallion Funds, used basket options to produce profits from 1999 to 2013 totaling more than $30 billion. The banks charged financing, trading, and other fees that, over the same period, produced revenues totaling about $570 million for Deutsche Bank and $655 million for Barclays. Basket options were clearly a lucrative line of business for the participants.

But this money-maker was built on an interlocking series of fictions. The key fiction is the option itself – the idea that this structure was really an option, when in fact what it did was give hedge funds the profits from buying and selling assets in accounts that the hedge funds themselves controlled. It was fiction to treat the banks as the true owners of the basket option assets, when the hedge funds controlled and executed all of the millions of trades in the accounts, the hedge funds paid the daily trading costs, and the hedge funds reaped the profits. It was fiction to suggest that the borrowed money that financed the trades was considered proprietary funds of the banks, rather than loans to the hedge funds. It was fiction to treat the profits from trades lasting days or even seconds as long-term capital gains deserving a reduced tax rate. And it was a fiction to pretend that hedge funds were not acting both as option-holder and as trade decision-maker. These were all fictions, but fictions with real-world consequences: they shifted billions of dollars in tax burden onto the backs of ordinary taxpayers, and they added billions of dollars in hidden risks to our financial system.

Congress and financial regulators can and should work together to stop these abuses.

The IRS should seek to collect taxes owed on billions of dollars in basket option profits unjustifiably claimed as long-term capital gains.

Federal financial regulators should make clear to banks that participating in abusive structures designed to avoid leverage limits and taxes is unacceptable, and penalize the banks that do.

The Financial Stability Oversight Council, working with other agencies, should establish reporting and data collection requirements to detect and stop abuse of structured financial products to circumvent leverage limits that safeguard our economy.

Finally, Treasury, and the IRS should remove impediments to audits of large partnerships, like hedge funds, 99% of which today escape IRS audits – meaning we are largely blind to how many other hedge funds may be using these structures to avoid risk limits and taxes.

These measures would help protect the interests of ordinary Americans who pay their taxes and must pay the price for tax avoidance schemes. It is these same Americans who would bear the burden of economic devastation that unaddressed systemic risks can cause.

I want to thank Senator McCain and his staff for their hard work in making today's hearing and our bipartisan report possible. The staff of this Subcommittee, majority and minority, through the years have been able to work together as one team. I'm very proud of them.

In: Structured Financial Products ...
Editor: Lenora Osborne
ISBN: 978-1-63463-785-5

Chapter 3

TESTIMONY OF STEVEN M. ROSENTHAL, SENIOR FELLOW, URBAN-BROOKINGS TAX POLICY CENTER. HEARING ON "ABUSE OF STRUCTURED FINANCIAL PRODUCTS: MISUSING BASKET OPTIONS TO AVOID TAXES AND LEVERAGE LIMITS"*

My name is Steven M. Rosenthal. I am a Senior Fellow at the Urban-Brookings Tax Policy Center, where I research, speak, and write on Federal income tax issues.[1] I have practiced tax law in Washington, D.C. for over 25 years, most recently as a partner at a major law firm. In private practice, I regularly advised hedge funds and other investors on the tax treatment of derivatives. In the 1990s, I was a Legislation Counsel with the Joint Committee on Taxation, where I helped draft tax rules for financial institutions, financial products, capital gains, and related areas. I am the former Chair of the Taxation Section of the District of Columbia Bar Association.

I would like to thank Chairman Levin and Ranking Member McCain and the Subcommittee for inviting me to testify.

Today, I will describe how two hedge funds (the Hedge Funds), with the help of two investment banks (the Banks), purported to convert short-term trading profits into long-term capital gains with derivatives—which lowered

* This is an edited, reformatted and augmented version of testimony presented July 22, 2014 before the Senate Permanent Subcommittee on Investigations of the Homeland Security and Governmental Affairs Committee.

the tax rate on their gains from 35% to 15% (the difference in rates for short-term and long-term gains for most of the years in question). I believe the funds stretched two key elements of the tax law to achieve their goal. The Hedge Funds (1) mischaracterized their investment arrangements as derivatives and (2) improperly deferred gains from their arrangements until final settlement. I believe the IRS should challenge both of these assertions—and need only defeat one. I also recommend legislation to address the misuse of derivatives more comprehensively.

I. The Stakes: Short-term or Long-term Capital Gains

The tax preference for long-term capital gains was established long ago. In 1921, Congress first lowered the rate for gain from the sale of property held for more than two years: from 58%, the top individual tax rate for the year, to 12.5%.

Congress cited the "lock-in" effect of high rates to justify the capital gains preference:

> "The sale of farms, mineral properties, and other capital assets is now seriously retarded by the fact that gains and profits earned over a series of years are under the present law taxed as a lump sum (and the amount of surtax greatly enhanced thereby) in the year in which the profit is realized. Many such sales, with their possible profit taking and consequent increase of the revenue, have been blocked by this feature of the present law."[2]

Today, our tax rules reduce the tax rate for gain from the (i) sale or exchange, (ii) of a capital asset, (iii) held for more than one year. But to determine whether gain from a sale or exchange qualifies as long-term capital gain, the tax law looks to the substance of the transaction, not the label a taxpayer puts on the transaction.

II. The Investment Transactions

The Hedge Funds are Delaware partnerships and were organized to "purchase, sell (including short sales), invest, trade and deal in securities and other financial transactions related thereto."[3] The funds pass their gains and losses through to their partners.[4]

Investment funds typically separate their investment assets from their operations. So, the Hedge Funds hold investments (including derivatives), but own no equipment or offices--and they do not employ any workers. Rather, they rely on their general partner, Renaissance Technologies LLC (Renaissance).[5] A general partner is "an agent of the partnership for the purpose of its business, purposes or activities."[6] Thus, Renaissance's efforts on behalf of the Hedge Funds are, legally, attributable to the Hedge Funds.[7] And Renaissance employed more than 250 professionals, 90 of whom hold math and science PhDs, mainly to develop and pursue the strategies for these Hedge Funds.

Starting years ago, Renaissance developed investment strategies for the Hedge Funds, which they describe as an algorithm. The strategies pursued statistical arbitrage—which exploits small, and fleeting, pricing anomalies of publicly-traded assets. The strategies were low-risk: they were both diversified and market neutral (with both long and short positions). But they required frequent trading—more than 100 thousand trades a day, and more than 30 million trades a year. Renaissance also sold stocks quickly: it sold 87% within three months, and more than 99% within a year.

In most respects, the Hedge Funds' trading was conventional, albeit frequent and extensive. The Hedge Funds identified assets that were mispriced and arbitraged those pricing anomalies.

But the Hedge Funds did not buy, hold, and sell the stocks directly. Instead, the Banks purported to buy, hold, and sell the stocks.[8] The Hedge Funds and the Banks used two interrelated contracts to structure the investment arrangement: First, a Bank agreed to pay a Hedge Fund the net profits from the trading of a basket of stocks in a designated account at the Bank (the "Basket Contract"). [9] Second, the Bank granted The Hedge Fund's general partner, Renaissance, the exclusive authority to buy and sell stocks for the designated account (the "Investment Management Agreement"). That permitted Renaissance to select the stocks to buy and sell, when to buy and sell, and how to route the orders.

To enter a Basket Contract, a Hedge Fund might deposit, say, $10 million, in the account at a Bank. The Bank also might contribute, say, $90 million, which permitted up to $100 million to trade (a leverage ratio of 10). The Basket Contract typically had a term of three years—but a Hedge Fund could "exercise" (i.e., cash out) the Basket Contract at any time. In fact, the Hedge Fund typically exercised the Basket Contracts after more than a year to qualify their gains as long-term. The Bank also could “knock-out” (i.e., terminate) a Basket Contract if the value of the account fell to or below $90 million. But the risk of a knock-out was remote, in part because the Banks had early trigger points to require the Investment Manager to sell positions, or reduce leverage, before losses fell to $90 million.[10] In fact, neither Bank terminated any of the more than 60 Basket Contracts of the Hedge Funds.

Upon a Hedge Fund’s exercise of a Basket Contract, the Bank paid the Hedge Fund the greater of (1) zero or (2) the return of the Hedge Fund’s $10 million deposit (less amortized fees for the Bank), increased by (i) the basket profits—which were the gains, interest, and dividends that had been earned in the account and reduced by (ii) the basket losses—which were the losses, interest expense, commissions and other trading costs that had been incurred and further reduced by (iii) an interest charge on the $90 million advance.[11] As mentioned earlier, in remote circumstances, a Bank could knock-out a Basket Contract early but, otherwise, the Hedge Fund would invariably exercise the Basket Contract, as the Hedge Fund could receive some value and would pay nothing to exercise.

As mentioned above, Renaissance, the general partner of the Hedge Funds, directed the trading in the designated accounts—not the Banks and not a third party. Under some Investment Management Agreements, Renaissance could trade without prior approval by the Bank. According to other agreements, the Bank could reject any trade prior to actual execution. But Renaissance sent the trades directly to the exchange, and did not did not notify a Bank of its trades in advance. Thus, there was no opportunity for a Bank to reject a trade, nor did a Bank ever reject or reverse a trade.[12]

In substance, the Basket Contracts and the Investment Management Agreements replicated a typical brokerage arrangement. That is, the Hedge Funds, through their general partner, Renaissance, directed the buying and selling of stocks for the accounts at the Banks, and the Hedge Funds profited from the trading.

But the Hedge Funds also achieved a substantial non-tax and tax advantage. As a non-tax matter, the Hedge Funds could borrow more than a regular brokerage customer, who often is subject to regulatory limitations.[13] As a result, the Hedge Funds increased their leverage and limited recourse to the Hedge Fund’s other assets. Under the Basket Contracts, the Hedge Funds averaged a leverage ratio of 12 or 13. For a typical brokerage customer account subject to Federal Reserve regulation, the maximum leverage ratio is 2.

For tax purposes, the Hedge Funds reported the profits from their rapid trading as longterm gain (from terminating a derivative they held for more than a year), rather than short-term gain from the sale of stocks held for a shorter period. At the time of most of these transactions, gain realized on the sale or disposition of capital assets held for more than a year was taxed at a top individual rate of 15%, compared to a regular top rate of 35% (now 20% and 39.6%[14]).

III. Basic Tax Issues for the Basket Contracts

In general, stock, derivatives, and other investments are capital assets. And, as noted above, gain from the sale of a capital asset that is held for more than a year is taxed at reduced rates.[15]

The Hedge Funds pursued a short-term trading strategy. Normally, their gains would be short-term. But the Hedge Funds wrapped the Basket Contracts around their investment strategies and claimed long-term gain upon exercise (after more than a year).

The Hedge Funds must overcome two hurdles to treat their gains from the Basket Contracts as long-term: first, the Basket Contracts must represent derivatives and not, in substance, the ownership of the basket of stocks in the designated accounts (which are bought and sold throughout the year). Second, if the Basket Contracts represent derivatives, and not the stock in the designated accounts, the Basket Contracts must not be fundamentally changed during the year (which would require gains to be recognized early).

For tax purposes, I believe Hedge Funds would lose both challenges—not win both. That is, I believe the Basket Contracts represent ownership of the basket of stocks in the designated account. And, were the Basket Contracts derivatives (and not ownership of the stocks), the Basket Contracts were fundamentally changed during the year.

A. Do the Basket Contracts Represent Derivatives—or the Ownership of the Stocks in the Referenced Accounts?

A derivative is a financial contract that derives its value by reference to other assets or indices—in the case of the Basket Contracts, the baskets of stock and other positions in the designated accounts at the banks. And derivatives vary: they include forward contracts, futures, options, notional principal contracts, and many other arrangements.

Businesses and investors use derivatives to manage price or interest-rate risk. For example, an airline might enter a forward contract to lock-in the price of jet fuel for the future— the forward would fix a price for a specified grade of jet fuel to be delivered later. Or an investor could buy a put option to hedge against a fall in the price of her stock—the put would entitle the investor to sell her stock at a pre-set price (which might, ultimately, be higher than the market price of the stock at the exercise date).

In recent years, as technology advanced, the use of derivatives expanded. Now investors and others use derivatives for a wide range of purposes, sometimes to replicate returns that are economically similar to holding an asset or a portfolio of assets.

The Hedge Funds reported their gains on the Basket Contracts as gains from derivatives—not accumulated gains from the ownership of an ever-changing basket of stocks in the designated accounts. But the tax law characterizes an arrangement based on its substance, not its form. So, does the Basket Contract represent a derivative that references the value of a basket of stocks—or the actual ownership of the basket of stocks, with the accumulated gains? I believe the ownership of the basket of stocks, for three reasons.

To start, the label of a contract does not matter, as the IRS explained in holding that a purchaser of a deep-in-the-money "option" effectively owned the referenced stock.[16] That was because the "option" was so likely to be exercised the taxpayer effectively assumed the benefits and burdens of owning the stock. The IRS added its ruling was "based on the application of the doctrine of 'substance over form,' [and] it will be applied whenever the substance of the transaction is the purchase of stock, not an option."

Second, to identify the true owner of stock, we must look through "wrappers." For example, a court looked through a "wrap-around annuity" to find that a taxpayer who directed the investment of funds for an account at an insurance company beneficially owned the investments, not the insurance company.[17]

Third, to identify the true owner of stocks, we must examine the benefits and burdens of the ownership of the stocks. With the basket of stocks referenced by the Basket Contracts, the Hedge Funds received all of the opportunities of gain from trading the stocks and incurred the burden of losses--until the Bank stopped the trading. The Hedge Funds also earned the interest, dividends, and other income from the stocks, bonds, and cash in the account—and paid the financing, commissions, and other expenses from the trading.

Finally, and unusually, the Hedge Funds, through Renaissance, selected the stocks to buy and sell for the designated accounts, when to buy and sell them, and how to buy and sell them (that is, the size of the lots to trade and the routing of the orders). As a result, the Basket Contracts, combined with the Investment Management Agreements, simply rewarded the Hedge Funds for their own trading efforts; the Hedge Funds did not derive their return from the performance of specified assets or indices, which is the hallmark of a derivative.

The Hedge Funds might assert their arrangement transferred some indicia of ownership of the stocks to the Banks but, these indicia were, in my view, economically trivial. The Hedge Funds apparently allowed the Banks to vote the stock in the accounts—but the right to vote publicly-traded stock, held for a short period, generally is worth very little. And the Hedge Funds permitted the Banks to loan the stock in the accounts, but customers with brokerage accounts also typically permit their brokers to loan their stock—and these customers own the stocks, or the right to the return of the stocks, in the account.

The Hedge Funds might also argue the economic substance of their investment arrangement differed from a regular brokerage account since the arrangement allowed the Hedge Funds to leverage their investments more than a regular brokerage account would permit. But the extra leverage, by itself, does not answer whether the arrangement is a derivative or ownership. In my view, the arrangement simply was a favorable way, from a leverage standpoint, to own stock.

B. If the Basket Contracts Represent Derivatives, Were the Basket Contracts Fundamentally Changed before Settlement?

The timing of gains is important under our tax system. Taxpayers must recognize income when they have "undeniable accessions to wealth, clearly realized, and over which the taxpayers have complete dominion."[18] Gain may arise either as "cash derived from the sale of an asset" or as "a result of exchange of property."[19] Thus, taxpayers must realize gain "from the exchange of property for other property differing materially either in kind or in extent.[20]

In the leading authority on the modification of a non-debt contract, the IRS explained:

> "A change in contractual terms effected through an option provided in the original contract is treated as an exchange under section 1001 if there is a sufficiently fundamental or material change that the substance of the original contract is altered through the exercise of the option. Under such circumstances, the old contract is treated as if it were actually exchanged for a new one."[21]

Thus, the IRS ruled that an employer that exercised an option to change the insured under a key person insurance policy must realize gain on the contract because the change in the insured changed the "fundamental substance" of the contract ("[T]he essence of a life insurance contract is the life that is insured under the contract"). The IRS added that "the result would be the same if the employer insured a person holding a particular position and, thus, no formal substitution is made when a new person occupies that position."

Likewise, the Hedge Funds modified their options every time Renaissance, their agent, changed the Basket Contract by changing the stock in the designated account. Renaissance's modifications became material during the term of the contract—most likely daily but, at least, every three months, after the turnover of almost 90% of the basket. And the modifications were fundamental to the Basket Contract. The reference assets or indices are the essence of the arrangement (and, more generally, of a derivative contract).

The Hedge Funds might counter their investment shifts occurred automatically, pursuant to a trading algorithm. But the Hedge Funds' agent, Renaissance, controlled these shifts—not an algorithm operating unchecked. Importantly, Renaissance's highly-trained employees constantly worked on and modified the algorithm—always exploring and adding new price signals, which set the trading parameters.

Finally, each time the Hedge Fund's agent, Renaissance, sold an investment at a gain, the Hedge Funds locked-in more trading profits. And the Hedge Funds could cash out their accrued profits any time they chose to do so. As a result, the Hedge Funds acceded to wealth, clearly realized, over which they had complete dominion. The Hedge Funds should recognize their gains currently, not await the settlement of a Basket Contract.

IV. A Uniform Tax Treatment for Derivatives: Mark-to-Market

Congress established a capital gain preference to relieve the lock-in effect of holding property that accreted in value over time. Congress did not lower the rate for gains from short-term trading—or countenance wrapping a derivative around short-term strategies. So, as a matter of tax law and policy, the IRS should not allow taxpayers to transform their short-term profits into long-term gains through the alchemy of derivatives.

I believe the IRS can, under current law, challenge successfully the most extreme strategies with derivatives or purported derivatives (such as the ones in front of this Subcommittee). But the IRS has limited resources to challenge the wide variety of derivative-related strategies, which often are complicated and abstruse. So, in my view, Congress should address the taxation of derivatives comprehensively—and reflect the income from derivatives more clearly.

To do so, I believe tax accounting ought to follow financial accounting for derivatives, which requires companies to mark-to-market their derivatives at year-end (i.e., to measure the value of their derivatives at market at year-end).[22] The current taxation of derivatives is complicated and inconsistent. There are different rules for different derivatives, for different uses of the same derivative, and for different taxpayers. As a result, two derivatives that are economically the same may be taxed quite differently. For many years, investors have exploited these tax differences to manipulate the character, timing, or source of their income to reduce their tax liability.

To account for derivatives for financial reporting, companies struggled for a long time for a variety of reasons:

i. the effect of derivatives was not transparent in basic financial statements;
ii. the accounting guidance for derivative instruments and hedging activities was incomplete;
iii. the accounting guidance for derivative instruments and hedging activities was inconsistent and
iv. the accounting guidance for derivatives and hedging was difficult to apply. In 1998, to address these problems, the Financial Accounting Standards Board (the board) issued Statement of Financial Accounting Standards No. 133, *Accounting for Derivative Instruments and Hedging Activities*.[23] These rules required companies to measure all assets and liabilities on their balance sheet at "fair value," which is

> very similar to "fair market value" for tax. When first issued, these rules were widely considered the most complex accounting standards ever promulgated by the board. Now, more than 16 years later, these rules have been widely-implemented, are familiar to the accounting community and are working well.

Last year, Chairman Camp of the House Ways & Means Committee released a discussion draft to reform the tax of derivatives by marking them to market at year end. Earlier this year, the Chairman revised his tax reform proposals—and, again, proposed a mark-to-market to tax derivatives. I believe this step is overdue. It would greatly reduce the amount of time and energy that taxpayers and the IRS devote to the taxation of derivatives, an enterprise that has been demanding increasing effort in recent years.

End Notes

[1] I am testifying at the request of the Subcommittee, by letter dated July 9, 2014, from Chairman Carl Levin and Ranking Member John McCain. The views I present here are my own and not those of the Urban Institute, the Brookings Institution, or any other institution or person.

[2] H.R. Rep. No. 67-350, at 10-11 (1921)

[3] The Hedge Funds are Badger Holdings LP and Mosel Equities LP, with identical objectives in their limited partnership agreements.

[4] Their partners are other partnerships, known as feeder funds, which are tailored to meet the tax and non-tax objectives of different categories of investors, including tax-exempt entities, foreign investors and others.

[5] Each Hedge Fund gave Renaissance "complete and exclusive responsibility for managing and administering the affairs of the partnership."

[6] Del. Code Ann. Tit. 6, sec. 15-301(1).

[7] Sun Capital Partners III LP v. New England Teamsters & Trucking Industry Pension Fund et al., 724 F.3rd 129, 147 (1st Cir. 2013) (the efforts of a general partner, and its affiliates, to manage a portfolio company are attributable to the partnership)

[8] The Banks were Barclays Bank PLC and Deutsche Bank AG.

[9] The Banks labeled the contracts "Barrier Options" or "Basket Options," but I believe "Basket Contracts" better describes the contracts. An option is a right, but not the obligation, to buy or sell designated property at a fixed price. And the right may or may not be exercised. Here, the Hedge Funds were virtually certain to exercise the Basket Contracts (at a price of zero)—so, in my view, they were not options.

[10] The Banks also imposed trading parameters that further limited the possibility the Bank could lose money (e.g., the Banks limited the concentration of investment in a single company or industry).

[11] The Banks profited through fees and financing charges. Otherwise, the Banks were indifferent—any loss (or gain) on the Basket Contracts was offset by the gain (or loss) on the stock in the account.

[12] The Banks compiled a list of stocks which the Hedge Funds could not purchase because the Banks could not hold the stocks for regulatory reasons. From time to time, the Banks might add another stock to the list—which, in theory, could cause the sale of that stock.

[13] For example, the Federal Reserve, with Reg. T, requires an investor to post an initial margin of 50% and to maintain a margin of 25% thereafter.

[14] There is also now a 3.8% tax on net investment income, whether short-term or long-term, for higher-income taxpayers. Code sec. 1411.

[15] A derivative also is subject to sec. 1234A, which provides that "[g]ain or loss attributable to the ... termination of a right or obligation . . . with respect to property which is (or on acquisition would be) a capital asset . . . shall be treated as gain or loss from the sale of a capital asset." An investor's gains from the termination of a derivative with respect to stock are capital.

[16] Rev. Rul. 82-150, 1982-2 C.B. 110, 111. In my view, the Basket Contracts are not options for tax purposes, as the Hedge Funds would almost certainly exercise these "options." For tax purposes, there must be a "substantial likelihood" that a taxpayer will not exercise a contract for the taxpayer to treat the contract as an option, regardless of the label of the contract. See Rev. Rul. 85-87, 1985-1 C.B. 268. Although a Basket Contract is not an option, it might, in theory, be another form of derivative (for example, a cash-settled forward contract). The tax rules are similar.

[17] See Christoffersen v. U.S. 749 F.2d 513 (8th Cir. 1985) ("We cannot too often reiterate that 'taxation is not so much concerned with the refinements of title as it is with actual command over the property taxed—the actual benefit for which the tax is paid." quoting Griffiths v. Comm., 308 U.S. 355, 357-58 (1939)).

[18] Commissioner v. Glenshaw Glass Co. 348 U.S. 426 (1955).

[19] Helvering v. Bruun, 309 U.S. 461 (1940).

[20] Treas. Reg. sec. 1.1001-1(a).

[21] Rev. Rul. 90-109, 1990-2 C.B. 191. In 1996, the IRS "did not alter the 'fundamental change doctrine articulated in Revenue Ruling 90-109" for non-debt instruments when it adopted regulations for modifications of debt instruments. T.D. 8675, 1996-2 C.B. 61.

[22] I first compared the tax and financial accounting for derivatives in Rosenthal and Price, Tax and Accounting for Derivatives: Time for Reconciliation, Tax Notes 895 (1999).

[23] The board codified FAS 133 at Accounting Standards Codification ("ASC") 815.

In: Structured Financial Products …
Editor: Lenora Osborne
ISBN: 978-1-63463-785-5

Chapter 4

STATEMENT OF MARTY MALLOY, MANAGING DIRECTOR, BARCLAYS. HEARING ON "ABUSE OF STRUCTURED FINANCIAL PRODUCTS: MISUSING BASKET OPTIONS TO AVOID TAXES AND LEVERAGE LIMITS"*

Good Morning. I am Marty Malloy, and I currently serve as Managing Director and Head of Barclays' European Prime Services unit. From 1998 to 2008, I headed the equity finance team of Barclays' Prime Brokerage group. In this capacity, I oversaw the execution of the Colt transaction with Renaissance Technologies. In the last eighteen months, I have met with the Subcommittee staff on several occasions in an effort to assist your review and analysis of the Colt transactions, and I am here today as a further continuation of my and Barclays' cooperation.

Barclays and Renaissance first entered into the Colt transaction in the fall of 2002. Renaissance, a highly sophisticated, well-regarded, and extremely successful hedge fund, was already a customer of the Bank at that time. Renaissance proposed aspects of a structure that ultimately became Colt in connection with ongoing discussions regarding potentially expanding its

* This is an edited, reformatted and augmented version of a statement presented July 22, 2014 before the Senate Permanent Subcommittee on Investigations of the Homeland Security and Governmental Affairs Committee.

business relationship with Barclays. Over the past twelve years, Barclays and Renaissance have entered into a number of Colt options.

The mechanics of the options can be summarized as follows:

- Barclays sells to a Renaissance subsidiary (Badger) a series of cash-settled options, which reference a basket of securities held by a wholly-owned subsidiary of Barclays (Palomino).
- The basket (also known as the reference portfolio) was funded by Barclays from the funds received from Renaissance as the premium for the options, plus the leverage financing provided to Palomino by Barclays.
- Renaissance determines the composition of the basket and the overall investment strategy, pursuant to an Investment Management Agreement, and subject to numerous limitations in that document.
- Renaissance employs a "statistical arbitrage" investment strategy, and utilizes the buying and selling of both long and short positions.
- Any income derived from the investment activity in the reference portfolio accrued to Palomino.
- Each time Renaissance elected to exercise an option, the value was determined by reference to the value of the Palomino portfolio.
- Originally, these options had a maximum period of three years and more recently they have had a maximum period of eleven months.

This was a commercial transaction from which Barclays earned fees in a number of ways. On options trades like this one, the Bank realizes income from the spread on our execution of our principal trades. Additionally, Barclays benefited from being able to both pledge as collateral and lend out the securities held by Palomino.

Before putting on the first Colt option, Barclays subjected the transaction to an extensive internal review process and consulted with both internal and external regulatory and tax experts. The extensive governance and approval process employed both at the early stage of this transaction, as well as when subsequent options were considered and approved, will be discussed further by my colleague, Gerard LaRocca, in his testimony.

While Renaissance has a stellar track record and reputation as an investment manager, the Colt transaction, like any transaction, poses certain risks to the Bank. In particular, Barclays bears gap risk associated with being the holder of the basket of securities. These risks are mitigated by particular features of the transaction, including Barclays' right to unilaterally unwind the transaction if losses exceed the amount of the premium paid by Renaissance on any existing option. There is also a monitoring system to oversee performance of the reference portfolio, and certain limitations such as concentration and skew limits. For example, over a period of several days in August 2007, this portfolio, like others using a statistical arbitrage strategy, suffered higher than expected losses. While the portfolio eventually rebounded, and the losses did not exceed the limit levels that would have triggered an automatic unwind of the transaction, Barclays' resulting concern led us to impose several additional risk mitigating limitations on the transaction.

While Barclays had the risks and protections I just described, the Colt transaction was unique in at least one important way in that it was non-recourse. In other words, unlike other transactions in which the Bank provides financing, with the Colt transaction we cannot pursue legal remedies from Renaissance in the event the portfolio suffers losses in excess of the amount of premium paid. So the risk of loss on the portfolio once the option premium is exhausted remains entirely with Barclays.

It is my understanding that the fundamental question raised by this Subcommittee is whether, historically, Renaissance has applied the correct tax rate to its earnings from the Colt options. It is also my understanding that this question has not yet been decided by the IRS. Although the IRS issued generic legal advice in 2010, it is my understanding that this type of legal advice does not set out official rulings or positions of the IRS and may not be referenced in other documents as precedent. Since the issuance of the advice, the IRS has issued no further guidance or decision on these transactions. Although Barclays feels strongly that this transaction was subject to sufficient and significant internal and external review to ensure it complied with applicable tax laws and regulations, ultimately the question of, "what tax rate should Renaissance pay?," is a matter to be resolved between Renaissance, as the taxpayer, and the IRS. It is not uncommon for taxpayers, large and small, to have occasional disputes regarding the amount of tax that they owe, and a fulsome process exists, both at the IRS and in the courts, to resolve such disputes.

I hope my testimony has been helpful, and I will do my best to answer the Subcommittee's questions. I should note, however, that although I have been involved with many aspects of this transaction over the course of its execution at Barclays, I have not been responsible for the deal's day-to-day operations since May 2008, more than six years ago. Nonetheless, to assist the

Subcommittee, the Bank has done its best to collect as much information related to this transaction as possible and therefore, at times, my testimony and answers will reflect not my personal knowledge, but what I have been informed of by others working for the Bank.

In: Structured Financial Products … ISBN: 978-1-63463-785-5
Editor: Lenora Osborne

Chapter 5

JOINT TESTIMONY OF BARRY BAUSANO, PRESIDENT, AND SATISH RAMAKRISHNA, MANAGING DIRECTOR, DEUTSCHE BANK SECURITIES, INC. HEARING ON "ABUSE OF STRUCTURED FINANCIAL PRODUCTS: MISUSING BASKET OPTIONS TO AVOID TAXES AND LEVERAGE LIMITS"*

Chairman Levin, Ranking Member McCain, and Members of the Subcommittee:

On behalf of Deutsche Bank Securities Inc., we respectfully submit the following joint written statement by Barry Bausano and Satish Ramakrishna.

Barry Bausano is currently the President of Deutsche Bank Securities Inc. and Co-Head of Deutsche Bank's Global Prime Finance Business. Mr. Bausano is based in the New York office of Deutsche Bank and has worked at Deutsche Bank for approximately twelve years.

Satish Ramakrishna is currently Managing Director and Global Head, Risk & Pricing for Global Prime Finance, Deutsche Bank Securities Inc. Mr. Ramakrishna is based in the New York office of Deutsche Bank and has worked at Deutsche Bank for approximately sixteen years.

* This is an edited, reformatted and augmented version of testimony presented July 22, 2014 before the Senate Permanent Subcommittee on Investigations of the Homeland Security and Governmental Affairs Committee.

This testimony is submitted in response to the Subcommittee's invitation to provide a written statement regarding barrier option contracts, which Deutsche Bank called MAPS, an acronym for Managed Account Products. MAPS was an option with the advantages of providing clients with increased leverage, limitations on downside risk, and market anonymity. Derivative financial instruments are a critical component of global finance as they allow participants to alter risk and the distribution of returns relative to holding the underlying investments. For the reasons discussed below, Deutsche Bank strongly believes that it acted at all times responsibly, indeed proactively, in its ongoing consideration of MAPS in the light of evolving views regarding the regulatory landscape surrounding derivative products, and that its conduct demonstrates the Bank's strong commitment to be well within the bounds of the law.

We further understand, however, that the IRS has expressed concerns with a particular type of barrier option contract and the potential for associated long-term capital gain treatment as set forth in an IRS Generic Legal Advice Memorandum, or GLAM, issued November 12, 2010. Importantly, in 2010, Deutsche Bank was not entering into barrier option contracts as described in the GLAM. Indeed, Deutsche Bank had ceased offering a product based on agreements similar to the ones described in the GLAM in 2008, when Deutsche Bank, in consultation with outside counsel, independently restructured its MAPS product. Despite having no knowledge of any IRS intention to release the GLAM, or that the IRS was even auditing barrier option contracts, Deutsche Bank proactively addressed virtually every factor considered in the GLAM approximately two years before the issuance of the GLAM. The restructured Deutsche Bank product is referred to in this testimony as New MAPS.

It is important to note the limited scope of the use of New MAPS at Deutsche Bank. From 2008 through today, Deutsche Bank has entered into New MAPS options with only one client, Mosel LP, a Renaissance Technologies LLC affiliate. And even with that one client, Deutsche Bank has entered into only one long-term option since the IRS's issuance of the GLAM. That option was negotiated prior to the GLAM and entered into on the business day following the GLAM's issuance—and only after Deutsche Bank conferred with outside counsel to confirm that New MAPS was not the same structure as the product described in the GLAM. Indeed, and importantly, shortly after issuance of the GLAM, Deutsche Bank reassessed its participation in barrier option contracts. Despite its belief that New MAPS was in compliance with applicable laws and regulations, Deutsche Bank decided that it did not wish to risk being associated with any controversy over the tax treatment of MAPS. Therefore, it decided to cease entering into any New MAPS transactions with a duration of more than one year.

We believe that Deutsche Bank acted appropriately at all times with respect to the barrier option contracts it offered. Deutsche Bank affirmatively and proactively undertook steps to ensure compliance with applicable tax and securities laws and regulations. While we understand the Subcommittee is studying tax policy in this area, and such issues are worthy of discussion, there should be no question that Deutsche Bank did its best to ensure compliance with the laws and regulations as written and understood by the subject matter experts at the time. We do note, however, that it is a widely accepted principle that tax consequences differ among various financial instruments. New MAPS, which was an option, was treated by Deutsche Bank in accordance with the tax rules relating to financial derivatives at all times.

The following is a more detailed description of Deutsche Bank's participation in MAPS.

THE MAPS PRODUCT

In 1998, Deutsche Bank acquired certain business lines of National Westminster Bank, or NatWest. One such acquired business line offered MAPS to certain hedge fund clients of NatWest. MAPS continued as an important but limited offering of Deutsche Bank after the 1998 acquisition, as it safely met the demand for increased leverage for a limited set of clients whose trading strategy was suitable for such a product. In MAPS, a client holds an option over a basket of securities, long and short, held by Deutsche Bank. The basket is traded by an affiliate of the option holder using the option holder's own trading strategy, but within strict parameters set by Deutsche Bank. Accordingly, MAPS was offered to and executed with only a limited group of institutional clients that followed balanced trading strategies that consistently fit within those parameters. Unlike many of its peers at that time, Deutsche Bank did not have a well-developed prime brokerage offering that met client need for increased leverage. MAPS allowed Deutsche Bank to compete for the business of those clients that wanted increased leverage and had trading strategies suitable for such a product.

Significantly, MAPS was not marketed by Deutsche Bank as a means of helping clients avoid or minimize taxes. In fact, when Deutsche Bank initially sought legal advice in connection with offering MAPS as a product, it did so to ensure that the structure was an option under the securities laws, and not because of any questions about the tax treatment of the option.

As noted above, MAPS itself was fundamentally an option on a trading strategy. The option buyer and holder, a hedge fund, paid a premium to Deutsche Bank to purchase the option. If the strategy did not generate gains in excess of the initial premium, the buyer simply paid for the cost of the option and use of Deutsche Bank's capital and received the remaining value in the option at maturity. However, if the strategy generated positive returns, the buyer received the amount of those returns, less the costs and fees for the option paid to Deutsche Bank. The Bank engaged an investment advisor affiliated with the option holder to run the trading strategy within strict parameters and to purchase in the Bank's own account the securities or positions that comprised the strategy as a hedge to the option.

While Deutsche Bank's exposure under the option was hedged, MAPS was not without risk to the Bank, particularly absent the controls we put in place. If the value of the securities held in the proprietary account fell below the barrier price of the option, the Bank bore all losses.

NEW MAPS

In August 2007, hedge funds employing a statistical-arbitrage, market-neutral strategy experienced what has come to be known as the "quant quake." The quant quake occurred over four days when it is believed the liquidation of a single quantitatively constructed portfolio triggered a domino effect across numerous "quant funds" running similar leveraged, market-neutral strategies. Many of those funds suffered enormous losses, with some incurring double-digit losses within a single day. Deutsche Bank clients utilizing the MAPS product in August 2007 (a total of six clients at the time) largely employed a leveraged, statistical-arbitrage, market-neutral strategy and were among the affected funds. Historically, these funds – because of sophisticated algorithms to balance long and short positions – had not experienced significant swings in performance. Therefore, they were viewed as low risk. The quant quake demonstrated that such funds were riskier than believed because of the high correlation in positions held by the different funds employing similar strategies.

As a result, in late 2007, the Bank's risk managers began to consider ways to provide the Bank with better protection if the value of the portfolio of securities the Bank was holding relating to MAPS suddenly dropped. At the same time, those in the Bank's control functions, including legal, tax, and compliance, were assessing MAPS in light of ongoing dialogue and observations concerning the regulatory landscape surrounding derivatives products. Those efforts were merged together as Deutsche Bank worked to restructure MAPS and develop "New MAPS" in 2007 and 2008.

The MAPS restructuring included the following changes:

- First, New MAPS included key risk-reduction terms that provided the Bank with certain rights at declining levels of account value— first to require the investment advisor to reduce its leverage, second to take over the management of the portfolio, and third to assume control and liquidate the positions being traded by the investment advisor in Deutsche Bank's proprietary account.
- Second, the New MAPS agreements further provided that the securities traded for each option would be held in separate sub-accounts, and the options staggered. This reduced the risk that a loss in value in one account would de-value options in other subaccounts.
- Third, New MAPS was changed from an American to a European-style option, which could not be terminated early without forfeiting a significant portion of the premium.
- Fourth, the investment advisor's duties to the Bank, which were set forth in an Investment Advisory Agreement, were clarified under New MAPS, and the fee paid to the advisor was changed to conform to standard market practices for investment advisors.
- Fifth, in New MAPS, Deutsche Bank ensured that it expressly retained important rights relating to the underlying securities, including distribution rights and voting rights.

In addition to these changes to the product, the Bank took steps to improve internal controls and limit the Bank's risk under New MAPS. Performance of the securities traded in the subaccounts was monitored on an intra-day basis, allowing for almost immediate detection of subaccount changes in value. Such monitoring enabled Deutsche Bank to assume complete control of the relevant portfolio in the event of an applicable threshold breach.

Deutsche Bank also ensured that the revised option price calculation accurately compensated the Bank for its risks and costs, including the costs of utilizing the Bank's capital. Pricing was done through the use of traditional option-pricing methods and the strike price was adjusted so that the cost of the option and the financing cost of the portfolio were reflected in the strike price of the option. Specifically, the option was priced based on an analysis of the risk that the Bank was assuming by entering into the option, as well as the time value of the capital the Bank was using to purchase the securities that comprised the portfolio.

In sum, Deutsche Bank priced the MAPS option as an option, managed it as an option, and documented it as an option. It did so because MAPS was an option and the Bank was compensated, and managed its risk, accordingly.

Precisely because it was an option, MAPS offered a number of unique advantages to clients. As the Subcommittee is aware, one of those advantages is that gains on options with durations of more than one year are treated as long-term capital gains. In this respect, MAPS was not different from any other long-dated option. However, the MAPS product offered many economic and other significant non-tax advantages for the option buyer.[1] Structuring financial products to meet client needs for risk and return is a necessary function of capital markets.

We identify the following three non-tax advantages of New MAPS that we consider most significant for purposes of this statement. First, as discussed above, Deutsche Bank was comfortable providing the option buyer with greater leverage at the fund level than it would have allowed in a traditional prime brokerage relationship. This was because the Bank had greater visibility, control, and protections in place relating to the underlying trading activity than it did in a prime brokerage account. Indeed, MAPS provided the option holder with leverage of up to eighteen times the premium compared with what the Bank could safely provide in the closest prime brokerage alternative, enhanced prime brokerage. Second, the MAPS option limited the client's downside risk to the premium it paid to purchase the option. Third, the client could pursue its trading strategy anonymously, because any market transactions associated with the trading strategy were made by Deutsche Bank, in Deutsche Bank's own name.

On the leverage point, it is important to emphasize that, while MAPS permitted clients to obtain leverage greater than other products offered by the Bank, the risk associated with such increased leverage was managed pursuant to the transactional terms. As discussed above, those terms were revised in connection with the 2008 restructuring to allow for improved management of the risk. MAPS, therefore, did not expose the Bank to excessive risk. In addition, unlike a traditional prime brokerage account, in MAPS the securities are owned and held by the Bank, providing the Bank with transparency into the portfolio and the ability to control the account's holdings, as well as the right to vote the securities. Moreover, New MAPS was entered into with only one hedge fund customer, Renaissance, a fund that pursued a market neutral investment strategy and that had historically consistent returns, thus reducing, albeit not eliminating, market risks.

DB Responds to the GLAM, and Discusses MAPS with its Regulators

Although discussed earlier in this statement, Deutsche Bank's actions after IRS's issuance of the GLAM on November 12, 2010, merit separate discussion and specific consideration.[2] Following the release of the GLAM, the Bank discussed the GLAM with its outside tax counsel, and counsel affirmed that the GLAM did not change their prior views on the New MAPS product. Nevertheless, and despite the Bank's view that New MAPS was outside the scope of the GLAM, the Bank decided it would no longer enter New MAPS options with its one remaining New MAPS client. It did so out of a desire to avoid being associated with any controversy over the tax treatment of MAPS that might result from the GLAM.[3] The Bank made this decision even though New MAPS was entirely consistent with the requirements of the Bank's Non-Prosecution Agreement with the U.S. Department of Justice.[4]

Conclusion

In sum, with respect to MAPS, Deutsche Bank affirmatively took steps, on its own initiative, to ensure that its conduct was well within the boundaries set by applicable legal requirements. Deutsche Bank: (1) ceased entering into the transaction described in the 2010 IRS GLAM two years before the GLAM was issued; (2) entered into New MAPS with only one client from the end of 2008 through the 2010 GLAM; and (3) completely stopped entering into New MAPS transactions with a duration of more than one year shortly after issuance of the GLAM. This is so, even though, as of today, neither the IRS nor any court or regulator has found that a New MAPS option (or indeed, any Deutsche Bank MAPS option) did not qualify as a derivative for tax, securities, or any other purposes. Deutsche Bank believes strongly that it acted appropriately in entering the New MAPS options when it did, and that it acted conservatively and responsibly when it decided to stop entering them for reputational reasons after the issuance of the GLAM.

Thank you for this opportunity to submit this written testimony, and we will be prepared at the hearing to address the topics raised in your letter of July 9, 2014.

End Notes

[1] Indeed, there were clients of Deutsche Bank that entered into MAPS trades that did not seek the long-term capital gain treatment of the option discussed in the GLAM, as those clients never traded a MAPS option with a tenor of more than one year.

[2] It bears noting that a GLAM, by its terms, is not to be cited or relied on as precedent.

[3] Renaissance subsequently expressed a desire to engage in New MAPS trades having a tenor of less than one year. Deutsche Bank agreed because such trades do not present the opportunity for the counterparty to claim long-term capital gains treatment for any gains and therefore do not present the same reputational risk. In addition, following the GLAM, Deutsche Bank briefly discussed with Renaissance an alternative to MAPS in the form of an option linked to the amount a trading strategy outperformed the S&P 500 Index. Although this concept was discussed in good faith with Renaissance, it was widely recognized within Deutsche Bank that it was highly unlikely the revised structure would overcome the reputational risks that caused the Bank to cease entering New MAPS. In any case, the project was abandoned well before it reached a stage where the potential reputational impact would have been reviewed by the Bank's tax and legal functions.

[4] New MAPS was consistent with the requirements of the Non-Prosecution Agreement because it was supported by an appropriate legal opinion and because the transaction, to this day, does not appear as a listed transaction or in any category that is prohibited by the NPA or DB's internal policies. In addition, it bears noting that the Bank discussed the MAPS product with certain regulators as early as 2007, and it discussed the MAPS product with the Department of Justice, the IRS, the SEC, and the Independent Expert Deutsche Bank retained as part of the NPA. All of these discussions took place well before this Committee began its investigation. Indeed, the Bank communicated with the Independent Expert about MAPS at a meeting on February 3, 2011, and discussed the MAPS product with the Department of Justice and the IRS at several meetings in 2012 and 2013.

In: Structured Financial Products …
Editor: Lenora Osborne
ISBN: 978-1-63463-785-5

Chapter 6

JOINT STATEMENT OF PETER F. BROWN, CO-CEO, MARK SILBER, CFO, AND JONATHAN MAYERS, COUNSEL, RENAISSANCE TECHNOLOGIES LLC. HEARING ON "ABUSE OF STRUCTURED FINANCIAL PRODUCTS: MISUSING BASKET OPTIONS TO AVOID TAXES AND LEVERAGE LIMITS"*

Chairman Levin, Ranking Member McCain, and members of the Subcommittee, we appreciate the opportunity to be here today to speak with you and to answer your questions on behalf of Renaissance Technologies LLC ("Renaissance"). We will do our best to explain to you who we are as a firm, what our approach to investing entails, and why we believe that our activities were and are appropriate under current law.

Below we discuss the topics you have asked us to address. As you know, we have also supplied your staff with information that further addresses these topics in document responses and in interviews over the last year and a half We appreciate having had the opportunity to meet with your staff on a number

* This is an edited, reformatted and augmented version of a statement presented July 22, 2014 before the Senate Permanent Subcommittee on Investigations of the Homeland Security and Governmental Affairs Committee.

of occasions to discuss this matter, and we hope that you have found our engagement cooperative and responsive.

We want to be clear: Renaissance's Medallion fund entered into barrier options with Deutsche Bank and Barclays, both large and sophisticated counterparties, for substantial non-tax business purposes. When we exercised an option held for more than a year, we reported any resulting gains as long-term capital gains, in accordance with current tax law. We reported gains on options held for less than a year as short-term capital gains. If the law changes in the future, we will of course comply. We also understand that there are questions about the level of leverage allowed in arrangements with our counterparties. Under current law, derivative instruments permit higher leverage than many other forms of investment. Again, if the rules concerning leverage change, we will comply.

The IRS has been reviewing these options for over six years now. Renaissance has been cooperating fully with that review and is working through this issue within the IRS's process. Ultimately, we expect to prevail. However, if it is determined that Renaissance's view is incorrect, we will fully comply with that determination. We recognize as well the responsibility and authority of Congress to take a careful look at this matter and to consider any related policy matters. We have been transparent with our regulators and hope we can also answer your questions today.

RENAISSANCE – BACKGROUND AND BUSINESS MODEL

Renaissance was established for the purpose of producing superior financial results for our investors by adhering to mathematical and statistical methods in the design and execution of trading strategies. We were founded and are principally owned by scientists and we generally hire physicists, mathematicians, astronomers, and computer scientists.

Renaissance's equity trading and advisory activities bring added liquidity to the equities markets, reduce inefficiencies, and improve capital formation. We collect all the publicly available data we can find that we believe might bear on the movement of the prices of tradable instruments—news stories, analysts' reports, energy reports, crop reports, weather reports, regulatory filings, accounting data, and, of course, quotes and trades from markets around the world. Our models use this data to make predictions about future price changes. Although we use different strategies in managing our different funds, all of our strategies depend on the output of our data-driven models. Of particular note for today's discussion is the fact that our models do not factor in tax rates when making trading recommendations.

Medallion has achieved exceptional returns over the years, but we are mindful that past success is no guarantee of future performance. We also understand the need for thoughtful regulation and laws to govern the operations of the financial system as a whole, and we are committed to being a constructive participant in the dialogue about what those regulations and laws should be.

THE USE OF BARRIER OPTIONS BY MEDALLION

Deutsche Bank proposed a barrier option transaction to Renaissance in the late 1990s. It did not do so with a focus on tax benefits. The barrier options that Deutsche Bank proposed allowed Medallion to obtain leverage on a non-recourse basis that could not be obtained through any other product. Medallion entered into its first barrier option with Deutsche Bank in September 2000 and later entered into similar options with Barclays so as to diversify its counterparty risk.

The model developed by Renaissance for Medallion makes predictions that are profitable only slightly more often than not. Moreover, the predicted price movements can be easily overwhelmed by external events. To compensate for these factors, the model generates a large number of recommendations, so that by virtue of the mathematical principle known as the law of large numbers, the variability of the returns produced by the model is greatly reduced.

However, because the model's recommendations are expected to be profitable only slightly more often than not, the rate of return obtained by applying the recommendations to an unleveraged portfolio would be very small. Leverage magnifies the effect of positive changes in the overall value of the portfolio on the rate of return, and this effect is greater the higher the level of leverage employed. Medallion's barrier options with Barclays and Deutsche Bank provide the high leverage necessary to take optimal advantage of the predictions made by Medallion's model. This leverage is entirely permissible and appropriate under current law. As the Joint Committee on Taxation has recognized, "[d]erivatives are critically important tools in the risk management process," and "[o]ne commercial reason for the popularity of derivatives is that derivative contracts typically afford a party much higher leverage than would be commercially possible (or permitted by relevant margin regulations) if the party were to establish a position in the underlying physical."[1]

In addition to leverage, a key benefit of these barrier options is that they provide Medallion with protection against losses that might occur when trading at high leverage. Models often work well, but the markets have many times taught participants the lesson of humility. Long Term Capital Management in 1998 and numerous banks and hedge funds caught up in the sub-prime crisis in 2008, for example, put too much trust in their models and were not wary enough of what we have come to call Black Swan risk. This is the risk of an event that lies far enough outside previous experience that it cannot be anticipated by existing models. Black Swan events can have catastrophic outcomes. For a model-based high-leverage strategy like Medallion's, mitigating Black Swan risk through loss protection is therefore crucial. We witnessed the importance of this in 1998 when Long Term Capital failed, and again when the dot-com bubble burst in 2000.

The barrier options offered by Barclays and Deutsche Bank are non-recourse, which means that Medallion's downside risk is limited to the premium paid when the option is first purchased. No other investment structure of which we are aware provides both high leverage and loss protection. As noted above, the options were not marketed to Renaissance for their tax benefits, and Medallion's decision to purchase the options was driven by a desire to obtain the leverage and the loss protection that they offered. In fact, Medallion currently enters into loss protection barrier options with terms of less than one year, even though these can only produce short-term capital gains.

Our decisions to exercise the barrier options were driven by business imperatives. For example, the average holding period of the Deutsche Bank options from 2000 to 2009 was 455 days, not the 366 days that might be expected if the holding periods were purely tax-driven.[2] After the August 2007 "Quant Quake," we exercised a Barclays option after only a few months and reported the profit as short-term capital gain; in early 2009, we exercised another Barclays option after only a few months during the market turmoil surrounding the financial crisis and again reported the profit as short-term capital gain. It is true that when new tax rates were enacted in 2012, we, like many other investors, sought to recognize gains inherent in our options before the new rates took effect. But this is simply the sort of prudent planning that our investors would justifiably expect us to undertake.

We are prepared to discuss issues of tax policy during the hearing in more detail. The Supreme Court recognized over 30 years ago that when a taxpayer enters into a transaction for real business purposes, with real economic substance, to manage real risks, the form of that transaction should be respected for tax purposes.[3] In our case, our primary business purposes for purchasing these options were, and continue to be, leverage and loss protection.

HOW THE BARRIER OPTIONS WORK

Each barrier option references the performance of a notional basket of securities, called the reference portfolio, generated by Medallion's trading model. There are other, publicly available options today that reference changing baskets of securities, such as options on the "Dogs of the Dow" or the S&P 500. When our model performs well, the fund profits, aided by the superior leverage available through these options. Upon exercise of the option, Medallion is entitled to a cash settlement payment generally equal to the net positive performance of the reference portfolio. If the model performs poorly, the option limits Medallion's downside risk, because Medallion's maximum possible loss is the amount of premium paid to purchase the option. We know of no other way to obtain this combination of leverage and loss protection.

Each option contains a barrier provision, pursuant to which the option automatically terminates if the value of the reference portfolio falls below a specified level, even momentarily. Thus, the barrier provision prevents Medallion from benefiting from a rebound in the value of the reference portfolio after such a decline. The barrier feature of the options helps the banks manage their risk; without this feature, the banks likely would not enter into the options. The U.S. Tax Court has specifically said that options with barrier provisions, such as ours, are taxed as options.[4]

The barrier options provide Medallion with critical loss protection and superior leverage, but these benefits come with a price. Because Medallion does not own the underlying instruments that make up the reference portfolio, it would have no claim to any of the assets its counterparty might hold to hedge an option should that counterparty suffer a Lehman Brothers-like collapse or default on the transaction. Instead, Medallion would be in line as just another of the counterparty's general creditors, with no guarantee of recovering any portion of the value of the option. Stated more directly, choosing the option form for our transaction meant we gave up the meaningful ownership rights, including bankruptcy protections, that we would have had in a prime brokerage relationship.

It is common for banks that enter into derivatives contracts to hedge against risk of loss by taking offsetting positions in the referenced instruments. Although nothing in the option agreements with either Deutsche Bank or Barclays required either to maintain hedge accounts, it is not surprising that each bank would choose to hedge its risk by actually holding the positions in the reference portfolio in bank-owned accounts. Renaissance was hired by the banks as an investment adviser to help facilitate the hedging process. At the banks' request, Renaissance executed the hedging trades on the banks' behalf, but it had no control over the positions thereafter; the banks had the power subsequently to lend out or even to sell the positions thus acquired.

How the Barclays and Deutsche Bank Barrier Options Changed over Time

Although the details of the barrier options have been modified slightly over the years to adapt to the unique demands of each bank, the Barclays and Deutsche Bank barrier options held by Medallion today are essentially identical in many important respects to the first barrier options Medallion purchased from these banks. Each option has required a single up-front premium payment. Each option has provided for cash settlement generally equal to the net positive performance of the reference portfolio at the valuation date, and each option has included a barrier provision. The underlying reference portfolio for each option was generated by Renaissance's trading algorithm. Neither bank was required to maintain a hedge against the reference portfolio for any option. Each bank explicitly preserved its unrestricted ownership of any positions in its hedge for each option.

The 2007 "Quant Quake" demonstrated convincingly that the strategies of different quantitative funds were correlated, and thus that the risk faced by even the best-run funds was significantly greater than previously thought. In particular, a forced liquidation by any fund could have cascading effects on other funds, resulting in greater losses for all. Newly sensitized to these concerns about risk, from 2007 until late 2008, Deutsche Bank and Renaissance renegotiated some of the terms of their barrier options prospectively. We negotiated for changes clarifying the parties' responsibilities in the event that an option hit a barrier and needed to be unwound. Deutsche Bank negotiated for, among other things, a change to a European-style option, which meant Medallion had no right to exercise an option prior to its stated maturity date, and for a non-refundable component of the premium that locked in a portion of Deutsche Bank's profits up front. These changes had real economic effects. Both we and Deutsche Bank exercised sensible business diligence, including discussions with our outside advisors, to understand the implications of all aspects of the changes, including those potentially related to tax.

In the wake of the "Quant Quake," we also modified prospectively our barrier options with Barclays. The relatively modest changes made to the Barclays barrier options addressed risk issues. We also are aware that in 2009 Barclays amended the articles of association of Palomino, the company through which it held its hedges to the options. We understand that this was done by Barclays for UK accounting purposes, but that it did not affect Barclays' status as the owner of the hedge positions for bank regulatory and other purposes. We entered into a letter agreement with Barclays in 2009 confirming our understanding that the Palomino changes did not affect the parties' rights and obligations under the option documents.

Tax Treatment of the Options

You have also asked more broadly about the tax treatment of barrier options. Renaissance has historically consulted with outside advisors on the tax treatment of the options at issue here and is comfortable that its tax treatment of the options is correct under current law. As noted above, the IRS has been reviewing these options for over six years. Renaissance has been cooperating fully with that review, and ultimately we expect to prevail. We hope you understand that we are unable to discuss the legal advice we received in more detail today without risking waiver of legal rights to which we are entitled in connection with this ongoing IRS proceeding. We hope also that the proceeding will move quickly as we and the IRS have a shared interest in obtaining a final determination of this matter.

It is common for parties to an agreement to allocate between themselves the burdens of various risks, including tax risk. Medallion's agreements with Barclays provide that Medallion bears the risk that the IRS will determine that Barclays should have reported the options differently. Medallion's agreements with Deutsche Bank do not contain a similar provision.

In 2010, the IRS issued Generic Legal Advice Memorandum ("GLAM") 2010-005, a nonprecedential internal analysis of the tax treatment of a barrier option based on summary facts set forth in the GLAM. Renaissance carefully reviewed the GLAM when it was released and did not believe that its description of the facts accurately reflected Medallion's barrier option transactions—particularly as to the risks associated with the transactions. We continue to believe that today. Should the IRS wish to change the tax treatment for barrier options, it could promulgate new rules to this effect—something that it has not done to date.

CONCLUSION

Medallion enters into barrier options to address the business imperatives discussed above. We believe we have reported the income from these options in accordance with current law, and are eager for a speedy resolution of the matter now before the IRS. We look forward to studying your report and will be pleased to address questions you may have.

End Notes

[1] Joint Committee on Taxation, Present Law and Analysis Relating to the Tax Treatment of Derivatives (JCX-21- 08), March 4, 2008, available at http://wwwjet.gov/x-21-08.pdf.

[2] The first Deutsche Bank barrier option, which was an operational test trade in 2000, is excluded from this calculation.

[3] Frank Lyon Co. v. United States, 435 U.S. 561 (1978).

[4] Garcia v. Commissioner, 101 T.C.M. (CCH) 1388, 1390-1 (2011).

In: Structured Financial Products ...
Editor: Lenora Osborne

ISBN: 978-1-63463-785-5

Chapter 7

STATEMENT OF GERARD LAROCCA, CHIEF ADMINISTRATIVE OFFICER, BARCLAYS. HEARING ON "ABUSE OF STRUCTURED FINANCIAL PRODUCTS: MISUSING BASKET OPTIONS TO AVOID TAXES AND LEVERAGE LIMITS"*

I am Gerard LaRocca, and I serve as the Americas Chief Administrative Officer of Barclays Bank PLC. Along with my colleague, Marty Malloy, you have asked us to assist the Subcommittee in its review of certain issues related to the Colt transaction, entered into between Barclays and our customer, Renaissance.

As with all other complex transactions, from the outset of Colt, the Bank undertook a comprehensive transaction review and approvals process to ensure that the transaction was subject to proper scrutiny. This included review by the Bank's internal governance functions, including our regulatory, tax, risk and legal departments. In addition, the Bank conferred with and sought review from a prominent law firm with significant tax expertise, and that firm issued a tax opinion to both Renaissance and the Bank. This tax opinion was later reaffirmed by separate law firms for both the Bank and Renaissance. Further, with respect to questions related to the Bank itself, we obtained separate

* This is an edited, reformatted and augmented version of a statement presented July 22, 2014 before the Senate Permanent Subcommittee on Investigations of the Homeland Security and Governmental Affairs Committee.

regulatory and tax opinions. Finally, Barclays disclosed its participation in the transaction to our auditors and our regulators, both here in the United States and in the UK.

As you can see, we did not take this matter lightly and were ultimately comfortable engaging in the transaction. Significantly, this was a transaction with a highly sophisticated and highly regarded counterparty. Renaissance's successful track record is well known.

As I understand it, the question raised by the Subcommittee concerning this transaction seems to be: "What is the proper tax rate to apply to profits earned by Renaissance through the exercise of its options?" Fundamentally, this is a matter to be handled between Renaissance, as a taxpayer, and the IRS. And as we sit here today, it is my understanding that the IRS has yet to answer that question.

While the IRS has not decided the appropriate tax treatment for these transactions, eighteen months ago Barclays elected—voluntarily and proactively—to change an element of the option contracts central to the tax analysis. Beginning in 2012, Barclays embarked on an extensive, bank-wide internal review known as TRANSFORM, on which I will provide more details in a moment. As a result of that review, early last year we informed Renaissance that any future option would only be for a period not to exceed eleven months. Historically, Colt options were for a period of three years, and Renaissance exercised those options at different times— some less than one year, some more than one year. By modifying the options to expire if not exercised within eleven months, Barclays eliminated any uncertainty that may have existed regarding the applicable tax rate. Since Barclays made this decision, Renaissance has entered into an option with this shorter term.

You have asked me to discuss the impact of a 2010 IRS advisory memorandum known to tax lawyers as a GLAM, including the Bank's decision last year to change the tenor of the options going forward. Before addressing these developments, I want to first state that all of this did not occur in a vacuum. Like other financial institutions, Barclays has faced numerous challenges in recent years. Our Bank has endeavored to meet these challenges head on, and at times resolving them has resulted in significant changes, both in process and in personnel at the Bank. Today, we have new leadership and feel strongly we are moving in the right direction, transforming the way we do business.

The Bank began its transformative process with a series of bank-wide reviews. First, Barclays launched Project Mango, an internal review of our investment banking operations. Next, Barclays commissioned Sir Anthony

Salz, an outside consultant, to conduct an independent review of Barclays' business lines, culminating with the publication of the Salz Report. Finally, Barclays embarked on the TRANSFORM program, an internal review aimed at establishing the conditions necessary for the Bank's long-term success, including the implementation of the thirty-four point roadmap for change detailed in the Salz Report.

As part of TRANSFORM, the Bank adopted five overarching tax principles that now apply to all tax transactions. It is against this backdrop that we considered what impact, if any, the GLAM should have on our participation in the Colt transaction.

In December 2010, Renaissance made what had become a routine request to enter into a new option. In light of the GLAM's recent publication and prior to moving forward, we specifically consulted with Renaissance, their legal advisors and our own legal advisors regarding the impact of the GLAM on the transaction. After extensive internal consideration and consultation with external advisors, Barclays approved the issuance of a new option. In so doing, we agreed to continue to monitor relevant IRS announcements going forward, and to revisit the decision from time-to-time if Renaissance sought to put on new options.

In February 2013, the Bank issued its new tax principles and undertook a review of existing tax transactions, including Colt. Central to our discussion here, one of the principles provides that Barclays will not structure transactions of a type different than tax authorities would expect. The end result of our review was a decision that, going forward, we would limit the tenor of any new Colt options to a period of eleven months. Of course, the IRS had not made any final determination as to the appropriate tax treatment. In fact, it is my understanding that the GLAM does not set out official rules or positions of the IRS and may not be referenced as precedent. However, the Bank made a proactive and voluntary choice to shorten the terms of these options so as to ensure we met the tax authorities' expectations. This was a decision that, in our view, brought the transaction into conformity with our newly adopted tax principles. By doing this, the Bank committed not only to following specifically applicable laws, but also to refrain from engaging in any transactions that, while legal, might not meet the expectations of the relevant taxing authorities.

We understand that taking this stance may mean that, going forward, we will have to decline certain transactions that are both commercially attractive and legal, causing us to possibly lose out on business. But we believe cultivating exemplary culture at the Bank, and instilling the highest sense of

Purpose, Value and Behavior, are fundamentally necessary to help us achieve our goal of becoming the "Go-To" Bank in the years to come.

Therefore, any questions the Subcommittee may have about these transactions do not relate to the Barclays of today, or the Barclays of the future. These are transactions from the past, about which we are still awaiting a decision by the IRS.

Thank you for the opportunity to provide this testimony. I am prepared to offer my assistance, but note that I was not personally involved in a number of the topics that you have raised; therefore, my knowledge may be limited, and my testimony here reflects not only my firsthand knowledge, but also what I have learned from my colleagues at the Bank. I look forward to answering the Subcommittee's questions.

INDEX

E

F

G

H

I

J

L

M

S

T

U

V

W

Y